On Creating a Usable Culture

On Creating a Usable Culture

Margaret Mead and the Emergence of
American Cosmopolitanism

Maureen A. Molloy

University of Hawai'i Press
Honolulu

13 12 11 10 09 08   6 5 4 3 2 1

Library of Congress Cataloging-in-Publication Data
Molloy, Maureen.
    On creating a usable culture : Margaret Mead and the emergence
of American cosmopolitanism / Maureen A. Molloy.
        p. cm.
    Includes bibliographical references and index.
    ISBN 978-0-8248-3116-5 (hardcover : alk. paper)
    1. Anthropology—United States—Popular works. 2. Anthropology
in popular culture—United States. 3. Anthropology in literature.
4. Cosmopolitanism—United States. 5. World War, 1939–1945—Social
aspects—United States. 6. United States—Social life and customs.
7. Mead, Margaret, 1901–1978—Criticism and interpretation. I. Title.
    E184.A1M63 2008
    973—dc22

                                    2007048336

Designed by Leslie Fitch and the University of Hawai'i Press Production Staff
Printed by The Maple-Vail Book Manufacturing Group

This book is dedicated to the memory of my mother, Margurite Lillian (Toddy) Molloy, who, in ways that cannot be counted, made it possible;

And to my granddaughter, Taylor Nyomi Sutton, for whom it was written.

Contents

Acknowledgments   ix

1   Introduction   1

2   The Problem of American Culture   19

3   The "Jungle Flapper"
    Civilization, Repression, and the Homogenous Society   42

4   "Lords of an Empty Creation"
    Masculinity, Puritanism, and Cultural Stagnation   62

5   "Every Woman Deviating from the Code"
    Cultural Lag, Moral Contagion, and Social Disintegration   83

6   "Maladjustment of a Worse Order"
    Temperament, Psychosexual Misidentification, and the
    Refuge of Private Life   107

7   On Creating a Usable Culture   134

    Notes   143

    References   175

    Index   193

Acknowledgments

For a small book, this one has taken a long time to complete, and many people have contributed to the process. I would like to thank first my co-researchers, Drs. Phyllis Herda and Lee Wallace, who were part of the Sexual Encounters Project funded by the Marsden Fund of New Zealand, which sponsored the research. My thanks also to the University of Auckland for the support and, especially, the leave from regular academic duties in order to research and write the book, and to the Department of Anthropology for subsidizing permissions and photographic reproductions. Dean of Arts John Morrow provided much needed last-minute clerical support. Carolyn and Terry Burke and Yvonne Marshall and Andrew Crosby accommodated me at various points in my research. Mike and Jo Molloy rescued me at a crucial moment. Thanks also to colleagues at the Centre for Research in Women's Studies and Gender Relations at the University of British Columbia, at which I wrote the original drafts of several chapters.

I appreciate the many archivists and librarians who assisted in finding the sources. Most especially, I am grateful for the help of the late Mary Wolfskill, who guided and encouraged me as she did many Mead scholars over the years. She is greatly missed. Librarians and archivists at the Alexander Turnbull Library, the London School of Economics, the American Philosophical Society, Vassar University, Columbia University, the University of Chicago, the University of California at Santa Cruz, and the Nebraska State Historical Society helped locate sources and photographs and smooth the way in obtaining permissions.

I would like to thank Mary Catherine Bateson and the Institute for Intercultural Studies for permission to quote from material and publish photographs held in the Margaret Mead papers at the Library of Congress and for speeding the processes of obtaining all the permissions needed, the London School of Economics for permission to quote from the papers of Bronislaw Malinowski, the American Philosophical Society for permission to quote from the papers of Franz Boas, Ms. Ann McLean and the Alexander Turnbull Library for permission to quote from the letters of Reo Franklin Fortune, Mr. Alan Kroeber for permission to quote from the letters of Alfred Kroeber, Professor Gerald D. Berreman of the University of California at Berkeley for permission to quote from the letters of Hortense Powdermaker, Columbia University for the photograph of Randolph Bourne and permission to publish it, the University of Chicago for permission to publish the photograph of W. F. Ogburn, the University of Pennsylvania for permission to publish the photograph of Van Wyck Brooks, Vassar University for permission to publish the photographs of Ruth Benedict and Franz Boas, Professor Ronald Hicks of Ball State University for permission to quote from the letters of Clark Wissler, and Mrs. Lucy Dos Passos Coggin for permission to quote from *1919* by John Dos Passos.

Many academic colleagues have read and commented on the work over the years. Thanks to Dolores Janiewski, Sharon Tiffany, Gerald Sullivan, Nancy Lutkehaus, Margaret Caffrey, Robert Kiste, my colleagues in the Social Anthropology Writing Group at the University of Auckland, and most especially to Judith Huntsman, without whom the book would not have been published.

Finally, I extend my deep appreciation to Doug Sutton, who encouraged and supported this work from initial application to final draft.

1 Introduction

THIS STUDY SEEKS to explain the shape of Margaret Mead's early popular ethnographies and the professional and popular responses to them as cultural phenomena. It asks the question: what was it in American culture between the wars that was articulated in Mead's early work in such a way as to secure it and her enduring place in the public imaginary? If Mead spoke to America, then just as surely America spoke to and through Mead. Thus, my focus is not on Mead's anthropology of the various indigenous groups she studied. Rather, I consider her de facto anthropology of America, a significant part of each of her early ethnographies, and the raison d'être for them all. "Who or what was this America?" is the question that informs this book. Running through Mead's work is a sustained commentary on the self and its relation to the larger society. It is one of the arguments of this study that the self as represented is not just any individual but is in some sense both an American self and the self of America.

In the first two decades of the twentieth century, as many writers have noted, there was a new self-consciousness of what it meant to be American.[1] What that nation/self might be or what it might become was the subject of much debate. Intellectuals and artists converged on New York City and began to explore the nature and meaning of culture in the United States, calling for the development of indigenous arts and literatures. By the 1920s, nativism, a new conservatism, modernism, new forms of religious fundamentalism, and a discourse of intellectual and artistic alienation all in some sense contested a definition of what America was and what it could or should be. The economic crisis of the 1930s intensified these debates, precipitating a reconsideration of many fundamentals, especially the economic system and its relation to democracy, freedom, prosperity, and what was by then a broader definition of culture. These contestations were explicitly about "America," and what shape, place, and direction individuals might assume in the country Gertrude Stein was to call "the mother of twentieth-century civilization."[2]

Within these contestations, issues of gender and sexuality loomed large.[3] The New Woman of the late nineteenth and early twentieth centuries, with her economic independence, her moral fervor to change the world, and her implicit sexual "inversion," was superseded in the 1920s by women such as Mead and Amelia Earhart. These new New Women were trumpeted as able to perform in male domains while remaining, publicly at least, intrinsically feminine in their deportment. However, even these earnest, achieving New Women were in some sense anachronistic by the time they appeared, being, if not quite displaced, then certainly supplemented by a new female figure, the flapper. Trenchantly heterosexual, hedonistic, amoral, and dismissive of rather than opposed to traditional moral regimes, the flapper posed a different kind of challenge to the social order than had the New Woman. While the latter often stepped aside from domesticity to pursue the higher ends of the modern self—autonomy and worthy pursuits—the flapper flaunted the moral order, pursuing instead sex and fun, albeit with the ultimate aim of marriage.

And it was not only definitions of the feminine that were undergoing change, although it is these that tend to be emphasized in the academic literature. Cultural commentary after 1910 and in the 1920s was characterized in particular by a critique of "business America" with its obsessive pursuit of money and material ends, standardization of consumer goods, forms of work and leisure, and machine-driven economy. Male intellectuals and artists, while repudiating the de-individualizing trends of industrial capitalism, struggled to find new definitions of masculinity in a country that, they felt, defined art as a woman's pastime and scholarship as effete. Nina Miller has argued that "the most visible experience of the situation we are calling modern was one of male crisis, and the most quintessentially modern response was a clearly marked style of masculinity, . . . more as a sense of anxious bewilderment than glib mastery." [4] Feminine incursions into traditional male arenas of work and the more marginal and risky forms of leisure, such as jazz clubs and speakeasies, exacerbated masculine anxieties.

New ideas about sex and its relations to freedom were central to this destabilizing of gender roles and definitions. The centrality of sex to selfhood was consolidated theoretically in the first decades of the twentieth century and almost simultaneously disseminated and absorbed into popular culture. The burgeoning science of sex, promulgated most famously in the writings of Havelock Ellis and Sigmund Freud, legitimated discussion of these issues and provided analytic frameworks that spilled out of the medical literature and into intellectual, middlebrow, and popular culture. The New Woman and the flapper were contentious figures, not just because they challenged traditional notions of female behavior but because they were also seen to be casting off unhealthy repressions that led to maladjustments, complexes, and neuroses. America, already characterized by its various mind-cure religions, cults, and therapies, took up psychoanalysis with a vengeance.[5]

While numerous scholars have explored the role of psychoanalysis and psychology in framing cultures of modernity and the meanings of modern selfhood in the twentieth century,[6] the formation and impact of the other social sciences has received less attention. Studies of anthropology have tended to focus on that discipline's formation in and complicity with earlier phases of Euro-American imperialism and colonialism. Yet anthropology and anthropologists, especially in the eastern United States, were centrally engaged in debates about the nature and meaning of modern life. Elsie Clews Parsons, Franz Boas, Ruth Benedict, and Edward Sapir, each a mentor of Mead, participated in vigorous, not to say ferocious, debates in nonacademic venues about the meanings of domesticity, sexuality, race, and culture. Of these three, only Parsons has had her life and work definitively studied in terms of her location in and contribution to emergent modernity and modernism.[7] Micaela di Leonardo's *Exotics at Home* examines Mead's and other anthropologies in the context of emerging American modernity. However, while di Leonardo devotes considerable space to Mead's work and, like many others, points to her inconsistencies and to gaps in her scholarship, she falls on one side of the all too common dichotomy of Mead scholarship—hagiography versus excoriation. Her conclusion, that "Mead spent a half-century lecturing Americans and others on changing cultural patterns while sedulously avoiding dealing with the harsh realities of power, discrimination, oppression, exploitation,"[8] leaves the reader wondering whether an anthropology of Mead might not try to understand Mead as being at least as much a product of her time as she was a (deficient) moral agent for American imperialism.

It is somewhat ironic that the only other major attempts to deal with the relationship between American modernism and anthropology come out of literary studies.[9] Most notably, these include Marc Manganaro's and Susan Hegeman's explications of the links between modernist poets, novelists, and critics, and anthropology. Manganaro, reading Bronislaw Malinowski, Ruth Benedict, and Zora Neale Hurston alongside T. S. Eliot, James Joyce, and the New Critics, traces "the development of the modern culture concept . . . as a complex whole," which can and should be read synchronistically, "with myth as a newly professional way of reading."[10] Susan Hegeman traces thematic links between the modernist fiction and poetry of T. S. Eliot, Sherwood Anderson, Hart Crane, and others, the cultural nationalist critics, such as Randolph Bourne, Van Wyck Brooks, and Waldo Frank, and the anthropological writings of Franz Boas, Edward Sapir, and Ruth Benedict, to argue that the idea of culture emerged in the first half of the twentieth century as an "estranged perception of collective identity," in which spatiality replaced temporality as a way of "explaining the specific experiences of alienation and difference Americans felt" under conditions of modernity.[11] Although their explications of the thematic resonances between anthropology and modernist literature are insightful, their focus on the texts misses the very fundamental anthropological point that there were real relationships, both temporal and social, among some of these authors and therefore among their texts. This is especially true of those whom Hegeman considers. Many of their social relationships centered on Columbia University. Bourne, who did his degree at Columbia, for example, was a close friend of both Brooks and Elsie Parsons before his death in 1918, and listed Boas as one of his favorite teachers.[12] Two decades later, the connections between the cultural critics and the anthropologists persisted: Mead's close friend Lawrence Frank had been a friend of Bourne at Columbia and continued to be a friend of Parsons. Brooks's protégé Constance Rourke was a student of Franz Boas. Brooks wrote his influential polemic *America's Coming of Age* twenty years before Ruth Benedict wrote *Patterns of Culture*, and she almost certainly read either the book itself or commentaries on it, or participated in discussions about it, perhaps even with Edward Sapir, to whose work Hegeman compares it. The thematic resonances between the texts Hegeman considers are more than the result of an abstracted developing modernism. They come out of a close set of discussions, sometimes face-to-face, sometimes via print, among a relatively small group of people passionately committed to developing and shaping "American culture."

Whereas Mead's teachers and mentors forayed into public debates, none but Mead made the intersection between social science and "middlebrow" culture the principle focus of their professional lives. She was virtually unique in picking up the educative mission from the older generation of anthropologists. As the discipline grew and institutionalized in the 1920s and 1930s, fewer of its members continued to see it in terms of contributing to the debates on contemporary American life. Mead alone located her work primarily in that space where, she believed, academic study could inform and improve everyday life. From the beginning of her career she was committed to educating "professionals"—especially social workers and teachers. Her third[13] academic publication, written when she was twenty-six and newly returned from Samoa, set out the agenda for her career, an agenda which, as far as I can tell, did not change much for the next fifty years: "By the study and analysis of the diverse solutions which other members of the human race have applied to the problems which confront us today, it is possible to make a more reasoned judgment of the needs of our own society. . . . Only by giving the students in normal schools and teachers' colleges the very best equipment for thinking about social problems can we hope to have teachers who will give their pupils a ground-work for constructive thought instead of a series of rules of thumb."[14] Although she is commonly identified as an anthropologist, until the early 1930s she saw her work as comparative psychology and education. In 1927, for example, she wrote William Fielding Ogburn that anthropology was "just something to think with. I'd be as happy in psychology or any other social sciences, or anything that was good to think with."[15] Throughout her career, her study of so-called primitive peoples was always couched in terms of what the modern West—especially the United States—could learn from their example.[16] The subtitle of *Coming of Age in Samoa* says it all: *A Study of Primitive Youth for Western Civilization*. Although not unique among her anthropological peers in writing for the popular media, she gained a unique position as the arbiter of this particular academic discipline in the public sphere, a position she made for herself and secured in the years covered by this study.

To locate Mead's work in its intellectual and cultural milieu and to ask what issues in American life it addressed and, perhaps more importantly, with what concerns it resonated, is simply to address Mead's writings as cultural artifacts—to anthropologize them. This is not a new kind of work. Libraries are full of texts that do this with writers of fiction, poetry, plays, and film. And, indeed, in the reading about the period between the wars, which has informed this study, I have often found studies of poetry and fiction more useful and have certainly found them more plentiful than studies of other kinds of writings contextualized in this way. It has been one of the recurrent disappointments in my reading that each time I found a text that purported to address "writers" or "woman writers" of the twenties and thirties, the term "writer" almost inevitably meant either novelist or poet. It seldom meant journalist or social scientist, of whom the twentieth century produced a number who are notable, influential, and, not incidentally, good writers. This abiding distinction between "literature" and "science," fiction and fact, is not, of course, innocent. As James Clifford reminds us, "[s]ince the seventeenth century . . . Western science has excluded certain expressive modes from its legitimate repertoire: rhetoric (in the name of 'plain,' transparent signification), fiction (in the name of fact), and subjectivity (in the name of objectivity). The qualities eliminated from science were localized in the category of 'literature.'"[17]

One of the curious features of the "new interdisciplinarity" engendered by the fluorescence of cultural studies is how seldom the objects of knowledge, the "data," or the modes of analysis cross disciplinary lines. A quick search of the literature on "the nation," for example, reveals that this object of knowledge has been more or less captured by literary and film studies. Novels, poems, plays, and films are examined to reveal the ways in which nation is inscribed in the fictive or creative texts of a particular time and place. The social sciences remain as cultural studies' necessary but repressed Other: necessary because cultural studies depends utterly on the detailed empirical work of historians and social scientists for "context," and repressed because that dependence is seldom acknowledged theoretically and because the privileged position of "literature" as the carrier of culture remains virtually unchallenged. There are very few studies that consider nonfiction authors as "writers" whose texts merit the same careful attention to image, theme, metaphor, strategy, and context. In the social sciences, anthropology and anthropologists have constituted a notable exception to this rule. James Clifford, George Marcus, and Clifford Geertz, in their important and controversial books, began examining the writerly accomplishment of ethnographic authority.[18] A couple of throwaway lines on Mead in *Works and Lives,* in conjunction with Derek Freeman's attacks on her work, have spawned a series of articles on her writerly craft and rhetorical strategies.[19] Mead, who had early aspirations towards poetry and fiction, regarded herself as a serious writer and crafted her books and articles with a keen ear for rhythm and eye for image. Her conflation of the modes of science, literature, and journalism was a reason for both her popular success and the ambivalence and hostility with which many of her professional colleagues regarded her work. The quality of her prose aroused suspicion, if not wrath, in the hearts of her fellow anthropologists, who are reported to have commented on her status as a "novelist" or "artist" rather than scientist.[20] It is therefore fitting that Mead's work should be contextualized in terms of her writerly strategies: because she regarded herself as a writer; because the intersection between "science" and "the public" was the locus of her work; and because she challenged the modernist boundaries between science, literature, and journalism while simultaneously depending on these same boundaries to maintain her public authority.

The entanglements of author, reader, and the culture or cultures within which they operate and to which they speak are not straightforward. The death of the author, to paraphrase Mark Twain, has been greatly exaggerated. Mead's works cannot be read without attention to authorial intent. She was, above all, a self-styled and self-conscious public intellectual who wrote for "ordinary people" and for change. In addition to being a molder of popular ideas, she was an avid consumer of intellectual public culture. She was a passionate reader of poetry and a distinctly anthropological reader of novels, which, as we shall see, often stood in for ethnography of the contemporary West in her work. But above all she relished the many little magazines that flourished in New York in this period, and her letters from the field repeatedly beg her family and friends to send them to her. Unlike many of her peers, who were actively distancing themselves from the nonacademic presses in order to reinforce the boundaries between journalism and science, Mead not only wrote extensively for a variety of magazines but also mined them for the themes of her work. Although most noted for her engagement with issues of adolescence and sexual identity, she wove many of the other debates of the 1920s and 1930s—about materialism, the role of the intellectual, the standardization of American society, the need for strong leadership in crisis—through her writings in remarkable coincidence with the shifting concerns of the times.

Even as this book explores Mead's handling of those concerns, it also tracks a change in her theorization, which paralleled a significant shift in the meaning of "America" and "American" during the interwar years. Ostensibly focused on the "native," each of her early studies provides a template for Mead's version, and vision, of America, and this changed significantly over the ten years covered here. This change is tied to Mead's developing theory of the relationship between personality and culture. Over this period Mead's theoretical position moved from an overriding insistence on cultural determinism to an emphasis on how "basic" temperaments fare in different cultures. Although a number of scholars have noted that "Boasians, Mead included, did not deny biology as much as they wanted to know 'the exact conditions that biology imposed,'" [21] the change in emphasis from culture to biology between *Coming of Age* and *Sex and Temperament* is striking. Furthermore, the movement begins to emerge well before the trip to New Guinea, during Mead's fieldwork among the Omaha in the summer of 1930. This change in the charting of the relationship between "culture" and "selfhood" parallels a wider set of complex shifts and contradictions in the meanings of "self," "culture," "identity," and ultimately "nationhood" that were occurring in the United States at the time.

The philosopher Charles Taylor has identified two conflicting themes that underpin the modern subject—a "disengaged, particular self, whose identity is constituted in memory." [22] One theme, which I have called *eventuation,* sees "the shape of a life simply the *result* of . . . happenings as they accumulate." The second, which I call *actualization,* sees "this shape as something already latent, which emerges through what comes to pass." As Taylor explains, both understandings of the shape and meaning of an individual life are inescapable: "We are made what we are by events; and as self-narrators, we live these through a meaning which the events come to manifest or illustrate." [23] This tension between eventuation and actualization ramifies through many of the discursive forms of modernity, underpinning the emergence of both the novel and the autobiography. However, it also pervades the social sciences, not least through the many nature-versus-nurture debates that have been central to the disciplines of anthropology, education, sociology, and psychology. *Coming of Age in Samoa,* of course, was a pivotal text in this debate, seen as coming down wholly on the side of nurture, culture, or event rather than essence, nature, or biology.

This discursive framing of the self, conflicted between event and essence, ramifies far beyond the discussions of the person, or personal subjectivity. Modern notions of selfhood or subjectivity arose in conjunction with broader historical and symbolic changes. The idea of the nation itself was constituted in the same sets of changes in the meanings and chartings of time and space, which Taylor, following Benedict Anderson, identifies as central to modern selfhood.[24] These include preoccupations with origins, with unity and the repression of difference, with boundaries and interiority. This imbrication of nation and self has spawned an array of scholarly works that have explored the ways in which the nation is narrated, revealing not only the overlapping forms between novel and nation but also the ways in which the story of the nation is told and retold at least as much, and perhaps much more effectively, in literature as it is in history books. One of the considerable pleasures of contemporary cultural scholarship has been the charting of the ways in which expressions of selfhood—subjectivity, ethnicity, sexual identity, for example—not only emerged through a similar set of narrative forms—novel, history, psychoanalysis—but also share their structures.

It is not surprising, then, that thematic struggle between essence and event in modern selfhood shapes also the meanings of nationhood. Between the wars in the United States, this struggle coalesced in the seemingly opposed ideas of "race" and "culture." In the social sciences, these ideas have been seen as more diametrically opposed than their intertwined histories would suggest. Robert Young has demonstrated that all three modern meanings of culture—a general process of intellectual, spiritual, and artistic development; the way of life of particular peoples; and the realm of intellectual and artistic activity—arise together out of the conflictual economy of capitalism. Furthermore, he argues that each is implicated in the meaning of the other and that all three are implicated in the simultaneous development of notions of race.[25] When Boas introduced the modern anthropological concept of culture in *The Mind of Primitive Man* in 1911 to signal a neutral equivalence of the ways of life of all peoples, the word was already hopelessly entangled with notions of racial hierarchy. The qualifier—primitive—already undercut Boas's antiracist agenda. This entanglement between culture as way of life, on the one hand, and race, on the other, mirrored the more obvious class hierarchy intrinsic to the meaning of culture as the "higher arts." The two meanings of culture grew out of the first and earlier meaning, "a general process of intellec-

Franz Boas, photograph courtesy of Vassar University Library

tual, spiritual and aesthetic development"[26] and, when held together rather than opposed to each other, they collapse again into it, each being an implicit hierarchy that privileges higher or greater development along some line of progression.

If culture and race have always been mutually implicating, the ways in which they are entangled are complex and changing. Indeed, Young argues that their very entanglement, complexity, and contradictions ensure their durability. Even those scientific theories most directly aimed at severing the links end up reinforcing them. Walter Benn Michaels contends that such a reinforcing process was occurring in the United States in the 1920s. In his study of American nativism in the 1920s, *Our America,* he explicates the shifting meanings of race and culture, essence and event, heredity and history, in the meanings of "America" and

"American." He argues that "American" changed in meaning over the course of the 1920s, away from something that was achieved (through immigration, naturalization, assimilation, hard work, etc.) towards something much more akin to race or biology or family—something into which one was born or that one inherited. This argument itself is not revolutionary. However, Michaels argues something more profound: changes in the notion of culture, and the emergence of associated ideas of cultural identity and cultural relativism were central to this change. These latter ideas depend on a prior notion of "race," however broadly construed. He argues that by the end of the 1920s, "culture" had become disarticulated from "beliefs and practices," a change he describes as "*deriving* one's beliefs and practices *from* one's cultural identity" instead of "*equating* one's beliefs and practices *with* one's cultural identity."[27] The former means that culture is no longer what one does, thinks, or believes but has become something separate from the self and indeed from the social group. Culture became something that could be destroyed, lost, stolen, just as it could be found or reclaimed. Culture is thus objectified: "We are not Jews because we do Jewish things, we do Jewish things because we are Jews."[28] Given this formulation, culture and cultural identity also can ultimately be claimed only through some form of inheritance, which ultimately must be construed as "biological" or "racial."

While one could take issue with Michaels's history of the notion of culture (Young might argue that what Michaels identifies as a development or trajectory is simply a chicken-and-egg problem), the implications of the changes he charts have yet to be explored in terms of anthropology itself. American anthropology was, of course, central to the formulation of "culture" and "cultural relativism" during the 1920s and 1930s. The equivalent value of all cultures, and thus of all humans, is an idea that received its most articulate theoretical expression through the work of Franz Boas and the anthropologists he trained at Columbia University. It developed precisely in opposition to racist assumptions of the biological inferiority of some peoples that had been one of the outcomes of imperialist applications of Darwin's theory of evolution. The centrality of anthropology to this process is curiously muted in Michaels's book. He ignores Mead's work, relegates Boas to a long footnote, and cites only Edward Sapir's essay "Culture: Genuine or Spurious"[29] from among the vast array of anthropological texts that contributed to the theorization of culture during the decade. However, Mead's writings were much more directly formative than were Sapir's in the wider scheme of things. Indeed, they were arguably the most central empirical texts that shaped popular ideas on culture and cultural relativism, and, not incidentally, shaped how these issues related to the personal lives of Americans during these two decades and beyond.[30] In this, they were supplemented, but not surpassed, by the best-selling *Patterns of Culture*, by her friend Ruth Benedict.[31] If Manganaro and Hegeman are concerned with the "modern culture concept," with a focus on texts that circulated within rarified or professional fields, then this book is more closely aligned with Michaels's in its emphasis on something less well defined than a concept: how the modernist ideas about culture were transformed into vernacular understandings of culture through the vehicle of Mead's work. It is striking, therefore, to find in Mead's work the very shift in emphasis from eventuation (culture) to actualization (temperament, thwarted or actualized, but not modified, by culture) that Michaels identifies in his study of nativist literature and polemics of the 1920s.

Issues of sex and gender were central to the development of racial ideas and

Ruth Benedict, photograph courtesy of Vassar University Library

theories. From Anderson's argument that ideas of race developed from class and aristocratic notions of blood, Young and Michaels, and also Ann Laura Stoler,[32] Anne McClintock,[33] and many others, have demonstrated the pervasive and multiple links between these two ideational formations. Anxieties about hybridity, degeneration, and race suicide[34] mingled with fantasies of the harem and the South Sea Isle to produce inextricable inter-implications of a sexualized racism and a racialized sexuality. But what of culture? If race and culture are mutually dependent, then what are the implications of gender, sex, and sexuality in the formation of modern notions of culture? Certainly, some aspects are obvious. Women had (and one might argue continue to have) an ambivalent relation to culture as refinement or the higher arts. They were excluded from being makers of high culture and considered unable to reach the highest plains of artistic, intellectual, and spiritual refinement. However, women served as gatekeepers to these realms, to the point where, in the United States, at least, high culture itself became viewed as feminized.[35] Modernist movements were impelled, at least in part, by men's attempts to claim or reclaim creative space and intellectual endeavor as legitimately masculine, not to say manly.[36] George Santayana's association of the "genteel tradition" with Puritanism provided a fruitful and ongoing target for young moderns.[37] Seeing themselves caught between the feminized repression of New England gentility, the anti-intellectual pragmatism of an outdated pioneer mentality, and the de-skilling and de-individualizing (and thus emasculation) of the machine age, modernist men from Herbert Croly and Van Wyck Brooks to Waldo Frank and H. L. Mencken sought to create a new meaning for (high) culture as the redemptive realm of modernity, and as fit work for men. It is not surprising then that the tables were turned and, as Andreas Huyssen has demonstrated, mass culture was consistently represented as feminized in cultural, political, and aesthetic discourse of the early decades of the twentieth century.[38]

The associated advents of a professional anthropology and a respectable psychology provide a crucial link in understanding the relationships between culture (as way of life) and sex. Descriptions of sexual practices had been, since the Enlightenment at least, a necessary, if not obsessive, part of the reports of non-Western peoples, signaling ambivalently their liberation from the constraints of civilization, or their degraded primitive status.[39] By the time Boas articulated the idea of culture as the way of life of a particular people, the meaning of culture had been pre-loaded, so to speak, with sex. The New Psychology, psychoanalysis, provided the theoretical link between a primitivism already well entrenched in modernist (high) arts and cultures as distinct ways of life. Freud's association of the primitive with the unconscious enabled associations between the child, the woman, and the primitive to be formally articulated to the unconscious as well. Culture, in its anthropological meaning, already saturated with sex, became simultaneously a marker of a pre-civilized sexual freedom and a contemporary constraint on that freedom. Elsie Clews Parsons's teachings and writings on the family, marriage, and sex were important in bringing anthropology into the public intellectual debates on these issues. But it was Mead, arguably, who is most responsible for widely consolidating the anthropological notion of culture with variability in sexual practices, in the United States at least.

Mead's popular ethnographies of the 1920s and 1930s trace a trajectory of a progressive disillusionment with "culture," articulated through discussion of sexual practices. In *Coming of Age in Samoa,* culture signifies the possibilities for change or for more-fulfilling ways of life.[40] However, in *Growing Up in New Guinea,* Mead represents culture both as inhibiting change and freedom, and as perverse to the extent that it develops, then fails to capitalize on, individual strengths.[41] Mead's disillusionment, not with individual cultures but with "culture" itself, deepened in the summer of 1930, which she spent researching the lives of Omaha women in Nebraska. Frustrated by the "social tragedy" she observed, Mead struggled, unsuccessfully, with the effects of America's internal colonization. Hampered by a model of culture as a unified, functionally integrated "whole," she was unable to come to terms with the social havoc she found in Nebraska in any way that made sense in terms of her imperative to find lessons for America. Her private correspondence began to consider the question of temperament as separate from the influences of culture. In the introduction to *The Changing Culture of an Indian Tribe,* she defines a focus on "the relationship between original nature and social environment" as one of two principle contributions of ethnology to social science.[42] A prolonged personal crisis in New Guinea between 1931 and 1933 consolidated this move. Temperament, not culture, emerges as the privileged element in her work from this period. In *Sex and Temperament in Three Primitive Societies,* culture is fully articulated as that which creates deviance by not allowing individual, innate temperament to develop according to its natural predilections and potentialities.[43]

This book, then, examines these themes in Mead's four early "popular" ethnographies, the related articles that drew on this ethnographic material, and the anthropological, critical, and popular responses to her work. It explicates how her writings reflected the intellectual debates and social milieux in the period 1925–1935. Mead was, by anyone's measure, an incredibly productive writer.[44] In the years 1925–1935, which are the focus of this book, she published seven monographs (writing three between mid-1929 and mid-1931 alone) and seventy-seven articles and book reviews in the academic, elite, and popular presses. Although this book is structured around her four general ethnographies, they stand as a gloss for the many shorter articles that she wrote for the popular, middlebrow, and academic presses. Indeed, to understand both the meanings that Mead gave to her work, and the meanings that might have been inferred from them, these articles must be taken as central to Mead's project and the response to it.[45] The monographs include the three for which she is best known—*Coming of Age in Samoa* (1928), *Growing Up in New Guinea* (1931), and *Sex and Temperament in Three Primitive Societies* (1935). Each of these went through between twelve and seventeen editions by the time she died in 1978, and each was translated into between twelve and twenty other languages.[46] She also wrote three much more orthodox anthropological treatises, at least one of these in order to prove to her anthropological colleagues that she could do "real" anthropology—that is, kinship, economics, and material culture.[47] The seventh, *The Changing Culture of an Indian Tribe*, her only non-Pacific monograph of that period, was written for quite a different reason: impelled by a grant to Mead's employer, the American Museum of Natural History. It occupies a peculiar position in her oeuvre—unusual in its provenance, unsure of its audience. It is included in this study for two reasons: because it was during her fieldwork with the Omaha that she began to formulate her theory of the relationship among temperament, personality, and culture, and because of its failure to ignite the popular imagination. It is the "other" to her more widely known works and as such tells us much about their popularity.

In encapsulating dilemmas of American selfhood, Mead's reputation among her professional peers as a "lady novelist" can perhaps be put to the test, not in terms of the facticity of her ethnography but in terms of her writerly strategies. If, as Taylor insists, the modern self is experienced and constituted as a "story," then Mead was a consummate storyteller. A good story has two aspects—a compelling plot and engaging characters. The plot of Mead's stories is the most compelling story of all—the self's transition from childhood to adulthood, and the struggles that shape that transition.[48] Each of her books addresses in some way those twin obsessions of modernity: how we have become what we are, and how we might become what we should be.

That this transition is focused on the child is something we have come to take for granted. But the modern investments in the child—as the quintessential form of the self, as the carrier of the history of the species, as the repository of innocence—have their own histories.[49] Carolyn Steedman uses the notion of "personification" to detail how "the figure of the child" came, over the period 1780 to 1930, to stand for or carry the meanings of "the self." Personification, "the giving of human shape to abstract ideas and notions,"[50] is stronger and more intrinsic than metaphor, more condensed and historical than archetype. I draw on Steedman's idea of personification to argue that Mead's most popular ethnographies were compelling at least in part because she built each one around a central character—a personification of the self's journey from childhood to adulthood. In these cases, the self is not necessarily female, as is Steedman's child figure, but in the three books that had popular success, the central figure is a child struggling towards adulthood. The Samoan girl, the Manus boy, and, more complexly, the deviant in *Sex and Temperament,* were each forged to highlight the dilemmas of selfhood Mead was addressing. Not quite archetypes, these figures personified a problem of "coming into being" not only in their own culture but more importantly in America. And it was not just American individuals who were struggling to "come into being" but also the nation itself. The Indian woman in *The Changing Culture of an Indian Tribe* is a complex exception; ironically, she is much more adult and culpable, and this may be one factor in the book's notable lack of popular success. However, she is a strongly delineated character type and as such gives a particular focus to the story of degeneration Mead penned in relation to the "Antlers." Sex is the lynchpin in each of these narratives of the relationship between self and culture: it epitomizes the essential status of the protagonist. The free love of the Samoan girl, the repressed Puritanism of the Manus boy, the disordered delinquency of the Antler woman, and the heroic struggle of the deviant caught in an alien culture condense and signify the relation of the individual to his or her society.

If the strength of Mead's books lies in her ability to take the foundational plot of the modern self and give it character, then the key to their reception is in the extent to which they held out hope. In all her work, but most particularly in *Sex and Temperament,* Mead drew on an aspect of the self that many theorists have identified but that has been eclipsed by other emphases in contemporary theory. This is the notion of modern selfhood as a constant state of development, an always coming into being. Each of her books tells the story of a particular coming into being. This emphasis not only on origins but on potentials is the aspect of Mead's work that most clearly addressed American concerns. For what Mead held out to America was, ultimately, a promise—that life could be better, that fulfillment was possible, that humanity had already crafted the cultures that allowed humans to develop in a variety of ways, and that these ways could be incorporated into American life.

The next chapter of this book describes the intellectual debates that provided the basic framework for Margaret Mead's writing during the period 1925–1935, and, indeed, set the character of her lifelong educative mission. Termed variously "the New York renaissance," or the "cultural nationalist movement," or even, "the beginnings of American modernism," these debates were prompted by the desire to create an indigenous arts and letters in the United States that would remedy what were perceived to be the ills that beset it: materialism, Puritanism, the Frontier Mentality,[51] alienation, chaos, lack of integration, lack of higher purpose, and discontinuity between America's industrial power and the state of its culture—a concept, of course, that had not yet been fully articulated into its present-day meanings. This debate was influenced by the advent of psychoanalysis after Freud's visit to Clark University in 1911. From that point, the tensions between therapeutic liberation of the self and the impetus towards socially meaningful cultural creation marked the debates on the problem of American culture in distinctive ways. Mead was to draw on both these tendencies in American cultural criticism to formulate the lessons she drew in her books.

Coming of Age in Samoa (1928), written and published at the height of the Roaring Twenties, is the focus of chapter 3. Mead took that most problematic figure of the twenties—the "flapper"—and asked whether she was a cultural or a natural phenomenon. *Coming of Age* was a spectacular success; both its publisher and its author were amazed by its reception. The reasons for this success are to be found in the way Mead encapsulated 1920s ambivalences about progress and loss, science and communal values, the possibilities for happiness and the superiorities of civilization in its story. The Samoan girl, and indeed Samoa itself, represents the sort of society of which cultural theorists such as Herbert Croly and Van Wyck Brooks had dreamed: one in which "[t]he individual becomes a nation in miniature, ... [and t]he nation becomes an enlarged individual."[52] As such a representation, Mead's Samoan girl, sexually free and without any value conflicts, epitomizes the loss ensuing from civilization. In Freudian terms she represents the pre-oedipal self that is whole, without repression, innocent and undamaged. She stands in marked contrast to the flapper, who epitomized not only loss of innocence but also loss of unity between the individual and the community.

Chapter 4 examines the second of Mead's ethnographies, *Growing Up in New Guinea* (1931), a product of the cusp of the prosperous twenties and the Depression. Mead's grasp of both her ethnographic material and the New York intellectual milieu is much surer than it was in *Coming of Age*. *Growing Up in New Guinea* is a mature and self-conscious work that traverses a wide range of issues, most of which come out of the agonized self-conceptions of 1920s intellectual and artistic life. The book hinges on a crisis in masculinity: not the self-deprecating masculinity of the Algonquin Round Table or the womanizing freedom of Greenwich Village[53] but the paralyzed masculinity of the businessman, sexually repressed, conformist, indebted, trapped. These themes of the 1920s are, however, articulated around the crisis of the early 1930s. In particular, the calls for strong, innovative leadership to guide the country back to prosperity were becoming increasingly desperate as businessmen and politicians were revealed as incompetent, helpless, ineffectual, and corrupt. The Manus boy, in his transition from lively, free, and intelligent boyhood to sexually repressed, miserable, indebted adulthood, provided a mirror for America at the beginning of the Depression. Mead wove these themes together to argue for a new masculinity that was strong, nurturing, and innovative, and unafraid to go against prevailing cultural mores.

The Changing Culture of an Indian Tribe (1932), the most anomalous of Mead's books, is the subject of chapter 5. It is her least well known work, being located in the American Midwest, far from her usual ethnographic locus in the Pacific. It received little public attention when it was first published and little academic attention subsequently. It provides a compelling contrast to the exoticized and eroticized "natives" of the other three ethnographies. Mead, whose Pacific ethnographies are marked by denial of Euro-American imperialism's effects, was unable to refute colonization's impact on the "Antlers." The book's reception reflects both the difficulties America had in coming to terms with its internal empire and Mead's dismissal of the study's usefulness for anthropology because the culture was "broken." By the early 1930s, Mead had embraced a functionalism drawing on both British anthropological influences and the Young American cultural critics' yearning for an integrated, un-alienated society. She used William Ogburn's influential notion of "cultural lag" to argue that the problem with Antler society was that it clung to traditional values even as its material base had changed drastically under the influence of European settlement. The Antler woman—diseased, sexually delinquent, yet clinging to and guarding traditional culture—was a frightening metaphor for the breakdown of American civil society in the early 1930s, when both socialist revolution and fascism were being touted in the intellectual and popular media. In many ways it is the best of Mead's early works, but its message is bleak. It was praised by her anthropological colleagues but passed over quickly at the nadir of the Depression and in the decades that followed.

Sex and Temperament in Three Primitive Societies, the focus of chapter 6, is a child of the New Deal, a reconstructive project not only for America but also for Mead herself. This book is closer in tone to *Coming of Age in Samoa* than it is to the hectoring faultfinding tone of *Growing Up in New Guinea* or the depressive, hopeless tone of *The Changing Culture of an Indian Tribe.* Mead's return to a call for openness to individual needs and aspirations, a liberality of culture, and flexibility in gender definitions was a tonic for America as it began to pull itself out of the crisis. After a prolonged period of depression, illness, and emotional break-down in New Guinea, Mead determined to have a child and build a family life, seeing that as the "private solace" of those who were in other ways unable to come to terms with their culture's restrictive gender roles. The book describes the gender roles of three societies, which fortuitously provide the most salient contrasts for America. Its true focus, however, is on the "deviant" within each culture—the person whose innate temperament set him or her at odds with the cultural expectations of his or her society. It is a story of how culture perverts the potential of individuals, but much more importantly it is a tale of individual survival against cultural and social odds. It is a message of endurance in the face of adversity, and its call for ongoing cultural change to foster individual potential was, like that of her other books, a message of the times.

Finally, chapter 7 ties together these themes, arguing that Mead's turn to a more essential version of the self in relation to culture was intimately connected to two "absences." The first is her lack of any endogenous or nuanced theory of the genesis of human variation, such as a more rigorous understanding of psychoanalytic theory might have afforded. The second is her implicit belief in the existence of homogenous, integrated, smoothly functioning cultures not subject to internal processes of change. Thus, Mead lacked, at the level of both the individual and the socio-cultural, any theory of endogenous change. Therefore, variation in human "personality" or responses to life could generally be found only in that realm she understood to be outside history and outside culture—that is, biology. I go on to argue that it is fortunate that Mead did not publish or further pursue (except in private) her "squares" theory of human types. Rather, she re-emerged into the public sphere after Bali and the Second World War as a major force for a cosmopolitan, democratic ethic. This was to be her enduring legacy.

2 The Problem of American Culture

TRADITIONAL HISTORIOGRAPHY COLLAPSES the decades from 1919 to 1939 into a general "between-the-wars" time span or differentiates this period into the Roaring Twenties and the Hungry Thirties. As a frame for understanding the cultural history of the United States and Margaret Mead's role within it, neither periodization works particularly well. Although her work under consideration here spans only a decade, its intellectual roots must be traced back two decades to the beginnings of what has been called the cultural-nationalist movement in the United States. If one comes backwards, as I did, from Mead's writing to the critical writings on American culture in the second and third decades of the twentieth century, it is remarkable the extent to which the America, and indeed the native peoples, that she presents in her early books are to be found there fully formed. For it was the debates around the poverty and paucity of American culture, arts, and literature that provided Mead with the analyses on which she hung her comparisons between "natives" and "Americans."

Various dates can be set for the beginnings of this long debate on the state of American culture, but for the purposes of this book, the years 1909 and 1911 are crucial to understanding Mead's intellectual influences. The first saw two important events: Sigmund Freud's visit to Clark University[1] and the publication of Herbert Croly's Progressive manifesto, *The Promise of American Life*.[2] Two years later, in 1911, Franz Boas published his first book of popular anthropological writing, *The Mind of Primitive Man*, the first time the idea of culture as distinct lifeways appears in his writing.[3] Also that year, the philosopher George Santayana gave a landmark lecture at the University of California at Berkeley. Entitled "The Genteel Tradition in American Philosophy," it set the terms for the debate on American culture for many years to come.[4] And in the same year, Randolph Bourne, then an adult student at Columbia University, published a series of articles in the *Atlantic Monthly* and the *Columbia Monthly* that were subsequently collected and published under the title *Youth and Life*.[5] The rethinking of America around the idea of culture had begun.

The publicity around Freud's visit precipitated a widespread and rapid diffusion of psychoanalytic theory into professional, intellectual, artistic, and popular culture. It can fairly be said that psychoanalysis had a major influence on both popular culture and intellectual agendas for at least the next twenty years. Sandford Gifford attributes its immense and almost immediate popularity to three factors: the nation's "therapeutic optimism," the Progressive era's environmentalist approach to social problems, and that era's coincident climate of sexual and political reform.[6] Another, more specific factor was the Mental Hygiene movement. Founded in 1908, the year before Freud's American lectures, this movement grew quickly into a powerful organization with privileged access to government funding and with influential physicians as its spokesmen. It characterized psychological problems as "structured within the individual, . . . medical in nature and . . . preventable through the practice of hygienic activities."[7] To these factors, John C. Burnham, the preeminent historian of psychoanalysis in the United States, adds America's preoccupation with "the latest, the newest, the most modern." He cites Leo Stein's statement that America felt less "attainted" by psychoanalysis. According to Stein, "We feel it as discoveries in a new and interesting field rather than as something that tears deeply at our vitals."[8]

The first explications in popular magazines appeared in *Good Housekeeping* and *Everybody's Magazine* in 1915.[9] In the same year, two books on psychoanalysis written for general readers, James Putnam's *Human Motives* and Edwin Holt's *The Freudian Wish*, were published.[10] Numerous articles and popular books followed, some written by physicians and trained psychoanalysts, some by amateurs cashing in on the trend. Novels and dramas that exposed the prevalence and dangers of "repression" and the miraculous cures that could be effected through analysis soon made their appearance. By 1924 the Mental Hygiene Association and other psychiatric organizations were being swamped with requests for books and information.[11] Throughout the 1920s, newspapers and mass-circulation magazines used terms such as "neuroses," "complexes," and "maladjustment," as if these "phenomena" were self-evident and the processes that generated them widely understood.

And what was generally understood to have caused them was repression—particularly, but not only, repression of sex. As Malcolm Cowley put it in his exegesis of "Greenwich Village doctrine": "We are unhappy because we are maladjusted, and maladjusted because we are repressed." The corollary was that "every law, convention or rule of art that prevents . . . the full enjoyment of the moment should be shattered and abolished."[12] Repression led to the second evil, which psychoanalysis was understood to have identified—"hidden motives." The uncovering of hidden motives and the removal of repression were held out as the keys to self-knowledge and freedom from constraints. Repression was broadly understood as social constraint, rather than the Freudian sense of the repression of the unacceptable desire for the mother that precipitates the formation of the unconscious. In a country where freedom had been the defining term for 150 years, it suddenly took on a new meaning—for freedom was now not just a political and economic right. It now meant health, well-being, "normalcy." Casting off repression was no longer just a personal pleasure: it became a social duty.

Herbert Croly's book, *The Promise of American Life*, was influential in a different way. Although it sold only seventy-five hundred copies, it had "immediate and extensive influence on what historians have come to call the Progressive era." [13] Thomas Bender calls Croly "the precursor of the modern intellectual in New York . . . [t]he youngest and most emancipated of the traditionalists . . . the oldest of the emergent young intellectuals." [14] For Croly, the strength of American democratic theory was that "[t]he people [are] to be trusted rather than suspected and disciplined. They must be tied to their country by the bond of self-interest. Give them a fair chance, and the natural goodness of human nature would do the rest. Individual and public interest will . . . coincide, provided no individuals are allowed to have special privileges." [15] However, Croly argued that the assumption that individual and public interest will coincide, an assumption that had made possible much of America's prosperity and freedom during the nineteenth century, no longer served the nation now that the continent had been fully explored, all "free" land had been claimed, and technological advances had rendered the Atlantic Ocean "merely a big channel." The new economic and political circumstances, he argued, meant that the material acquisitiveness and overweening individualism, which had served America well during its pioneering phase, had resulted in "a morally and socially undesirable distribution of wealth." [16] In order to realize "the promise of American life" this individualism had to give way to a self-subordinating discipline and commitment to social and also individual good. The sense of "glorious national destiny" must become a sense of "serious national purpose." [17] Croly envisaged a democracy that "would not only provide material welfare" but would create a culture that would consist of "an ardent and intelligent cultivation of the art of living." [18]

Although Croly's call to discipline and commitment to social good echoed so-called Puritan sentiments, his vision of the relationship between nation and individual, and in particular the central role of the artist and the intellectual in effecting this vision, touched the hearts and minds of the young cultural critics beginning to articulate the sense of alienation and social chaos that was to underpin social thought for the next twenty years. Challenging the separation of individual and state, he argued that true individualism, as opposed to mere competitive particularity in pursuit of money, will come about only if men develop exclusive but disinterested goals, through which they pursue excellence. In this way, each finds a special niche or function within the nation such that the distinction between national and individual interest disappears and "[t]he individual becomes a nation in miniature, . . . [and] [t]he nation becomes an enlarged individual."[19] In order to achieve this, he argued, the political and economic systems must be subject to more regulation, but the intellect must be set free, a formula that appealed to the young intellectuals who were beginning to argue for the development of an indigenous American cultural and intellectual life.

The book propelled Croly, until then the editor of the *Architectural Record*, into the center of the wealthy liberal-left circles of New York. In 1913 the heiress and social activist Dorothy Whitney Straight[20] and her husband, Willard, suggested he start a journal. Drawing on her circle of like-minded wealthy liberals (including Elsie Clews Parsons) Dorothy Straight raised the funds ($100,000 for the first year alone) needed to maintain the journal for five years until it could become self-sustaining, and personally underwrote the journal for much of the next twenty years, finally setting up a trust for its support in 1935.[21] Founded in 1914, the *New Republic* was one of the principle organs of Progressivism, supporting Roosevelt at first but switching to Wilson before the 1916 election. Its influence was at its peak during the early years of the Wilson administration, when it was regarded by some as an unofficial government organ. It published many of the influential American and English intellectuals of its day, including John Dewey, Van Wyck Brooks, Walter Lippman (a coeditor), and Randolph Bourne, and later, Lytton Strachey, Virginia Woolf, and Lewis Mumford.

Within two years of Freud's visit and the publication of Croly's book, the link between repression, Puritanism, and the state of the arts and literature in the United States erupted into a debate on American culture. In his lecture "The Genteel Tradition in American Philosophy," George Santayana described Americans as irrevocably split between "American Will" or "aggressive enterprise" and "American Intellect" or the "genteel tradition," the latter too rarified, convention-bound, and feminized to engage in the political and social issues at home and abroad.[22] Puritanism quickly became the bête noir of the cultural critics, even more responsible than Frederick Turner's Frontier Mentality for all that ailed the nation. The same year, Randolph Bourne began to publish a series of essays in which he decried the stultifying effects of Puritanism on the younger generation. Gathered into a book entitled *Youth and Life* in 1913, these essays became the first manifesto for youth.[23] Bourne castigated the older generations for mistaking moralizing for

Van Wyck Brooks, photograph courtesy of the University of
Pennsylvania Library

religion and for using ideals of duty and service to defend their intellectual lazi-
ness and self-interest. He exhorted the young to eschew duty, service, prudence,
and humility and ordered them, "Dare! Take risks." Radical, cultural criticism
had found a target—Puritanism. The cry went up for the young to create a daring,
new, and distinctively American arts and literature that would integrate individual
and society, politics, economics, and the arts—a big-C Culture that would enrich,
revolutionize, and integrate the small-c culture of daily life. A movement had been
born. Variously called the cultural critics, the Young Americans, the cultural nativists, the Lyrical Left, the 1915 generation, the driving intellectual force behind the
New York Little Renaissance, a group of young men centered in Greenwich Village, began to write prolifically and seriously about the state of American "culture"

and to propose new ways of articulating art and life. Their goal was eloquently expressed by Waldo Frank in the "Announcement to Authors" for the movement's more admired magazine, *Seven Arts:* "It is our faith and the faith of many that we are living in the first days of a renascent period, a time that means for America the coming of that national self-consciousness which is the beginning of greatness. In all such epochs the arts cease to be private matters, they become not only the expression of the national life but a means to its enhancement."[24] Bourne, a man of ferocious intellect, unceasing idealism, and uncompromising commitments, has been regarded, perhaps because he died so young, as the central intellect, and certainly the one whose most important writings have best stood the test of time. After finishing a degree at Columbia, where he studied with John Dewey, Frederick Woodbridge, and Charles Beard, in addition to Franz Boas, Bourne was awarded a fellowship to study town planning in Europe. Traveling there in 1913 and 1914, he was impressed by the egalitarianism and intellectualism of French culture, and the French concern for aesthetics. On the other hand, he was horrified and angered by England, which he characterized as a "stupid, blundering, hypocritical beast."[25] His experiences there reinforced his determination that young Americans must rid themselves of their colonial disposition to defer to England and Anglo-Saxon values. In Germany for the outbreak of war, Bourne was also disillusioned by the way in which young Germans rallied to the war, pouring into the streets and singing patriotic songs. This was not the youth he had idealized, a youth that would turn away from the cant of its elders and forge a new future.

Bourne returned, relieved, to New York, where he was soon hired by the *New Republic* and given the education and town-planning briefs. He was to develop considerable expertise and to write prolifically on these topics, especially on education. However, he remained frustrated in his ambitions to write on politics and literature. Despite his feeling of being sidelined, he published numerous book reviews, an important article on Matthew Arnold, and a series on "the university."[26] But he was becoming increasingly disillusioned by the magazine's backing for the Wilsonian agenda, particularly as the president began to attack immigrants and move towards a decision to enter the war.

Bourne is most noted for two, or perhaps three, articles written at the height of his powers, when, as Waldo Frank said, war had driven him sane.[27] The first is "Trans-National America," published in mid-1916 not in the *New Republic* or *Seven Arts* but in the magazine that had launched his career, *Atlantic Monthly.*[28] The second and third, which really make up a single argument, are "The War and the Intellectuals" and "The Twilight of the Idols," both published in *Seven Arts* in 1917.[29] These latter are a ferocious attack on the war and on the American

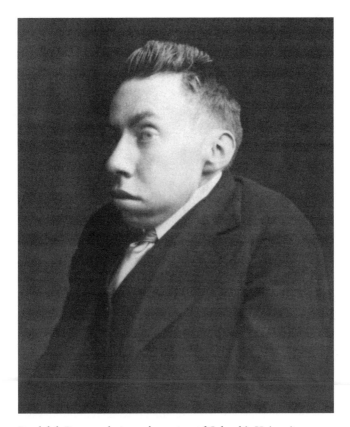

Randolph Bourne, photograph courtesy of Columbia University Library

intellectuals who rushed to justify and support it. The latter focuses especially on Dewey and the failure of his pragmatism to live up to the values that supposedly underpinned it. These articles, now widely cited, were responsible for the demise of *Seven Arts*, the withdrawal of Bourne's editorship of the *Dial* (insisted on by Dewey) and his complete marginalization in the *New Republic*, leading him to fear in the last months of his life that his ability to make a living by his pen was over.

There are two articles that stand out as prime influences on Mead; one seems to have provided the blueprint for her private life, the other for her public. The first is a chapter of *Youth and Life* entitled "The Experimental Life." Mary Esteve neatly sums up the particular fusion of disinterest and passion, aesthetics and politics, personal and public life that Bourne envisioned, espoused, and attempted to live:

On the one hand, the experimental life stands for "nonconformity," for "those who vary from the textbook rules of life" and whose "acts" are "new and very interesting hypotheses." Further, in this capacity experimental livers are favorably aligned with that which the world despises: "The world has never favored the experimental life. It despises poets, fanatics, prophets, and lovers." On the other hand, Bourne confers on the experimental life a markedly sober valence. Instead of celebrating as one might expect the passionate anti-conventional pursuit of fanatic experiment, Bourne characterizes the experimental disposition as "calm disinterestedness" and "detached enthusiasm," such as befits a person interested in "sports and games." Such a disposition is "unaffected by considerations of the end, and views the game as the thing." It is also the disposition of those who elect "to take life not with their naked fists, but more scientifically—to stand with mind and soul alert, ceaselessly testing and criticizing, taking and rejecting, poised for opportunity, and sensitive to all good influences."[30]

This ideal combination of reasoned, dispassionate scientific approach and willingness to experiment and take risks marks both Mead's personal and professional lives.

The other article that is most likely to have influenced Mead is "Trans-National America," now widely regarded as the foundational exposition of a cosmopolitan vision for the United States. "Trans-National America" is a critique both of the theory of the "melting pot" and of the growing xenophobia in the United States, unleashed by the country's entry into war. Wilson himself had lashed out at "hyphenated" Americans, avowing that "[a]ny man who carries a hyphen about him carries a dagger that he is ready to plunge into the vitals of this republic."[31] As a counter, Bourne argued that so-called hyphenated Americans were the nation's future and hope: "America is already the world-federation in miniature, the continent where for the first time in history has been achieved the miracle of hope, the peaceful living side by side, with character substantially preserved, of the most heterogeneous peoples under the sun."[32] It is thus unique in being "the first international nation," not a melting pot but an interweaving of the "threads of living and potent cultures."[33] America alone, therefore, had the potential, and indeed the duty, to lead the world in the cosmopolitan enterprise, using dual citizenship and the movement of its immigrant citizens back and forth between the United States and their natal lands to educate those nations that lag behind.

Bourne argued that America had the potential to lead the world in this regard because it was not weighted down with an indigenous tradition. Bourne noted, "In our loose, free country, no constraining national purpose, no tenacious folk tradition and folk-style hold the people to a line."[34] By casting aside the dominant but repressive Anglo-Saxon culture, America could develop a federation of cultures, preserving what was best of each national tradition while creating a new, fluid, living transnational culture and politics. For him, the Midwestern states of Wisconsin and Minnesota were the model. There German, Polish, and Scandinavian immigrants had "self-consciously labored to preserve their traditional culture" while contributing "wisdom, intelligence, industry and social leadership . . . to the greater glory and benefit, not only of themselves but of all the native 'Americanism' around them."[35] They had not been assimilated but had assimilated the Anglo-Saxon.

Bourne argued that America's lack of a unified history and culture was both a blessing and an opportunity. His experiences in Europe in 1913 and 1914 had convinced him of "the extraordinary toughness and homogeneity of the cultural fabric" of the countries he visited. Primed by Boas's anthropology, he emerged committed to take "each one with entire seriousness" and judge it "not in American terms, but in its own." However, he was also aware of the power and resistance to change that these "homogeneous" cultures represented.[36] He saw the absence of a tradition as enabling freedom rather than stifling the development of an indigenous American culture.

This position on the value of tradition was a point of friendly disagreement between Bourne and his friend Van Wyck Brooks. Brooks, educated at Harvard, but like Bourne a native of New Jersey, was also in search of a new articulation of American life and art. In 1913 Brooks republished his *Wine of the Puritans*. Originally issued by a vanity press in England in 1908, the book was largely ignored in the United States, except at Harvard, where it impressed the young T. S. Eliot, and possibly inspired George Santayana.[37] However, in the wake of Santayana's influential essays, there was now more-fertile ground for Brooks's thesis that all of American life was underpinned by a basic and crippling division. He argued that the Puritan tradition was like old wine in new bottles; when the bottle explodes under the pressure of new conditions, the material body of the wine falls to the ground, while the aroma passes into the air. "The aroma, or the ideal, turns into transcendentalism, and the wine, or the real, becomes commercialism." "In any case," he commented wryly, "one doesn't preserve a great deal of well-tempered genial wine."[38]

Brooks was to pursue this dichotomous characterization of America for most of his life, but undoubtedly his most famous dualism organizes his most influential work, *America's Coming of Age*,[39] published two years later at the height of the New York Renaissance. In this work, Brooks argued that America was caught between two modes of thinking and living, which he characterized as highbrow and lowbrow. For Brooks, this distinction permeated all phases of life: "Between university ethics and business ethics, between American culture and American humor, between Good Government and Tammany, between academic pedantry and pavement slang, there is no community, no genial middle ground."[40] This schism, Brooks argued, effectively stymied the development of an indigenous cultural life.

The Wine of the Puritans begins with Chateaubriand's statement that "[p]oetry and imagination . . . are regarded in the United States as puerilities appertaining to the first and last ages of life. The Americans have had no childhood, and have, as yet, had no old age."[41] Unlike other countries, the United States was established by men deracinated from the soil, climate, and other surroundings that made them distinct. Because America was founded by adult men, it is, Brooks argued, a country without a childhood and thus without a history. This was a message he was to develop further in an essay published in the *Dial* in 1918. In "On Creating a Usable Past," Brooks argued that American writers were deprived of a history and tradition. He blamed the previous generation of scholars and literary critics, who accepted and participated in the moribund values of the society at large and therefore suppressed knowledge about writers of an earlier generation who might have expressed frustration with these values. This, in turn, he argued, deprived the current generation of writers of any "sense of brotherhood in effort and in aspiration"[42] with earlier writers who had confronted these values. To understand this position it is important to understand that Brooks, much more than Bourne, saw the individual as expressing his "race" or as springing from his nation as the flower from the soil.[43] The imagery of organicism—soil, roots, flowers, branches—is persistent throughout his early work. To deprive young writers of this history was, for Brooks, to deprive them of the very source of their talent and inspiration.

Clearly, these influential writers, although committed to changing the face of America and agreeing on the importance of culture, or art, as the mark of a full life, did not agree either on methods or on basic terms. Where Croly saw the unity of nation and individual coming out of individual pursuit of excellence, Brooks saw the relation between individual and nation as much more organic. For Brooks, the relationship between individual and society preceded individual choice or activities. Croly still worked with the idea of the self-made man, the man who shapes and is shaped by the events, culture, and opportunities America could provide; Brooks foreshadowed the shift to a more determined American: one who expresses an inherent "race." Bourne, on the other hand, while valuing "racial" or "cultural" difference, was committed to the idea of conversation, between individuals and between cultures. More democratic than either of the others, he trusted the call for freedom, believing that open conversation and removal of oppressive social and cultural systems and attitudes would enable all individuals to flourish and develop.

Casey Nelson Blake has argued:

> The confusion that Brooks' work generated had much to do with the often conflicting meanings that he, along with Bourne and Frank, attributed to culture. If pressed as to whether they sought to transform "high" culture or an entire way of life, all three men probably would have answered that the question was posed incorrectly, that it was impossible to imagine a renovation in culture in its Arnoldian sense without a corresponding change in social relations. The answer, in other words, was both. By moving back and forth from a notion of high culture as a secularized version of religious spirit to an equation of culture and everyday life, the Young Americans kept in tight dialectical opposition the two poles of their project in cultural criticism.[44]

But there were significant differences between the men engaged in this debate. In 1916 Bourne attacked the Arnoldian view of culture in an essay entitled "The Cult of the Best."[45] Bourne had seen Arnold-ism in action in England, where he had visited a socialist education program in a London slum where classics were taught to the poor in order to uplift them, a experiment he described as "one of the most marvelous demonstrations of the futility of the English mind that I know."[46] Showing his Boasian roots, he argued that culture could not be dictated; it had to be what one responded to on the basis of experience, something continuous with the rest of one's life.[47] Brooks tended to be more conservative than Bourne, more concerned with the creation of a unified national culture in which arts and letters could flourish, and perplexed about how that could be achieved in the face of cultural pluralism in the United States, whereas their erstwhile mentor, Croly, came increasingly to support the repression of cultural difference and the "Americanization" of immigrants.

Underpinning these debates about American culture were some key terms that recurred again and again. The most frequent rallying point was "alienation," a word that the young artists, critics, and intellectuals seized on as describing their relationship to the mainstream or "Main Street" America. The term often recurs in both the writings of the era and in the later biographies and autobiographies of these men. Van Wyck Brooks later described his lifelong corpus as devoted to "the problem of alienation in American history."[48] That sense of alienation derived from American provincialism, especially as it was manifested in outmoded Puritan values. The way out of that provincialism, with its attendant sense of alienation, increasingly came to be defined as cosmopolitanism or, as Bourne termed it, "trans-nationalism." In 1917, for example, Ezra Pound characterized the work of Henry James, Gustave Flaubert, and Ivan Turgenev as a fight against provincialism, and argued that their weapon in this fight had "largely been the presentation of human variety."[49] Anthropology, and the development of the idea of culture as way of life, clearly had a role to play in enabling the emergence of cosmopolitanism, providing both the theoretical concepts and the empirical evidence not only for human variety but also for the intrinsic and extrinsic value of other ways of life.

In his classic essay on the topic, David Hollinger defined cosmopolitanism as the desire to transcend the limitations of any and all particularisms in order to achieve a more complete human experience and a more complete understanding of experience. The ideal is decidedly counter to the eradication of cultural differences but counter also to their preservation in parochial form. Rather, particular cultures and subcultures are viewed as repositories for insights and experiences that can be drawn upon in the interests of a more comprehensive outlook on the world. Insofar as a particular ethnic heritage or philosophical tradition is an inhibition to experience, it is to be disarmed; insofar as that heritage or tradition is an avenue toward the expansion of experience and understanding, access to it is to be preserved.[50] As Nina Miller argued, "[T]he sense of freedom from ethnic limitations is critical to modernity's appeal."[51] However, the intellectuals and artists who craved that "distanced freedom" for themselves also depended on what they perceived as older communitarian ways of life for both the human variety that served as their knowledge base, and as the examples of un-alienated life towards which they wished to work, an attitude Miller has called "a pervasive modernist attraction toward communitarian values."[52]

The scale of the cultural-nationalist movement belies its impact. If, as I have posited, it can be said to have begun in 1909, then, institutionally at least, it was virtually over by 1918. And the 1909 date is certainly early: James Gilbert dates its beginning to 1911;[53] Edward Abrahams sees the 1913 Armory Show and Paterson Strike Pageant in Madison Square Garden as the signal "examples of the creative union of modern culture and radical politics."[54] The year 1915 has been identified as its apotheosis, the year of the New York Little Renaissance.[55] By 1916, U.S. entry into the war had fatally split what had been a loose but optimistic consensus that a cultural-cum-social renaissance could lead to more-meaningful lives for Americans. In 1917 *Seven Arts* closed as antiwar hysteria led to its funding being withdrawn; the more left-wing *Masses* was shut down as its editors were prosecuted (unsuccessfully) for sedition.

Columbia University had similarly been riven by the war. Boas, along with his pro-war colleagues Charles Beard and John Dewey, all formidable contributors to the intellectual foundation of American culturalism, rallied to support the distinguished Columbia scientist James McKean Cattell, fired for "sedition and treason" for issuing a public statement opposing conscription. Beard resigned in protest. When Boas's only anthropological colleague, Alexander Goldenweiser, was likewise fired for making antiwar statements, the Columbia anthropology department, a central font of culturalist thought, was irrevocably damaged, leaving Boas institutionally isolated and forced into dependence on wealthy patronage to maintain his teaching and research programs.[56]

But more than any other event, the death of Randolph Bourne in the 1918 influenza epidemic was seen as symptomatic of the end of an era: "For his contemporaries as well as for many intellectuals since 1918, Bourne's life represented an unfinished search for a new culture that would have enlarged personal freedom at the same time it supported collective social ideals. Few of Bourne's admirers did not interpret his passing as signifying the end of their own hopes for a cultural revolution in the United States."[57] He was most eloquently eulogized by John Dos Passos in his novel *1919:*

> This little sparrowlike man,
> tiny twisted bit of flesh in a black cape,
> always in pain and ailing,
> put a pebble in his sling,
> and hit Goliath squarely in the forehead with it.
> . . . If any man has a ghost,
> Bourne has a ghost,
> a tiny twisted unscared ghost in a black cloak
> hopping along the grimy old brick and brownstone streets
> still left in downtown New York,
> crying out in a shrill soundless giggle:
> *War is the health of the State.*[58]

The significance attached to the death of this one man points to another fact: if the time span of the cultural renaissance was short, then the human scale was likewise small. In the histories, the same names recur again and again—Bourne, Brooks, Croly, Frank, we have seen. To this list, intellectual historians add Walter Lippman, Walter Weyl, Hutchins Hapgood, Floyd Dell, John Reed, James Oppenheim, Harold Stearns, Max Eastman, Sherwood Anderson, Scofield Thayer, and sometimes Margaret Anderson, Crystal Eastman, Henrietta Rodman, and Alyse Gregory. Often in the background, but supporting them financially and contributing intellectually, were Elsie Clews Parsons, Mabel Dodge Luhan, Dorothy Whitney Straight (later Elmhirst), and the reclusive Mrs. Annette Rankine, who sponsored *Seven Arts* to give some meaning to her life and then, under pressure, withdrew her backing and committed suicide. Certainly, the biographies of fewer than fifty people would encompass most, and certainly all the most influential, of those who theorized, proselytized, and institutionally supported this cultural revolution.

Yet despite its small scale and short life, the cultural-nationalist movement significantly and permanently changed the face of intellectual and literary life in the United States and made a lasting impact on how a vast range of people came to understand themselves in terms of "culture." We have yet to understand how it is that "culture" passed into the vernacular during this period, but Margaret Mead was certainly one of the vectors of these ideas. Mead was to follow the debates on the nature of American culture, and the calls for the development of a distinctive new culture through the many magazines founded or reinvigorated in New York in the second decade of the twentieth century. She grew up in a household steeped in discussion about the economic, political, social, and cultural life of America. Edward Sherwood Mead, Margaret's father, was an avid reader of the little magazines and passed this habit onto his daughter. The call for the magazines in which these debates flourished is persistent through all her periods of fieldwork. From Samoa, she wrote family and friends: "Be it announced that MAGAZINES ARE WELCOME. I am being sent the NATION, NEW REPUBLIC, SATURDAY REVIEW, MERCURY, DIAL, ATLANTIC and the poetry magazines. But I'm in the market for any others of any date, especially LIFE, JUDGE, VANITY FAIR, THEATRE MAGAZINE, SHADOWLAND, VOGUE, and the COSMOPOLITAN." [59] While in New York, attending the theatre was her favorite leisure pastime, but in the field she devoted any spare time to reading poetry and the critical debates about American society, literature, and the arts. Novels were too consuming; she had no ear or talent for music and loathed all games and "unnecessary" physical exercise.

At college she and her friends were captivated by and engaged in the intellectual debates about Puritanism and American culture. As early as 1924, while still a master's student, she had submitted an article entitled "The Waste of the Protocracy" to the *Nation*. [60] Ruth Benedict admired Randolph Bourne, and Mead wrote an essay on *Youth and Life* for her. In a letter to Benedict, she wrote that she regarded him as having won "real victories over very live and vicious enemies, these battles . . . with which my generation has nothing do, but calmly accept the fruits of victory." Her summation of Bourne's accomplishments reads like a blueprint for her own work of the next decade and is uncannily similar to Hollinger's much later definition of cosmopolitanism: "Randolph Bourne's "won Battles" seemed to me to be first, distinctly American ones. He seemed to have fought through and conquered his provincialism, bringing with it a release from the little standards of material prosperity a sense of what a real national culture might mean, an understanding of other civilizations untouched by provincial bias."[61] Bourne's writings also influenced the values that were to govern her personal life. She believed he was able to control his emotional affections "without the unpleasant devices of Electra and Oedipus notions" and that he had "achieved tolerance and a sense of the place of Puritanism as a rather puerile access to Paganism rather than a veritable menace to be assaulted."[62]

Although Bourne died tragically young (he was thirty-two), he was immensely influential in the debates both before and after his death, being regarded as a martyr to his antiwar principles.[63] He published his most influential work in the short-lived but formative *Seven Arts*. Surviving only a year (1916–1917), this magazine set a standard that subsequent magazines strove to meet. Under the joint editorship of James Oppenheim and Waldo Frank, it published poetry, plays, short stories, and essays by the panoply of literary and critical greats of American arts and letters—Theodore Dreiser, Van Wyck Brooks, Carl Sandburg, H. L. Mencken, Eugene O'Neill, Amy Lowell, Vachel Lindsay, Sherwood Anderson, Gertrude Stein. The editors espoused the position that the arts were "a means not only to express the life of the community, but to build a community of spirit."[64] Almost anyone who was or was to become a figure on the American literary scene found his or her way into its pages.

Although other magazines stepped in to fill the gap, it was the *Dial* that became the more cosmopolitan heir to *Seven Arts* under the new editor/ownership of Scofield Thayer and James Sibley Watson, who purchased it in 1919. The *Dial*, however, eschewed the cultural-nationalist mission of *Seven Arts*, asserting a more modernist agenda of "a worldwide sharing of aesthetic experience . . . [based on] an appreciation of formal or technical beauty."[65] In 1917 Margaret Anderson moved what was to become the most infamous of the arts magazines, the *Little Review*, from Chicago to New York. Its spirited defense of James Joyce and *Ulysses* was to be the American literary court case of the decade, confirming all the worst visions of Puritanism held by the critical arts community. Like the *Dial*, the *Little Review* was truly modernist and cosmopolitan, its masthead proclaiming that it would make "no compromise with the public taste."[66] The philosophies of these magazines marked the shift away from the idea of "art" in the service of and as an expression of an indigenous American culture and towards a more truly modernist emphasis on formalism, elitism, and art for art's sake, both reflecting and contributing to the critical intellectuals' disillusionment with America's potential to foster or respond to new and liberating forms of cultural life.

Vanity Fair, founded, with the New Republic, in 1914 as its "chic and fashionable sister" (note the gender), was more mainstream than the Dial. Its mission was to "believe in the progress and promise of American life and . . . to chronicle that progress cheerfully, truthfully, and entertainingly." Modern Quarterly, begun in 1923, was a relative latecomer to the scene whose owner and editor, V. F. Calverton, regarded the magazine as an eclectic "clearing-house for all things modern." But perhaps the most influential in terms of setting the tone of the postwar years was the Smart Set, which was the voice of the man who, more than any other, came to personify the attack on Puritanism, Comstockery, ignorance, and superstition: Henry Louis Mencken. In 1924 Mencken and George Jean Nathan were offered the editorship of a new magazine, the American Mercury, in which they carried on their tradition of publishing modern literature and satirical social commentary. These were but a few of the magazines dedicated to critical social, political, and cultural commentary during the first decades of the twentieth century and in whose pages the war against the "genteel tradition," "repression," and alienation was waged. They were Mead's principal windows into the state of "American culture," especially during her formative years and during long periods of fieldwork.

As Margaret Mead entered college and began her professional and intellectual formation at the end of the war, the Progressive impulse to integrate American arts, economy, and politics into an "organic whole" had begun to disintegrate. A range of factors contributed to this: disillusionment following the war, the collapse of the League of Nations, rampant materialism, and "boosterism." The optimism that had fueled the young cultural critics began to fade. According to Gorman, by the beginning of the 1920s, "the link between literary–aesthetic and political radicalism in the United States generally had been severed,"[67] although, as we shall see, it revived briefly a decade later. In literature and the visual arts, a modernism based on formal aesthetic criteria displaced the cultural nationalists' call for indigenous cultural forms that would express the life of the people. This life, indeed, began to seem less attractive as the mass media grew and Puritanism and xenophobia, rather than receding, seemed to have the country in its grip. A cultural renaissance framed largely as a revolt against "repression," understood as big-C cultural and personal rather than economic or political, began to be posed as the alternative to the grand integrative schemes of the prewar period. Freud's psychoanalytic writings could be deployed to support the notion that the cure for what ailed America lay in the individual. Brooks, in an editorial in the *Freeman,* a magazine he helped found, espoused this change in emphasis: "We live in a new epoch; the time has come to perceive that through the self-fulfillment of its constituent individuals alone a nation can become great."[68]

Waldo Frank, whose *Our America*[69] was regarded as signaling the arrival of a new generation but in reality was the swan song of the cultural nationalists, argued that economic and political reform was impossible without a "revolution in attitude and vision."[70] He called for a thorough exploration of American civilization. Radical change in institutional forms must, he argued, be based on a thorough understanding of what constituted "America." Frank's inspired readings of Walt Whitman, Herman Melville, and, above all, Charlie Chaplin shaped the postwar generation's aspirations for national revival, fueled by a culture that, "like the kingdom of heaven, lies within us, in the heart of our national soul."[71] Like Bourne, Frank called for a cosmopolitan Americanism, in which nationalities would mingle but not lose their distinctive identities. Inspired by Frank, Harold Stearns drew together a group of academics and intellectuals over the winter of 1920–1921. Meeting fortnightly in his home, they developed a series of "state of the nation" essays on various aspects of the arts, knowledge, and life in America, published in 1922 as *Civilization in the United States.*[72] However, Frank's optimism was no match for the prevailing cynicism of the times. Most of the essays repeated Brooks's assessments of a decade earlier—scholarship is nonexistent, the arts are smothered by convention, intellectual life is feminized into applied social work, life is standardized and without adventure. Contributing luminaries, including Lewis Mumford, Henry Louis Mencken, Van Wyck Brooks, Robert Lowie, and Elsie Clews Parsons, agreed—"civilization in America" was a contradiction in terms.[73]

While intellectuals and artists despaired and many fled to Europe to free themselves of what they saw as the narrow, constrained provincialism of the United States, there were significant changes under way in the country. The number of high school and college graduates doubled over the decade; the percentage of women attending college trebled. The growing educated public proved a ready market for books, and the number of new titles published rose from just over six thousand in 1920 to more than ten thousand in 1929.[74] New publishing firms, such as Knopf, Boni and Liveright, Harcourt, Brace & Howe, and William Morrow, and older ones, like Scribner's, under new editorship, sought to publish the exciting modern literature and to broaden the market for their books.[75] The successes of Sinclair Lewis's "exposé" of the banality of small-town America in *Main Street*[76] and Fitzgerald's representation of the wanton habits of the young in *This*

Side of Paradise[77] were indicators of two facts: firstly, the intelligentsia was not the only sector of American society dissatisfied with "the genteel tradition"; and secondly, "getting cultured" was becoming a preoccupation with the expanding middle class.[78]

That "culture" in 1920s America meant rejecting small towns and provincialism, and taking on the aura, at least, of cynicism and fast living may also explain why these books were so popular. Whatever the reason, a culture industry began to target this new middle class. It created new ways of marketing—through book reviews, the Book-of-the-Month Club, and "great books" series, the latter two sold by subscription. The marketing strategies that underpinned these phenomena were identical to those used to sell toothpaste, clothing, and automobiles. Advertisements played on consumers' anxieties about their own expertise, ability to meet goals, and social inadequacy. Culture was a way of "getting ahead," a self-evident value that could improve your business, sex, and social life. Book clubs and book reviews assured consumers that they would have the "right" cultural tools at their fingertips, without the agonies of trying to judge for themselves. As publishers and the growing middle class anxiously observed (while also consuming) the rise of mass culture—movies, radio, and pulp magazines—"good books" answered the need for distinction and provided ways of making sense of the rapidly changing world. Included among these "good books" were those in the relatively new and prestigious field of popular social science, such as the anthropologist George Dorsey's *Why We Behave Like Human Beings*,[79] which was so successful it enabled Dorsey to quit his academic job and devote himself full-time to writing. "Middlebrow" culture began to take shape. This, above all, was the target audience for Margaret Mead's work.

Not everyone, of course, was in a position to embrace the new freedoms or the products of the new culture industries. For a large proportion of Americans, there was little freedom from want. Despite the booming economy, wages did not keep pace with production, and approximately thirty percent of all households struggled to keep food in the cupboard and a roof over the family's head.[80] The new emphasis on consumption and "personality" increased pressure on these households. They now had to struggle not just to feed and clothe youngsters but also to clothe them stylishly and to find funds for the range of new consumer social activities such as dances, clubs, automobiles, movies, and magazines. Adolescent girls, in particular, felt the pressure. Mothers went out to work to ensure that their children did not drop out of school because they couldn't "keep up"; young women left school to work in order to fund these all-important goods and activities.[81]

And while the Young Turks of modernism were railing against repression and calling for a new, distinctly American arts and letters, other less beneficent sentiments were also at work in the land. These impulses to morally and racially "purify" America found expression in three notorious legislative acts: The first was the Eighteenth Amendment, which consolidated at the federal level prohibition laws that had been accumulating at the state level for a decade. The second, the National Origins Acts (1921 and 1924), also known as the Johnson Acts, restricted access to the United States to the "northern races" by indexing immigration of national groups to their proportion of the U.S. population, first as it was in 1905 and then as it was in 1890. The third was the Tennessee Anti-Evolution Act (1925), which forbade the teaching of evolution in schools.[82] These Acts were symptoms of a more pervasive movement. For immigrant, African, and Hispanic Americans, the rise of new forms of racist nationalism was especially devastating. Even as the Harlem Renaissance provided hope that African Americans could, through the arts, attain a distinct and respected place in America, ordinary black Americans benefited little from the new economy. On the contrary, the Ku Klux Klan, revived in 1915, used pyramid sales to recruit members to the ideal of "pure Americanism." Between 1920 and 1924, it grew from a few hundred members to nearly four and a half million; intimidation, torture, and lynching instilled terror as a way of life in many communities, both in the South and in the Klan's stronghold states in the Midwest. Anti-immigration sentiment was prevalent, finding its legislative expression in the National Origins Acts and its most notorious judicial expression in the hanging of the Italian immigrants Nicola Sacco and Bartolomeo Vanzetti for treason in 1927. The call for a new and distinctively American culture had a powerful doppelganger in new forms of racist nationalism.

Margaret Mead fully inhabited the changing world of the East Coast middle-class intelligentsia, and the world just described was, in almost every sense of the word, her world. She came from two generations of college-educated professional women: her grandmother had been a teacher; her mother was educated at Wellesley, the University of Chicago, and Bryn Mawr. Her mother's sister, the acerbic Aunt Fanny McMaster, had been a social worker at Jane Addams's famous Chicago settlement house, Hull House. Mead's college years at DePauw, Barnard, and Columbia were enriched by the female romantic-cum-sexual friendships that are now recognized as not atypical of college women of that era. They were also beset by the fears and ambivalences that Havelock Ellis and Sigmund Freud had cast upon same-sex relationships. Mead and her friends read Freud, admired the free-spirited Edna St. Vincent Millay, and struggled and despaired over the seemingly irresolvable conflicts between their emotional and sexual commitments to women and men.[83]

Mead was also both personally and professionally immersed in the debates about immigration and Americanization. While at Barnard she took part in the protests over the Sacco and Vanzetti trial. For her master's research she returned to Hammonton, New Jersey, where Emily Fogg Mead had begun her doctoral work on the Italian immigrant population when Margaret was a toddler. Margaret's choice of this site was not merely to connect her professional life to that of her mother. The National Origins Act of 1924 was being debated in the Congress, and its particular target was the burgeoning immigrant Italian population. In Hammonton she collected household data and administered intelligence tests to three hundred children of Italian immigrants. She demonstrated that IQ scores correlated to "social status" and "language disabilities," and argued that they were also influenced by "that more subtle and less measurable aspect of environment" such as "different attitudes and habits of thought."[84] She was recruited to this task by the tireless antiracist Franz Boas, whose groundbreaking work had demonstrated that skulls of second-generation Italian children were larger than those of their parents.[85] Boas was heavily involved in the attempt to forestall the passage of the 1924 bill.[86] Margaret's findings that intelligence tests tested social, rather than inherited, traits, capped his thesis that environment, not biology, determined cranial capacity. In the hullabaloo about the sexual content of *Coming of Age,* we are sometimes apt to forget that it was prompted not by concerns about sex but by concerns about biological determinism and racism.

Mead's own struggles to make herself were inextricably entwined with her work. In 1925 she was a very unsure student working under the supervision of Franz Boas. By 1935 she was a national, and even international, figure, one of the earliest, if not the first, academic star. She had been elected to the National Academy of Sciences, was being asked to give keynote addresses to national and international conferences, and had chaired the Social Studies Committee of the National Review of the Secondary Schools Curriculum. She had carried out four periods of fieldwork (nine months in Samoa, nine months among Manus in the Admiralty Islands, four months among the Omaha in Nebraska, and two years working with three different peoples in New Guinea). This period is framed by the fieldwork and publication of her two most famous books—*Coming of Age in Samoa* and *Sex and Temperament in Three Primitive Societies.* The first took America by storm and established her as the most daring and controversial young scientist of her time. The last consolidated her reputation as someone committed to questioning the sexual taboos of the contemporary West, grounding her views in intrepid research among exotic savages and conveying her research in accessible books that reached a wide public.

While her career was meteoric, her personal life is better described as mercurial. These years begin a with a number of important decisions about her intimate relationships—to go to Samoa alone, leaving her first husband, Luther Cressman, behind; to forgo her romantic relationship with Edward Sapir and to consolidate her lifelong commitment to Ruth Benedict. These decisions were framed at least in part by a doctor's advice that she could never bear children, advice that shook the foundations of her marriage to Cressman and reinforced her determination to have a career in anthropology. More significantly, they include all the years of her marriage to and work with Reo Franklin Fortune, a New Zealand–born research scholar whom she met on the ship returning from Samoa in 1926 and married in New Zealand in October 1928. That meeting had tremendous effects on the intellectual direction and professional development of both Mead's and Fortune's careers and indeed on the course of American anthropology. Fortune, on his way to Europe to study psychology with Freud's disciples, went instead to Cambridge to study anthropology with A. C. Haddon, and thence to London to learn field methods from Bronislaw Malinowski. All his books came out of his intense periods of fieldwork with Mead, including the classic *Sorcerers of Dobu,* which provided the keystone for Ruth Benedict's ideas on the patterning of cultures.[87] Fortune, in turn, introduced Mead to Malinowski and A. R. Radcliffe-Brown, who sponsored their research in the Admiralties and New Guinea. Mead's engagement with these men and their ideas converted her from a kind of pop-psychology cultural determinism to an uneasy functionalism, which became one of the bases for the "culture and personality" focus of American anthropology. During the last period of fieldwork, she and Fortune spent four months on the Sepik River in New Guinea with another young Cambridge anthropologist, Gregory Bateson. By the end of that four months, Bateson and Mead had fallen in love. She divorced Fortune on her return to the United States and married Bateson in 1936 on the way to Bali, determined to forge another working partnership, but one, this time, that included children. By her own account, her marriage to Bateson began a new phase of her career.[88]

Mead's early professional development has been mapped in the many biographies and articles on her work and life and it is not my intention to repeat that information.[89] Suffice it to say, she was encouraged into anthropology by two of the major figures of American anthropology, Franz Boas and Ruth Benedict. Mead took classes from both Boas and Benedict while a student at Barnard College and followed them to Columbia for her graduate work. Boas's firmly antiracist culturalism and Benedict's lyric, impassioned interpretive style enriched Mead's essential pragmatism. Her commitment to these two figures never flagged; they were prime among the many loyalties she both held and commanded. However, although Boas may have set the frame and Benedict the tone, the energy, force, and direction were Mead's own. She had other influences, and these waxed and waned over the course of her career. The British influences via Fortune, Radcliffe-Brown, and Malinowski have already been mentioned. She was also influenced by "My dear Prof.," William Fielding Ogburn who made it possible for her to attend graduate school (which her father refused to fund) by employing her at the *Journal of the American Statistical Association.* She corresponded with Ogburn regularly, confided in him, listed him as someone she loved and admired, and sent him copies of all her books.[90] Later, another psychologist, John Dollard, became a close friend, and with him she explored the possibilities of Freudianism in a series of letters and in meetings with Karen Horney, Eric Fromm, and others. She wrote him almost weekly and saw him many times in 1934 and 1935 while she was writing *Sex and Temperament.*

Intertwined with these professional influences, and represented in all her books to a greater or less degree, are the personal and familial issues that Mead confronted during this period. Margaret Mead was the eldest child of Edward Sherwood and Emily Fogg Mead. He was a professor of economics at the University of Pennsylvania, she a sociologist, who, like many women of her time, had forsaken her own career for marriage and family. Margaret was born in 1901 and had an unsettled childhood as her father moved the family around the state while he set up extension education programs. Eventually, the family settled on a farm in Doylestown, Pennsylvania, where the children, including two sisters and a brother, were schooled irregularly and eccentrically. Margaret, who wrote several autobiographical essays in addition to *Blackberry Winter,*[91] recalled herself as a child who was quick, determined, restless, and directive. She likened her family to "refugees, always a little at odds with and well in advance of the local customs."[92] Mead spent much of her life maintaining herself just a little ahead of the mainstream but never again so far off the normative as to threaten her sense of belonging to, and indeed leading, the pack.

Mead's father, to whom she was to remain "dear little girl," both in her appellation and his, well into her thirties, was, according to Jane Howard, flighty, philandering, sarcastic, and distant.[93] Throughout this period, he was deeply alienated from his children. They seemed to crave his approval but allowed their mother to take the brunt of breaking the news about their unconventional lives. Mead's mother, whom Howard dismisses as a snob, was a deeply committed socialist, who approved of birth control, abortion, and ready divorce, although she was less sure about Catholics and the Scottsboro boys. She was, in many ways, much more liberal than Margaret and supported her daughters through divorces and affairs and her son through his difficult relationships with his father and outgoing sisters, protecting all from their father's harshness and disapproval. Although Margaret's early work has been seen largely in terms of child-rearing, sexuality, and women, she was equally concerned with masculinity and, specifically, with fathering, a fact that has been little recognized. Her difficult relationship with Fortune and her ongoing sexual friendships with Ruth Benedict and other women are reflected in her attempts to make cultural space for new forms of gender identity and behavior. The issues that she explores and the solutions she proposes arise not just from her fieldwork, or from her broader cultural milieu, but were issues with which she and those who were close to her were struggling daily.

3 The "Jungle Flapper"

Civilization, Repression, and the Homogenous Society

"SCIENTIST GOES on Jungle Flapper Hunt": thus the *New York Sun Times* introduced Margaret Mead, the young woman who was to establish anthropology in
the popular lexicon and entrench an unsuspecting Pacific Island people in the
popular imagination as the epitome of sexual permissiveness and bliss.[1] *Coming of
Age in Samoa,* the product of this "jungle hunt," is unique among anthropological
texts in its durability in both the popular imagination and academic debates. If
as Micaela di Leonardo suggests, Margaret Mead is the public's Ur-anthropolo-
gist,[2] then *Coming of Age in Samoa* is surely its Ur-text. Despite, or because of, its
contentious scholarly status, it retains a vivid place in the popular imaginary. The
reasons for this durability, however, have never been explored, perhaps because it
has been assumed that it was due to its sexual subject matter. However, although
it is tempting to argue that the popularity of *Coming of Age in Samoa* stemmed
from a combination of sexual prurience and accessible writing, backed by a good
publicity machine, that interpretation runs the risk of glibness. It too readily dismisses the possibility that the book reached more deeply into cultural meanings,
and it fails to address the tenacity of the book's hold on both public and academic
imagination. That tenacity lies deeper[3] than the book's well-known evocation of
the South Sea island sexual paradise and its "dusky maidens," or, perhaps, this
imaginative landscape contains more than meets the eye. Before one can understand the book's reception, let alone its place in popular culture, it is necessary to
focus not on Mead's scholarly credibility but on the social meanings that *Coming
of Age in Samoa* both tapped and fed into in the years 1925–1935.

The *New York Sun Times* headline compresses a lot of meaning into just one
line. In just six words, it encapsulates many of the contrasts and contradictions of
mainstream American culture in the 1920s—the faith in science and progress, the
fascination with the primitive and exotic, the problematics of female emancipa-
tion, and the sense that the world was America's oyster, an adventure waiting to
happen. The headline aptly captures the deep ambivalence that was characteristic
of America during the 1920s. The country was, Lawrence Levine argues, torn by "a
belief in progress coupled with a dread of change; an urge towards the inevitable

future combined with a longing for the irretrievable past; a deeply ingrained belief in America's unfolding destiny and a haunting conviction that the nation was in a state of decline."[4] When we think about the 1920s, we are apt to conjure images of speakeasies and jazz clubs, Model T Fords, young men in raccoon coats and young women in short skirts drinking gin and dancing the Charleston. In sharp contrast to the previous decade, the twenties seem modern, the real beginning of the twentieth century.

However, the 1920s were characterized not just by prosperity, technological advances, and loosening of social mores, but also by counter-movements that sought to re-inscribe a nostalgic vision of an older, more communitarian, more homogenous America. These latter forces found their most famous expression in Prohibition, but they also were characterized by a rise in anti-immigration sentiment, the reestablishment and growth of the Ku Klux Klan, and a surge of organized and vocal fundamentalist religious groups. This ambivalence between the new modernity and the yearning for an imagined tradition permeated all strata of society. Intellectuals deplored both the machine age and the provincialism of rural America; politicians and businessmen "boosted" American industry while decrying the immigration that provided their workforce; middle-class Americans mourned the loss of community while spending their leisure time in automobiles and movie theatres.

No figure better encapsulated both the exhilarating new freedoms and the destabilizing of established mores than the subject of Mead's "jungle hunt"—the flapper.[5] Frederick Allen Lewis, in his classic "informal history of the 1920s," *Only Yesterday*,[6] dedicates most of his chapter called "The Revolution in Manners and Morals" to changes in women's behavior: at home (where use of convenience foods and electric appliances skyrocketed and divorce rates doubled in two decades), in the workplace (as more and more women entered the clerical and service industries), in fashion (where the average woman's outfit in 1928 consumed only a third of the fabric it had fifteen years previously), and in leisure and sexual behavior. While the 1920s may be remembered for Prohibition, gangland wars, and jazz, it is personified in the figure of the flapper, with her aura of modernity, cynicism, and amorality.

Kenneth Yellis contrasts the flapper with her "foremother," the Gibson Girl.[7] The Gibson Girl, he argues, was the model of turn-of-the-century womanhood— wifely, stable, modest, a fitting marker of her husband's social success. However, it is at least as instructive to contrast the flapper with another female figure, one that, unlike the Gibson Girl, also condensed the meanings of unwelcome social change in America. The flapper's foremother, it might be argued, is more fittingly the New Woman, a figure who had been characterized as a social threat for at least two generations before the 1920s. The first generation of New Women was nurtured in the all-female colleges during the last decades of the nineteenth century until it emerged as a network of the first female professionals. These women staffed women's colleges and settlement houses, were social workers, writers, industrial reformers, feminists, and suffragettes. In addition to being supportive professional environments, women's colleges and settlement houses provided the opportunity for women-only families and households. Between forty and sixty percent of women who graduated from college between 1880 and 1929 never married (as opposed to ten percent of all American women).[8] This generation of independent women came under pressure at the beginning of the twentieth century with the advent of sexology. A nineteenth-century tradition of lifelong romantic friendships between women was disrupted by the new science of sex. Havelock Ellis, Ellen Key, and Sigmund Freud asserted or were interpreted as asserting that women's heterosexual drives were both natural and necessary for healthy physical and emotional life. However, they pathologized romantic and sexual relations between women. The radical New Women who flocked to Greenwich Village in the early twentieth century claimed heterosexual fulfillment as a right and a necessity, but female sexual and romantic relationships were increasingly stigmatized.[9] By the 1920s, the New Woman was on her way to oblivion: although more women attended college, more of them married; fewer went on to graduate school; fewer worked after marriage.[10] Articles in the popular press profiling professional women emphasized their femininity in addition to their achievements and often used domestic images to characterize their work. Feature articles on Mead, for example, inevitably remark on her diminutive stature and girlishness; she herself was not above equating anthropology with housework.[11]

The threatening female figure of the twenties, therefore, was not the earnest social reformer, nor the ideologically driven sexual experimenter, nor the new professional, but the flapper. Although "flapper" was sometimes subsumed under the rubric New Woman, and both terms connote women operating beyond the norms of traditional femininity, there were significant differences between the two. The flapper was a more widespread phenomenon than was the upper-middle-class, educated, (typically) white professional New Woman, or the even smaller number of radical New Women who inhabited "bohemia" in Greenwich Village. She was certainly more common than the elite wife of a tuxedo-wearing man, signified by the Gibson Girl. More significantly, the flapper was a product of mass culture, not higher education. Her clothing was factory produced in standard sizes or made at home, copied from designs in mass-circulation magazines; her models were not dress reformers or society-page fashion plates, but movie stars. And her primary aim was not freedom for self-development or the betterment of the world, but freedom and fun, albeit heterosexual fun with marriage as the end goal.[12] Fun was available in a range of forms both old and new. Speakeasies and jazz clubs were new forms of older institutions such as saloons. The latter, like the cigarettes and alcohol consumed in them, had been exclusive male preserves. Now, as Allen put it, "not only the drinks were mixed, but the company as well."[13] Other democratizing forms of fun were automobiles, motion pictures, radios (in one of every two households by the end of the decade), and an unprecedented number of magazines, especially those devoted to movies, sex stories, and true confessions and aimed principally at the female market.

The figure of the young woman as symbol of the 1920s is not a post hoc construction. The first best-seller of the decade, Sinclair Lewis's *Main Street,* begins with a glimpse of its heroine, Carole Milford (soon to be Kennicott), in a state of "suspended freedom" on the banks of the Mississippi. "Credulous, plastic, young; drinking in the air as she longed to drink in life." Such a "rebellious girl," Lewis declares, "is the spirit of that bewildered empire called the American Middlewest."[14] Carole's struggles with the small souls of small towns triggered a wave of identification among the emergent middle class, and "Main Street" came to signal everything that those with aspirations to "culture" were seeking to escape. However, it was not Carole Milford Kennicott, with her improving aspirations, who defined the spirit of the decade, but the young women who propel Amory Blaine to self-knowledge in F. Scott Fitzgerald's *This Side of Paradise,* published just months after *Main Street.* Myra St. Claire, Rosalind Connage, Eleanor Savage, Isabel, and Jill were girls "casually . . . accustomed to be kissed" who ate "three-o'clock, after-dance suppers in impossible cafes, talking of every side of life with an air half of earnestness, half of mockery, yet with a furtive excitement that . . . stood for a real moral let-down." They were the girls who led Amory to declare "the cities between New York and Chicago as one vast juvenile intrigue."[15] But more than anything, they were cynical about love. Rosalind rejects true love "cooped up in a little flat" for the reliable Dawson who will be good to their children and give her "sunshine and pretty things and cheerfulness."[16] Eleanor has already led her peers astray in a bohemian life and retired to a "despairing" "Indian summer of love" at the age of eighteen. Jill sleeps with Amory's friend in a hotel but has the sophistication (and presence of mind) to give a false name and address when caught by the police. Idealistic, married Carole Kennicott was anachronistic within months of being launched. The action had moved to the young, frivolous, smart, and fast.

Thus when Franz Boas set Margaret Mead's "problem" as "the psychological attitude of the individual [adolescent girl] under the pressure of the general pattern of culture," [17] he was asking her to reflect on what was widely perceived to be a social problem—the rebelliousness and loose morals of the young, particularly young women. Boas was too much of an anthropologist to be particularly concerned with the moral outrage, but he was interested in to what extent adolescent "sullenness," "sudden outbursts," "desire for independence," "excessive bashfulness," "crushes among girls," and "romantic love" were induced by cultural constraints. He did not, at least in writing, put pressure on Mead to resolve these questions in favor of cultural influences, and his letter to her suggests genuine curiosity about the question, rather than a prejudgment of the outcome.

The logistics and debates surrounding Mead's decision to work in Samoa have been well rehearsed in the many books on her and that research.[18] Her poor health and "high-strung" nature worried not only her lover, Edward Sapir, who tried to stop her from going, but also Ruth Benedict and Franz Boas. Boas resisted pressure from Sapir to forbid the trip, writing to Benedict that he would not, on principle, "interfere in such a radical way with the future of a person for his or her own sake [for] . . . if [Sapir] were right then, who should not be restrained?"[19] Benedict's advice was that Boas should use his authority to impress on Margaret the "duty of care and avoidance of risks."[20] Boas did so in a letter, which set out both her responsibility to look after herself and the intellectual issues she should tackle. He directed her to articles by Ruth Bunzel and Bronislaw Malinowski for models and finished with the gentle admonition, "Don't forget your health."[21] Buoyed with that good advice, she set out with Benedict across the continent by train at the end of July. After stops at the Grand Canyon with Ruth and in Honolulu for two weeks in order to consult with experts at the Bernice P. Bishop Museum, she arrived in Pago Pago at dawn on August 31. By breakfast time, she was ensconced in her hotel ("THE Hotel, children, where Rain[22] was staged"), . . . "glad to have dry land" beneath her feet, "and very pleasantly tucked away in a little round fold of the Pacific where time goes very smoothly and there seems to be always a breeze."[23]

She spent the first two months in Pago Pago living in a hotel, learning the language, and getting to know the various communities that comprised the little center of government. Her observations about expatriate Navy life are at least as perceptive as her comments on the hierarchies of race that determined social interactions in the town. During this time, she made several trips to villages along the coast in the company of the Navy doctor and his wife. Towards the end of October, she spent ten days in Vaitogi, living with a Samoan family. Here, after finding that she could "speak politely," the chief made her a *taupou,* or ceremonial virgin, of the village. She described the trip as the most "peacefully happy and comfortable ten days" of her life. However, it confirmed her conviction that she would have to live in an American household in order to work effectively. She wrote, "I was too sheltered. As a Taupou I could go nowhere alone, nor could I enter the houses of common people. But it was like visiting at a royal court, and excellent for getting practice in the language."[24] At the beginning of November, she moved to Tau in the Manu'a group and commenced life in the household of the Navy pharmacist, along with his wife, their two infants, and a radio operator, inevitably nicknamed "Sparks."

Almost immediately, it appears, she was surrounded by young people. She wrote to Franz Boas: "Natives of all ages and sexes and ranks drift on and off my porch in a casual fashion which would be out of the question if I were living in a native house. I have to lock the door to keep the adolescents out and yawn prodigiously to get rid of them at midnight."[25] They came by to bring her gifts, to borrow ink, paper, needles, and pens, to play games, read her magazines, tell her stories, take her fishing, but most of all they came to dance for her:

> They dance for me a great deal; they love it and it is an excellent index to tempera-
> ment, as the dance is so individualistic, and the audience thinks it is its business to
> keep up incessant comment. Between dances they look at my pictures, I am going
> to have to put Dr. Boas much higher on the wall, his picture fascinates them,
> and converse one with another about many and sundry things. And how I have
> perverted them. I have translated "Nice little green worm, nice little green worm,
> want to go to heaven?" . . . into Samoan. They love it.[26]

Despite the extreme heat ("This is a churlish climate at best,"[27] she wrote), her health was excellent and she had clearly found her métier.

Throughout her time in Samoa, Mead struggled with issues of method, analysis, and presentation of her results. Although she had studied anthropology, her research training was in psychometrics rather than ethnography or psychoanalysis. Later in life, she described Boas as defining her problem and her method of tackling it in an interview lasting perhaps three minutes. Although she devised a number of ways of recording "data" on the adolescents and on village life, she was struggling to integrate her vivid perceptions of the way of life she was observing with the scientistic tools with which she had been trained. In January she suffered a crisis of confidence about her work. She wrote Boas a long (and prescient, in the light of subsequent debates) letter in which she agonized over how to produce a scientifically transparent report from her study of fewer than sixty children: "Ideally, no reader should have to trust my word for anything, except of course in as

Margaret Mead standing between two Samoan girls, ca. 1926; photograph
courtesy of the Institute of Inter-cultural Studies and the Library of
Congress (Manuscript Division 50a)

much as he trusted my honesty and averagely intelligent observation. I ought to be able to marshal an array of facts from which another would be able to draw independent conclusions. And I don't see how in the world I can do that."[28]

She went on for three pages, giving examples of various, obviously inadequate, statistical analyses. Two weeks later, she wrote him again, throwing herself on his mercy: "I have no idea whether I am doing the right thing or not, or how valuable my results will be. It all weighs heavily on my mind. Is it worth the expenditure of so much money? Will you be dreadfully disappointed with me?"[29]

Boas reassured her by return mail: "I am very decidedly of the opinion that a statistical treatment of such an intricate behaviour as the one that you are studying, will not have very much meaning. . . . I rather imagine that you might like to give a somewhat summarized description of the behaviour of the whole group . . . and then set off the individual against the background."[30] By the time she received his letter, she had regained her confidence, and in mid-March she wrote him that her work was almost complete and that, due to the hurricane-induced famine, she was planning on leaving a month early.[31]

The last weeks were a round of *malaga* (trips) and ceremonials in which she was feted and bid farewell. The children came nightly to compose songs, which they wrote in her notebook: "Now comes the rub, which tune will fit. With three or four little black heads close together, they try this tune, then that one, try slurring this word and expanding that one, until finally a moderate fit is attained. I have one touching ballad written to 'Just Before the Battle Mother,' or rather finally sung to that tune."[32]

She left no account of her departure. In mid-May she sailed to Australia, where she boarded a ship to Europe. There she was to meet her husband, Luther Cressman, and attend the Society of Americanists Conference in Rome with Ruth Benedict. On board she was drawn to the company of another young scholar, Reo Franklin Fortune. Fortune, who had just completed a master's in psychology at the University of New Zealand, was on his way to Europe to study psychoanalysis. By the time they landed in Paris, they had fallen in love and he had decided instead to pursue anthropology. She spent an emotionally agonized summer. At Fortune's insistence, she broke a commitment to tour Southern Europe with Ruth Benedict in order to make time for Reo, a decision that was to scar her relationship with both parties well into the future. Torn between her husband and new lover, still emotionally involved with both Sapir and Benedict, Mead made the conservative choice and determined to return home to live with Cressman.

Mead and Cressman returned to New York in the autumn of 1926. Here Margaret took up her new post as assistant curator of ethnology at the American

Museum of Natural History. Despite the turmoil in her domestic and emotional life, she settled down with characteristic speed to write up her fieldwork, using Boas's framework. She quickly determined that she wanted to use the book to proselytize for anthropology and so she sought the advice of George Dorsey on how to tailor her writing for a popular audience. In December she recorded her progress to E. S. C. Handy, the ethnographer of Samoa at the Bishop Museum, to whom she had promised a more scholarly ethnographic text on Samoa: "I've only been back a couple of months and what with getting settled in civilization and starting work here, I've not had time to touch the ethnology at all. The adolescent girl however flourisheth and merely awaits Dr. Boas' return from Europe to be sent questing for a publisher. The need for mixing propaganda for the ethnological method and human interest somewhat obscures what ethnology is scattered through its pages."[33]

She soon sent the manuscript off and spent the summer in Germany, ostensibly looking at the Pacific collections in German museums. However, the trip had another purpose: a secret reunion with Fortune. By the end of the summer, they had decided to marry and do fieldwork together in the southwest Pacific. He returned to Cambridge in September to prepare for fieldwork among the Dobu; she to New York to end her marriage to Cressman and to hear the disappointing news that no publisher had accepted her book.

It wasn't until March 1928 that she was able to write to her mother: "William Morrow has taken my book. It will come out in the fall, I hope with an English edition at the same time. It's like having the first baby in a new hospital, the whole staff takes a personal interest. It's to have eight pages of illustrations."[34] This turned out to be a fortuitous and productive partnership for both Mead, the new author, and Morrow, the new publisher. Having seen the original manuscript, Morrow must have known he had an extraordinary author in Mead. Her writing style is both lively and evocative. There is no doubt that she both enjoyed in others' writing, and was able to communicate in her own, a rare, if perhaps not always accurate, sense of place and peoples.[35] It was he who set her on the road to becoming the most famous social scientist of her time. Mead was giving a course over the winter of 1927–1928 at the New York League of Girls' Clubs. Morrow suggested that she use her lecture material as the basis for an introduction and final chapter drawing out the implications of her findings for American society.

As she was completing her manuscript, she was preparing for her field trip to the Admiralty Islands with Fortune. The press picked up on her new trip and sensational headlines ("American Girl to Study Cannibals,"[36] "Will Shows Fear of Cannibals: Dr. Mead Inserts Clause in Case She Meets Death in South Sea

Study" [37]) appeared in newspapers and magazines across the continent, with some articles syndicated over and over again. In a move that must have thrilled her, she began to get requests for articles from the very magazines she so enjoyed reading. She wrote to her mother that *Smart Set* had asked her to do a series of articles at $150 a piece. With characteristic efficiency, she decided to do them while she was in Mexico getting her divorce. [38] Morrow was concerned about placing her work in such venues: "you should be cautious in arranging for magazine articles, and should take into account the possible attitude of your fellow-scholars whose opinions would count in connection with your future career as a scholar and scientist." Somewhat paradoxically, he also advised her to go with the wider-circulation magazines such as *Cosmopolitan* rather than the more restricted and critical *Smart Set*. [39] Despite Morrow's caution, Mead was determined to have an impact beyond academia. Although the *Smart Set* arrangement fell through, she prepared a number of other articles for publication in popular magazines during her absence. She departed for the South Pacific in late August, leaving the devoted and ever-patient Ruth Benedict to cut and collate, find photographs, liaise with editors, and disburse payments.

Days after her departure, Morrow announced the publication of *Coming of Age in Samoa* with endorsements from "four great authorities": Dorsey, Malinowski, Havelock Ellis, and the psychologist John B. Watson. Ellis called it "fascinating." Dorsey said it was "extraordinarily brilliant and unique." [40] The combination of a fashionable social problem, sex, an exotic location, and a girl adventurer proved irresistible to the American press. The response was sensational in both senses of the word. Attention-grabbling headlines announced the book: "Samoa Is the Place for Women—Economically Independent, Don't Have to Cook and Go Home to Dad When Husbands Get Tiresome" [41] and "Where Neuroses Cease from Troubling and Complexes Are at Rest." [42] It even inspired a cartoon in *Esquire* in which a young woman wearing only a hat and bracelet explains to her hostess, "But I came of age in Samoa." [43] Mead returned from the Admiralties in late 1929 to a backlog of requests for interviews, articles, and speaking engagements. She signed on with Science Service, an agency for placing articles in magazines and journals, and with Mary Squire Abbott, an independent agent, to handle any articles Science Service could not place. She contracted with yet another agent to secure and manage public-speaking and radio engagements.

The response of the popular press was, in general, uncritical, enthusiastic, nonjudgmental, and either earnest or humorous. Mead was praised for her scholarship and her courage in venturing so far afield. Her conclusion—that adolescent crises were cultural rather than biological—was widely and accurately reported and generally accepted as having important implications for modern families. However, whereas the popular press responded with a combination of enthusiasm, humor, and sensationalism, the response of her anthropological colleagues and the elite magazines was, even at this time, mixed. Alfred L. Kroeber was admiring; the powerful Robert Lowie, editor of the *American Anthropologist,* praised her new approach of focusing on a single problem but was skeptical of the links she drew between Samoan and American life and of her glossing over colonial influences.[44] Sapir, stung by her rejection, published an indirect but vicious attack in which he dismissed her work (and Malinowski's) as the "smart and trivial analysis of sex by intellectuals who have more curiosity than intuition." Not content with dismissing her work, he reviled feminists and lesbians, accusing them of frigidity and insatiable ambition, and completed the work with a direct personal attack accusing "emancipated women" of being little better than prostitutes.[45] However, other anthropologists were more accepting: Malinowski and Alfred Tozzer wrote both publicly and privately in praise of *Coming of Age.* Malinowski and Mead commenced a cordial professional correspondence that continued for the next two years and only later turned sour.

If some of the anthropologists were critical of her descriptions of Samoa, the elite magazines were equally unsure about her anthropology of contemporary America. Mencken wrote that *Coming of Age* was "[a] sweet story, but Miss Mead finds it somewhat difficult to apply its lessons to American life. . . . I believe that Miss Mead's book would have been better if she had avoided discussing the woes of American high-school girls and confined herself to an objective account of life in Samoa."[46] A letter to the editor of the *Saturday Review of Literature* pointed out that "[h]er American girl has a strict Presbyterian father, a haughty Episcopalian grandfather, an agnostic aunt, a mystic elder brother, an engineer uncle full of dyed-in-the-wool materialism, and quietistic mother studying Hindu philosophy. . . . [N]one of them earn their living by the sweat of their brow. None of them belong to the *hoi polloi*—or the subway rush."[47]

Mencken suggested that rather than homogenizing American youth, social scientists had better find out more about the diversity of American society: "[W]e know far more about the daily life of the Pueblo Indians than we know about the life of Mississippi Baptists. Whenever, by some accident, light is let into the subject there is gasping surprise, and even horror. This happened, typically, when a gang of slick city jakes descended upon the primitive mountain village of Dayton, Tenn. at the time of the Scopes trial, and found it full of Aurignacian men clad in dressy mail-order suits, with Bibles under their arms."[48]

This was a criticism Robert and Helen Lynd were to answer within the year with *Middletown*,[49] a book that has stood the scholarly test of time much better than has Mead's but which lacks the panache that catapulted hers into the popular imagination. Propelled by these responses—prurient, critical, wishful, or comic—*Coming of Age in Samoa* became a best-seller nationally and then became internationally renowned. Not everyone approved, but everyone had an opinion. In 1932 Morrow sold the rights to publish to Blue Ribbon Books, which produced cheap (one-dollar) copies of best-sellers. In 1933 *Coming of Age in Samoa* was nominated as one of the hundred best books by women "in this century of progress." Of the seven social science books selected, it is the only one that still has wide name recognition and remains the subject of lively and ongoing debate.[50]

Much has been written about Mead's evocative writing style and what Evans-Pritchard characterized as the "rustling of the wind in the palm trees" form of ethnography.[51] The accessibility of the writing drew comments from academic and press reviewers and was certainly a factor in the book's success. Couched in novelistic language is an account of the daily life of Samoan girls as they "change from babies to baby tenders, learn to make the oven and weave fine mats, forsake the life of the gang to become more active members of the household, defer marriage through as many years of casual love-making as possible, finally marry and settle down to rearing children who will repeat the same cycle."[52] Mead's description of the freedom and fluidity of sexual relations depicted a utopian paradise where "[f]amiliarity with sex, and the recognition of a need of a technique to deal with sex as an art, have produced a scheme of personal relations in which there are no neurotic pictures, no frigidity, no impotence, except as a temporary result of severe illness, and the capacity for intercourse only once in a night is counted as senility."[53] According to Mead, Samoans had not only a crisis-free adolescence, but had a way of life characterized by leisure, simplicity, and relative freedom from care for adults as well. In an unconscious paraphrase of Marx's famous maxim, Mead's Samoans followed "a morning of work and afternoon of sleep with an evening of song and dance."[54] By the time this article came out, its readers would have known what followed the song and dance—"the rhythmic beat of the surf, . . . the soft perfume of frangipani blossoms, [and] low-voiced protestations of love."[55]

The appeal of this vision of paradise seems self-evident. However, to understand its particular meanings in terms of the redefining of America in the 1920s, it is useful to step away from Samoa and sex and consider the ontology of the modern self. As many writers have noted, the modern self is conceived in spatial terms.[56] The "true" self is that which is inside, hidden, mysterious. The very interiority of the self constitutes a challenge to rational modernity, which means it is subject to technologies that purport to uncover or reveal it, most importantly to ourselves. The thematic of a selfhood created in childhood, lost to us, but able to be found, healed, or explicated had pervaded both popular understandings and professional theorization in the decades leading up to 1928. This was a relatively recent phenomenon: in psychology, case histories did not begin to include life histories until the 1890s, and it was only after Freud's visit to America that case histories began to attend to childhood and sexual life.[57] This points to a further dimension of the self: it is conceived not only in spatial terms but in temporal ones as well. The "interiorized self" is "created by the laying down and accretion of our own childhood experiences, our own history."[58]

Carolyn Steedman has argued that this conceptualization of the self as con-stituted by personal childhood history has a converse movement. In the period 1780 to 1930, what she calls "the figure of the child" came to personify the self over a range of literary forms and public policy debates. Steedman's exegesis of versions of this figure begins with the child acrobat Mignon in Goethe's *Wilhelm Meister,* and ranges over the novels of Walter Scott, and a plethora of German and Russian novels over a period of 130 years. She became familiar to popular audi-ences through settings of Mignon's songs by Beethoven, Franz Schubert, Franz Liszt, Robert Schumann, and other continental composers. She appears in the first popular melodrama and in 1866 was the subject of an opera by Ambroise Thomas. By the 1880s, Mignon was the subject of a series of novels, and in 1885 she had become a "One-Act Operatic Comi-tragique Burlesque," which was performed all summer in the Barnstable Townhall. By the end of the nineteenth century, there were countless representations of this orphaned androgynous child–woman with the mysterious past.[59] Steedman shows how an aesthetic that eroticized the "little-ness"[60] of the child's body and the "mystery" of the child's past not only echoed in literary forms and popular culture but permeated public debate about stage and street children.

Steedman began her research after finding Mignon used by Margaret McMil-lan, a British Labour Party activist who had fought to get working-class and street children onto the social agenda. McMillan did this specifically in an article pub-lished in 1911 entitled "Marigold: An English Mignon." Steedman writes that what was astonishing about this article, which drew on all the tropes that surrounded Mignon—her beauty, her damage by adults—was "McMillan's calm assumption that her W[orker's] E[ducational] A[ssociation] readers would *get* all this."[61] This aesthetic mapped increasingly onto concerns about and models of the self. The child-figure to which Steedman refers is not just any child but a specific constel-lation of attributes: almost always female, but often ambiguously embodied; little, although she may be any age from toddler to twenty-five; and with a mysterious history of damage by an adult, a history that, if not explicitly sexual, certainly has pedophilic undercurrents. This specific figure or personification, Steedman argues, condenses the meanings of modern selfhood with its attributes of interiority, historicity, sexuality, and mystery.

Hans Gumbrecht provides an example of this girl-figure in his innovative book *1926: Living on the Edge of Time*, an examination of the year in which *Coming of Age in Samoa* was written. Gumbrecht is making a point not about the self but about the representation of homosexuality in the novels and short stories of 1926. He notes that in these stories "implicit homosexual attraction" is inevitably associated with the "loss and recuperation of precarious intellectual certainty." He illustrates this with an episode from Thomas Mann's short story "Disorder and Early Sorrow," in which Dr. Cornelius, a professor of history, experiences an intellectual crisis brought on by an encounter between his daughter Lorchen and "a pretty youth," Max. Max has danced with Lorchen until she is hysterical and then has to be called in to calm her to sleep. The sight of Max leaning over Lorchen's bed evokes in Cornelius intense and ambivalent emotions—gratitude, embarrassment, hatred, and jealousy—and his sense of himself as a "reasonable" man is shaken. For my purposes, however, what is significant about this passage is that it is Cornelius's "almost Oedipal" feelings for his five-year-old daughter that make the story a more complex triangle than Gumbrecht's essay allows. Cornelius, reflecting on his love for his daughter, admits to himself, "for the sake of science," that the intensity of his feelings for her "undermines his intellectual rigor as a historian" and evokes in him feelings of animosity for the present "on behalf of true history." [62] In Mann's story, "intellectual uncertainty" appears first in relation to the girl child, the object of intense, almost incestuous feelings. The complex of ideas that Steedman identifies are at play in Mann's story: the dancing, eroticized child; a hint of incest—damage of the child by a parent; the centrality of history/science, both in the father's profession and in the form that his crisis takes.

Steedman's account of Mignon resonates uncannily with that of Mead's Samoan girl. The Samoan girl is constituted, as is the Mignon figure, in terms of surface and depth, history and time, wholeness and damage. She thus slotted into tropes of selfhood already in wide circulation, not just the stereotypic vision of exotic maidens but a trope that was at once more subtly embedded in popular culture and more consciously theorized in the versions of psychoanalysis propounded in both the popular and academic media. For if the Mignon girl-figure personified a self that is understood to be already damaged ("If we repress [our children], heaven knows what complexes their turbulent minds may develop," one reviewer wrote of *Coming of Age*),[63] both professional and popular versions of psychoanalysis in the 1920s proclaimed that this damage was avoidable. When in the final chapter of *Coming of Age in Samoa* Mead wrote that the larger Samoan family "seems to ensure the child against the development of the crippling attitudes which have been labeled Oedipus complexes, Electra complexes, and so on,"[64] she was able to do so without challenge from either the psychological professionals or the popular press. The Samoan girl proved the point, far beyond the limits of the case to which she was applied.

In considering how the relationship between the Samoan girl and the American self operates, one of the first things to be noted is that the Samoan girl stands in a simple relation to Samoa itself. Mead continually reiterated the continuity between the Samoan individual and the culture or society as a whole. This is one of the principal messages of the study: that where there is no conflict between individual and social values, there is no adolescent rebellion. Samoa was what Mead, following Bourne, called a homogenous society. This discursive homogeneity was such that what was said of the Samoan girl was often also what was said of Samoa. Conversely, Samoa and its adult members were juvenilized, if not directly by Mead, surely by the popular press, aided by Mead's descriptions of them: "The Polynesian is not a true adult; . . . he is rather an overgrown child, gay, happy, and thoughtless of the morrow."[65] Likewise, a review in the *Brooklyn Eagle* stated, "[*Coming of Age in Samoa*] takes us far into the South Sea Isles and bids our fancy rove, free and unrestrained among the child people of the Samoan group."[66] Samoa and the Samoan girl were interchangeable as discursive objects.

In contradistinction to the modern self, constituted by personal history, the Samoan girl and, indeed, Samoa itself were represented by Mead, and by those who reported on her work, as being both history itself and without history. Both Mead and reviewers invoked the well-documented association of the primitive with the past, in subtle and not so subtle ways. The widespread use of the terms "primitive," "simple," and "natural" as distinguished from "progress," "complex," and "civilized," were understood as locating Samoa as archaic: "It is not entirely primitive, nor yet is it debauched by the most pernicious forces of Western civilization."[67] But while Samoa stood for the past, it was, paradoxically, a timeless past. In an interview, for example, Mead is reported to have claimed that "[l]ife is peaceful, orderly and gracious in Samoa. . . . It seems timeless. Nothing has ever changed. Nobody is troubled. No voice is ever raised. It would be a fine place to die."[68] Even where there appears to be change, she argues this is only apparent and not real. In one of the few academic articles she wrote on Samoa, she made an impossibly confused argument, contending that because change is easy in Samoa it hardly happens at all: "the ever-yielding, ever-accommodating social structure has remained much the same, generation after generation, while [those] with original minds and social ambitions slid, sated with too easy victories, into undistinguished grooves."[69] Her refusal to acknowledge the very real amount of change, including the impact of the missionaries, and the American Navy presence, was a major feature of some contemporary and much current criticism.[70]

Suspended in a timeless past, Samoa was said to be a place without that source of modern ills: repression. "The Freudian diseases, of course, cannot occur in Samoa," wrote a reviewer in the *St. Louis Globe*.[71] Another, more humorously, commented, "[H]ere are erotics without neurotics; Oedipus is not Rex, and laughter goes hand in hand with desire."[72] Mead herself wrote that Samoan children "grew up painlessly and almost unselfconsciously."[73] Like its undamaged children, Samoa itself is undamaged. This place, simultaneously history itself and without history, is a place where repression, which modern psychology identified as fundamental to modern mental illness, deviance, and just plain unhappiness, cannot occur. Samoa is a place where the self is not damaged and where, notably, there is little consciousness of self. It should come as no surprise, given this complex of attributes, that Mead's Samoa and Samoans lacked that other defining feature of modern selfhood—depth or interiority. Samoan culture, she argued, was shallow, concerned with surface and form. This lack of depth was set in place in early childhood: "when the child is handed carelessly from one woman's hands to another's, the lesson is learned of not caring for one person greatly, not setting high hopes on any one relationship."[74] Lack of strong attachments in childhood led to a similar casualness about adult sexual relationships. They were, she argued, concerned with technique, ignorant of romantic love, contemptuous of jealousy. This "shallowness" was not confined to intimate relationships but was recapitulated throughout the structures of the society: "[H]owever much we may deplore such an attitude and feel that important personalities and great art are not born in so shallow a society, we must recognize that here is a strong factor in the painless development from childhood to womanhood. . . . So, high up on our list of explanations we must place the lack of deep feeling which the Samoans have conventionalised until it is the very framework of all their attitudes toward life."[75]

It was, ironically, the purported absence of pain, repression, and strong emotions that evoked the most divergent reactions between the popular and the elite press. In many of the newspaper reviews, "civilization" is understood to be the source of modern ills and the "blessings" of civilization mixed indeed: "The Samoans of Tau . . . know nothing of industrialism, bureaucratic abuses, modern warfare and the abolition of leisure."[76] However, the supposed absence of such pain and stress brought forth a strong moralistic reaction among commentators in the "elite" press. Aldous Huxley, for example, wrote, "Margaret Mead's picture of such a life . . . makes one wonder whether, after all, contentment may not be bought at too high a price. No great civilization has ever taken a cheerful view of life. . . . Not to pursue happiness, but to bear unhappiness with fortitude, has been the lesson of all the practical philosophers."[77] A reviewer for the *Psychoanalytic Review* agreed that

> while the savages have solved their problems apparently with very much more sense than we have and in a way to produce very much less conflict, that they are to all intents and purposes without neuroses and psychoses, still the fact remains that they are savages and that it is very possible that it is because of these easy-going solutions that they remain so. Civilization is not a process that comes upon us passively. It is the result of an active, energetic attack upon problems and situations. . . . [O]ne can not make war against any aspect of reality without taking the risks that go with such a course of conduct, and the results when success is not the outcome are in many instances neuroses and psychoses.[78]

Although no single piece, by Mead or others, engages all these motifs of time, depth, and consciousness, they recur across the various texts. This is, of course, not a new picture of "the native": it is a constellation that has been repeated through a variety of discursive practices. As Freda Kirchwey's review in the *Nation* put it: "[Y]ou will probably be astonished to discover how like a South Sea island that South Sea island can be."[79] However, it is a motif with systematic similarities and contrasts to the Mignon figure. What emerges is a girl-figure that is both the adolescent girl and Samoa itself. Unlike Mignon, who personifies the post-Oedipal self, this girl-figure is the prior self—before repression, before the personal history—which also is the personal mystery—has accrued. This is the self that is undamaged, whole, sexually free, and unselfconscious, without the interiority of the modern self. At best or at her most nostalgic incarnation, the Samoan girl represents lost bliss, unfettered sexuality. At worst or in her most moralistic incarnation, she represents the necessity of taming and disciplining sexuality in order to achieve modern selfhood and its correlative, civilization. She figures not just as savage but as loss—a loss of unrestricted sexuality, which is itself encoded as freedom.

What Mead suggested as a substitute or compensation for this loss was, not surprisingly, rationality, or what she termed "education for choice." In a complex society, she argued, the stresses of adolescence can be minimized not by ignoring complexity but by giving the young the intellectual tools they need in order to make intelligent choices among the array of values to which they are exposed. Indeed, this was to have been the principle message of the book. Even more significantly, she argued that the practice of science and rational, critical self-reflection was something that distinguishes the contemporary West from all so-called primitive societies: "[W]e . . . have one great superiority over . . . all primitive peoples. To them their customs are immune from criticism—given, ordained, immutable. They move unselfconsciously within the pattern of their homogenous, self-contained societies. We, caught almost as completely in a far more complex pattern, have acquired the ability to think about it." [80] Kirchwey's review aptly summed it up: Miss Mead "expresses a reasonable and civilized doubt of the Samoan attitude." [81] Reason and civilization go hand in hand.

Mediating the bucolic past and future progress was Margaret Mead herself. Just as there was a slide between "the Samoan girl" and Samoa, there was also a slide between Mead and the Samoan girls she studied. The most recurrent theme in contemporary descriptions of Mead is her youth. She was twenty-seven when the book was published, had been married, divorced, and remarried but was described repeatedly in the reviews as "exceedingly young," a "girl anthropologist" or "girl scientist," and as "the youngest anthropologist." Mead herself played on her youth and childlike appearance, emphasizing in both the book and in interviews and feature articles the importance of her smallness and slightness to her acceptance within the girls' groups in Samoa. [82] But the identification went beyond Mead's youthfulness. A number of reviewers, for example, wrote that the success of her research was due to the fact that she had "identified herself so completely with Samoan youth." [83] More-critical reviewers saw this identification as a drawback, such as the one who wrote, "Dr. Mead forgets too often that she is an anthropologist and gets her own personality involved with her materials." [84] Either way, her identification with the Samoan girl was reiterated. It was reinforced by the numerous pictures of Mead in Samoan garb, which appeared in newspapers and feature magazine articles, such as one in the *New Age Illustrated,* entitled "An American Princess in the South Seas." It and other articles told how Samoan families and/or chiefs had adopted her or made her a princess and how she had learned to dance and lived "cheek by jowl" with "natives," sleeping on the floor of grass huts. However, this was not just any Samoan girl, for "little Margaret" was also the "girl scientist," a "prodigy," going intrepidly where no white woman had gone before, living without the civilized amenities for the sake of science. Circumscribing the array of statements and images about Mead and her work is the language of science. Categorization, comparison, analysis, critique, objectivity, and rigor are words and ideas that couch all the descriptions of Mead's work in Samoa, whether these are positive or negative evaluations of her work. They located her both directly and by implication on the side of civilization.

"Samoa" thus evoked a complex set of reactions. It was interpreted, unsurprisingly, in different ways by different presses. Notably, the popular press read it with nostalgia for a simple and unfettered sexual economy, whereas the elite magazines reiterated the more civilized values of emotional depth, forbearance in the face of adversity, and a go-ahead, rational, problem-solving approach to life. These distinctive readings neatly encapsulate the ambivalence between nostalgia and progress that, Levine argues, was particularly characteristic of 1920s America. In a sentence that could have been written with reference to *Coming of Age* (but wasn't), he writes that Americans' fascination for filmic representation of "native" and black cultures enabled them to simultaneously "feel superior to those who lacked the benefits of modern technology and to envy them for their sense of community, their lack of inhibitions, their closer contact with their environment and with themselves."[85] *Coming of Age in Samoa* was launched at the height of this ambivalence over the values of the golden past and the promise of the golden future. Its problem, the flapper—with all her associations of freedom, modernity, and rejection of the constraints of traditional femininity—is the problem of lost generational, sexual, and gender certainty. Its solution, the application of science and education to the problems of social complexity and change, is an assurance that progress can and will win.

In this aspect of the work, Mead showed most clearly her investment in the Progressive and post-Progressive visions of society, with the former's emphasis on education and rationality and the latter's emphasis on cultural and personal rather than economic change. Overtly, Mead privileged these apparently contemporary American values. Her disquisition on the lack of true individuality in Samoa reflected Croly's and Brooks's concerns with the ways in which "true individuality" (Croly) or "true personality" (Brooks) can develop only when men in complex societies work "in pursuit of an exclusive interest, promoted by . . . a disinterested motive"[86] or "self-fulfillment" in pursuing "a life interest apart from his rewards, . . . an object of living."[87] For these men, the development of disinterested individuality would lead to "a nation in which each individual should find some particular but essential function" (Croly) or where "the individual could . . . express the better intuitions and desires of his age and place" (Brooks). Whereas for Croly the functionally integrated society grew from men developing their exclusive but disinterested interests, for Brooks the organic interrelationship between individual and society preceded the pursuit of self-fulfillment, "since the mind is a flower that has an organic connection with the soil it springs from," [88] a vision that, thirteen years before the publication of *Coming of Age in Samoa,* prefigured its precept of cultural determinism.

For the intellectuals of the late 1920s, the title of Mead's book would have clearly echoed Brooks's *America's Coming of Age.* However, in *Coming of Age in Samoa,* Mead did more than reiterate a somewhat out-of-fashion philosophy of American society. In portraying Samoa as a "homogenous" society, one in which there was no separation between an individual and his or her culture, she provided a concrete exemplar of the kind of unity of individual and society that Croly had hinted at and that Brooks had asserted. Samoa was more than a South Sea island sexual paradise; it was the embodiment of the dream that a previous generation of American intellectuals had nurtured in a more idealistic and hopeful time—a society in which, to quote Croly, "the individual becomes a nation in miniature, . . . [and] [t]he nation becomes an enlarged individual." [89]

To this Progressive vision, Mead added the popularized versions of psychoanalytic theory that had gained such currency since Brooks and Croly had published their landmark books. The Young American critics expressed their alienation from mainstream middle-class culture in terms of a clash of values, but by the mid-1920s that alienation had been personalized, largely around the notion of repression. In its transatlantic journey, "repression" lost its association with the unconscious and the Oedipal crisis and became any force that restricted the individual, thus giving rise, in the popular parlance, to neuroses and complexes. The populist version of psychoanalysis did have a particular cast in the United States. Freud had downplayed the darker side of his theory in his American lectures, emphasizing instead the "ameliorative, pragmatic qualities of health and good functioning." [90] Repression came to signify something injurious that could be eradicated, freeing the individual from unnatural and unhealthy restraint. The association between the primitive and a lack of constraint, especially sexual constraint was, as Kirchwey pointed out, not in any sense new. Mead's genius was to articulate this association to both well-established Progressive ideals and the particular ambivalences of the more populist sentiments of the mid-1920s. Although Mead was careful to elaborate the disadvantages of primitive homogeneity, the vision of Samoa as a place without strife, without psychological torment, and indeed with a great deal of pleasure and freedom, was the one that held the popular imagination. *Coming of Age in Samoa* was the first accessibly written, widely distributed but scientifically based account of such a society published in the United States. As such, it provided a template for other, future portrayals of societies against which America could be measured and, more often than not, found wanting.

4 "Lords of an Empty Creation"
Masculinity, Puritanism, and Cultural Stagnation

MARGARET MEAD LEFT New York in August 1928 with a crescendo of praise for *Coming of Age in Samoa* rising behind her. Her ultimate destination was not yet decided—somewhere in the Admiralty Islands off the coast of New Guinea—but her aims were clear: "to collect a body of detailed material upon the behavior of children in a primitive community for purposes of comparison with the large body of data which psychologists and educators are collecting concerning the mental development of children in our own civilization." [1] She returned almost exactly a year later, having completed the fieldwork that was to be the basis of her next best-selling book, *Growing Up in New Guinea*. [2] However, she returned to a very different New York. Having departed in a period of burgeoning optimism and economic expansion, she returned to find that optimism soon replaced by panic as the stock market wavered and then plummeted, culminating in Black Thursday, October 24, 1929.

As the heady spirit of the 1920s had shaped both the writing and the responses to *Coming of Age in Samoa*, so *Growing Up in New Guinea* was formulated on the cusp of the 1920s and the early months of the Depression. Although repeatedly criticized for her anthropology of the contemporary West, Mead was nothing if not an astute reader of the temper of the times. The deepening economic crisis and the country's first faltering attempts to understand and counteract it would have been at the forefront of her concerns as she wrote not only her book, which was completed by May 1930, but the many related articles she continued to produce until she left again for New Guinea in autumn 1931. In *Growing Up in New Guinea* and its many spin-offs, she was, once again, to deploy her anthropological material in order to highlight what she saw as America's problems. In the Manus boy, she created a vehicle that personified the crisis in confidence that the United States was undergoing at the turn of the decade.

As Mead drew together her monograph in the months between October 1929 and May 1930, the country struggled, unsuccessfully, to come to terms with the catastrophe that was unfolding. After the initial panic, the principal political response from both Washington and Wall Street was denial. President Hoover cut taxes and put half a billion dollars into public works, but both he and his business advisers continued to declare that the economy was fundamentally sound and that the problem was one of confidence, a ploy one critic suggested was akin to faith-healing the economy.[3] Early 1930 saw an upsurge in stock market activity, characterized mostly by mergers and the creation of holding companies. However, banks continued to collapse at an unprecedented rate; many factories and shops closed down. In April, as Mead was writing the final chapters of her book, the market began to slide again. By the end of the year, nearly fourteen hundred banks, representing nearly $900 million in deposits had folded (this number was to increase by another fifty percent in the following year).[4] As the country entered the second winter of the Depression, Hoover refused to provide federal aid to individuals on the grounds that such a move would undermine the American character and its traditions of rugged individualism, charity, and self-help.

Though the historiography of the years between the wars was shaped by the radical economic rupture that the Wall Street crash ushered in, there was, of course, also considerable continuity from one decade to the next. Cultural historians have noted a number of themes that recur in the personal documents, expressive culture, and social criticism of both decades. President Hoover was not alone in his firm belief in rugged individualism and the power of a positive attitude to cure the country's economic woes. Individualism and individual responsibility were deeply ingrained. This individualism was probably most succinctly expressed in that peculiarly American phenomenon: "the self-help and healing practices of the interconnected, quasi-religious, late nineteenth century movements known as Mind-cure, Spiritualism and Christian Science."[5] Mind-cure was epitomized by the likes of Mary Baker Eddy, its basis the belief that a positive attitude could and would overcome external odds. The Depression did little to change this attitude. Lawrence Levine has argued that, even in the grip of fear and desperation, people felt, almost despite themselves, a sense of personal responsibility for their plight. The American belief that hard work, thrift, and individual initiative led to success did not disappear, even in the face of overwhelming evidence that the problem was structural rather than personal. Levine notes that two of the top-selling books of the decade were Margaret Mitchell's *Gone with the Wind* and Dale Carnegie's *How to Win Friends and Influence People,* which shared the theme that attitude could overcome event.[6]

Strongly linked to this sense of personal responsibility was the shame that people felt at their predicament, a shame that affected men especially. The destabilizing of gender roles, epitomized by the flapper in the 1920s, became, if anything, more acute as the Depression began to bite. Although mechanization of labor, Taylorist work practices, and the acceleration of industrialization in the first decades of the century had undercut the traditional bases of individualist, self-sufficient masculinity, among all classes it had not substantially affected the most basic masculine role of family breadwinner. However, as farms dried up, businesses closed, banks collapsed, and even government jobs disappeared, the breadwinner role became increasingly jeopardized, and for millions of men it disappeared completely. A sense of shame and failure, Levine argues, almost in passing, was particularly acute for fathers whose inability to fulfill traditional responsibilities exacerbated familial tensions already intensified by the hardships the Depression imposed. The Depression's effects played out through gendered structures.[7]

Throughout both decades, there were countervailing trends to the traditional emphasis on hard work, savings, and thrift. There was a greater emphasis on consumption and pleasure in economic theories, in advertising, and in popular culture. This shift towards consumerism began to consolidate in the 1920s with the increase in prosperity, the invention of mass advertising, and the move from "character," with its emphasis on internalized attributes such as prudence, integrity, and stoicism, to "personality," rendered in terms of effect on others, with such traits as magnetism, persuasiveness, and charisma being the measure of the person.[8] These concerns and ambivalences were carried forward into the Depression years. In the 1930s, both expressive culture and alternative economic theories were advocating increased consumption as the nation's economic solution and the individual's key to security and fulfillment. Coincidentally, there was also a greater emphasis in popular culture on living for the present. Films such as *You Can't Take It with You* and books such as *Life Begins at Forty* expressed what many Americans were experiencing—that there was no sure route to material security or success and that the pleasures of the present may be all that one could count on. Between these two, sometimes complementary and sometimes contradictory, positions, "lifestyle" and its less materialistic cousin, which Mead was to term "the art of living," were coming into being.

These concerns and themes echo throughout *Growing Up in New Guinea* and the many spin-off articles Mead published in the professional and popular presses. Her commentaries on contemporary American life led to commissions to write a number of broadly comparative articles on more-general topics—adolescence, childhood, the family—for professional educational publications such as textbooks and *The Encyclopedia of the Social Sciences*. Although *Growing Up in New Guinea* did not get anywhere near the sensational response that *Coming of Age in Samoa* received, it was widely reviewed, and Mead and her research were the subject of feature articles in magazines such as *Travel, Scientific American,* and the *Woman's Journal.* However, *Growing Up* and the articles that drew upon the Manus fieldwork are very different from those that initially grew out of *Coming of Age.* Pervading these articles are anxieties of the times, an uneasy mix of intellectual themes from the 1920s—the problem of sustaining individuality in the face of standardization; the link between materialism and art—and themes more typical of the early Depression—the dysfunctionality of American society, the need for strong leadership for change. These concerns were condensed in the figure of the Manus boy and his transition from spoiled, but lively and intelligent, youth to unhappy, quarrelsome, but hardworking adult, an alter ego for contemporary America in its transition from the Roaring Twenties to the Hungry Thirties. Although at this point, Mead was still committed to the overwhelming influence of culture in shaping individuals, her distaste for the culture she found in Manus, her sense that it wasted the tremendous human potential it developed in its young, set the stage for a progressive disillusionment with culture that would eventually lead her away from seeing human individuality as a process of eventuation.

Although she left New York at the end of August, Mead did not begin fieldwork in Manus until the beginning of December. After a trip across the country and two weeks in Hawai'i, she sailed to New Zealand, where, on October 8, she married Reo Fortune in the Auckland Registry Office. The Manus trip had been engineered by Fortune, who had just completed a stint in the d'Entrecasteaux Islands that would become the basis of his classic study, *Sorcerers of Dobu.*[9] He chose the Admiralties as the location for their joint research project, intending to collect further material for his thesis on comparative religion. They had decided that Mead's planned study of "primitive" children's thought could be undertaken there as well as it could be in any other culture "unchanged" by European encroachment.[10] From New Zealand, the couple sailed to Sydney, where Mead met one of the emerging eminences of British anthropology, A. R. Radcliffe-Brown. Radcliffe-Brown was lecturing in the anthropology department at the University of Sydney and was, at the time, the principal academic gatekeeper of Australian and Melanesian anthropology. He had supported Reo's work in Dobu and recommended him to the Australian Research Council for further fieldwork in the Admiralties. Soon, however, Mead reported to Benedict: "Brown has now gotten to the point where I contrast the institutionalization of kinship in Tonga and Fiji with village institutionalization in Samoa and he is so mad that he was barely civil to me this morning, and didn't introduce me to Elkin who has just come back from the field. . . . He said, pontifically that the similarities between Tonga, Fiji and Samoa were much more interesting than the differences. He really is rather insufferable because he is so sulky and rude whenever he is crossed." [11]

By the time Mead and Fortune were ready to leave for New Guinea, the tensions between them and their mentor had intensified, and Brown withdrew support for English publication of her Manu'a ethnography, telling Mead that it was "the kind of thing which was more appreciated in America." [12] Disgruntled, but convinced of their righteous independence, Mead and Fortune left Sydney at the end of October on "the worst ship in the Pacific." They landed at Rabaul and then made their way along the coast in "a tiny, evil-smelling little tub" to Lorengau, the government station of Manus. [13] There they engaged an interpreter from the Peri village and thus their fieldwork base was decided. In the Peri (or Pere) village at the end of November, they settled in the government house, ordered a new house to be built, and began work.

Mead's bulletins to family and friends evince a growing confidence and engagement with the ethnographic detail. Unlike those from Samoa, which tended to be more personal and gossipy, those from Manus are richly ethnographic. The "Manus true" were a marine people. Mead described the Pere village as "a primitive Venice, the streets are waterways, the houses set on high poles over the water. The only land is found in a few tiny islands, inundated at high tide. . . . All life is conducted by means of canoes." [14] The Manus fished but depended upon their land-based neighbors for sago, fruit, vegetables, and other forms of sustenance and wealth. This dependence, however, was turned to advantage by the Manus, who controlled trade along the coast by virtue of their superior navigation skills and technology. Relations within and between Manus villages, and relations with their land-based trading partners, were fraught and antagonistic. Mead's letters are full of the practical difficulties of living in a culture where an elaborate etiquette of affinal avoidance and exhaustive rituals of divination set in train by illness or accident govern daily life.

After their own house was built, she and Fortune spent the days apart—he in the government house, working on the general ethnography, and she in their new one, working with the children. She described the working conditions as "perfect," noting, "The house abuts on a tiny island where the children play their games; on the other side of the house is the lagoon where all the waterplay goes on. A stone's throw away are two islands where the children swing and on top of which the little girls dance in groups without their grass skirts at sunset. The three year old children can go about alone in canoes so I have no trouble in collecting them minus their parents." [15]

The lives of Manus children provided a stark contrast to those of either American or Samoans, a contrast that was to structure Mead's subsequent writing. Manus, she wrote, "[is] a paradise for children. They have no work except to run errands and that involves paddling about in the water. The women take care of the babies so that the children are free. At low tide in the early morning they course about, shooting fish with tiny bows and arrows, dragging the water for minnows with a long piece of bark used in imitation of a net, or practicing just missing the other's feet with a piece of coral hurled through the water." [16]

The children were not the only ones in their element. Mead clearly loved this new fieldwork and loved, particularly, working with these high-spirited, independent babes. Her new house, she wrote her family, "[is f]rom morning to night . . . full of children, drawing, chattering, spatting, begging cigarettes from each other until one cigarette has gone the round of twenty. When the drawings are finished, they come to me to be dated and named, and then are deposited in a great wooden bowl which is already full to overflowing. At sunset I sometimes make bread or roast a chicken in a camp over on the little islet with twenty eager helpers shrieking, exclaiming, running to throw rotten eggs in the sea or fetch wood for a dying fire." [17]

That these children were principally boys is apparent from other accounts of her fieldwork: "By selecting the oldest boys of the adolescent group, youngsters of about fourteen, as house boys, we were able to attract all the rest of the children

Two Manus boys in a canoe, Pere Village, Manus, 1928–1929; photograph courtesy of the Institute of Inter-cultural Studies and the Library of Congress (Manuscript Division 115)

to our little patch of back yard. Each fourteen-year-old had a ten-year-old slavey, who in turn delegated the disagreeable aspects of his task to a six-year-old. Dinner was often prepared by some dozen small hands, one small boy tending each pot, faithfully blowing up the twig fire underneath it. The little girls were enlisted to pluck the wild pigeons and to fetch the fire wood."[18]

Girls were likely to be betrothed younger, and once betrothed—or at the latest at puberty—they were confined to the company of older, married women and set to work preparing the goods that would be exchanged in the various ceremonies involving their sisters-in-law or their own wedding. Constrained by strict rules of avoidance, their mobility and their ability to operate in mixed-sex groups was severely limited.

Before leaving for the Admiralties, Mead wrote to Bronislaw Malinowski, whose *Sex and Repression in Savage Society* had just been published.[19] She acknowledged the debt owed to him in the field he "originated, sowed, ploughed and made fruitful for those who should try to do the same kind of work."[20] Malinowski's delighted reply reached her in Manus and encouraged her to focus sharply on the details of kinship, building up from her studies of daily individual interactions, a picture of how kinship actually operated. The letters show Mead trying to engage in the theoretical issues raised by Malinowski's Freudian-inspired attempts to understand the relationships between structures of kinship and psycho-affective patterns.[21] However, the systematic reading and theoretical rigor required for that work was at odds with her tendency to broad sweeps, commonsense generalization, and her educative mission. In the end, she developed what might called a kind of dysfunctionalism, viewing Manus society not as a functioning whole but as a dysfunctional culture that was unable to harness to good effect the considerable individual strengths it cultivated in its youth.

At the end of March, Mead announced to her family that there would be no more field bulletins, as "work is getting faster and furiouser as the end of the trip approaches."[22] In July, Mead and Fortune decamped from the Peri village. She described the moving ceremony that marked their departure: "[T]he people gathered in the thatched pile house which we were deserting and stood there silent, huddled together, possessing no customary phrase for so drastic a leave taking. But as our canoe was poled, solemnly, by the elders of the village, . . . the people we had left behind beat out upon the great slit drum first the call which we had used to call our house boys and, second, the death beat."[23]

From Manus, Fortune returned to Dobu for a month, while Mead stayed in Rabaul with Mrs. Phoebe Parkinson, an American Samoan expatriate. After short sojourns in Sydney, Vancouver, and San Francisco, the couple established themselves in New York, where Mead returned to her curatorial duties at the American Museum of Natural History and Fortune took up a doctoral fellowship at Columbia University arranged for him by Boas. She settled down to write *Growing Up in New Guinea*. He worked on the *Sorcerers of Dobu*, which was to be his doctoral dissertation, delaying his general ethnography of Manus until the Dobu book was completed. The next two years were to be a period of intense productivity for both of them. As the economy ground down public and private institutions, including government departments, museums, and universities began to cut programs and staff. The museum began canceling expeditions and reducing salaries in early 1930. Academic and government jobs in anthropology were fast disappearing. It rapidly became clear that the only way the couple could construct a viable future together, in the short term at least, was in joint fieldwork where they could be together and where costs would be lower and covered by research funds. They decided to write their material up as quickly as possible, all the while applying to every possible source for funds for a prolonged period of field-based research. They tried to set up projects in Africa, Fiji, and Rotuma, in addition to New Guinea.

By May 1930, Mead had completed *Growing Up in New Guinea* and sent it off to William Morrow. In it, she described a lagoon-dwelling, trading people whose social organization was based on a cycle of intergenerational debt, sexual "repression," and inter-gender hostility. The children, she argued, were trained in three things only—to be physically safe in their watery environment, to respect property, and to observe a system of sexual and excretory taboos that resulted in extreme prudery. Other than these matters, they were completely indulged by their parents and, once safe, left to entertain themselves until betrothal or puberty for the girls, or marriage for the boys. Although the littlest girls enjoyed the same freedoms as boys, by puberty, at the latest, all girls were betrothed—a state that imposed on them a vast range of avoidance taboos in relation to their future husband and all his kin. From the time of their betrothal, they had to wear pandanus capes that they drew over themselves when a taboo relative was in sight. All houses had two doors so that women could make hurried exits without passing incoming affines.

Boys had a more prolonged adolescence, one marked by freedom and play in a "boys' house." However, their state changed abruptly and irrevocably at marriage. To finance their marriages, young men were forced into debt to older men, and thence into fishing and trade. All young people, Mead contended, were saddled, ignorant, and unprepared and suffered the burdens of adulthood—for the girls an oppressive array of in-law taboos, marital violence, and alienation from their children. Boys, with whom Mead became more concerned, were faced with almost unceasing monetary and social indebtedness. For them, adult life was a continual struggle, first to pay off the debts incurred to finance their marriage, and second to increase prestige and wealth through the financing of the marriages of their younger kin. Long betrothals, involving years of avoidance and shame, resulted in uncomfortable and often hostile marriages, from which there was little opportunity for escape, except through death. From tyrannical, free-spirited toddlers, Manus boys turned into litigious, unhappy, quarrelsome adults, "sexually repressed" and indebted to their uncles for the bride-price of wives they loathed. There were things she approved of in Manus culture, such as the emphasis on competence and success that made the smallest children capable of living safely on land or sea, and the close nurturing relations between fathers and children. But she found the culture in general rancorous, empty, and without grace.

In Manus, Mead found a society that she presented as having direct parallels with the United States and its capitalist economy, "a caricature in brown of contemporary American society."[24] Like Americans, the Manus were obsessed by business: "The news of the day was money, unpaid debts, bankruptcy, a new economic deal, the merger accomplished between two business men, or a contract successfully concluded between two traders."[25] And like the Manus, "Americans tend to spoil their children, to demand no work from them, not even to ask that they understand the veriest outlines of steel manufactory or soap-making, investment banking or civil engineering, upon which their bread and butter and the purchase of a popgun depend."[26] Following the pattern of *Coming of Age in Samoa*, the second part of *Growing Up in New Guinea*, entitled "Reflections on the Educational Problems of Today," draws out the implications of her findings for American parents and educators. The four chapters deal with respect for older generations, fathers' roles in the raising of boys, the cultural basis of imagination and art, and the strength and inevitability of tradition. Manus and American children, Mead argues, are "lords of an empty creation,"[27] having no respect for their elders nor the finer values of life nor, for the majority, any choice but to conform to the patterns that their particular cultures have laid down for them. She found in the Manus a surrogate America, where spoiled, undisciplined children turned into indebted, unhappy adults. A more direct connection to a still Puritanical nation in the throes of the Depression cannot be imagined.

The response to the book within anthropology was mixed. Her friend Ruth Benedict praised it in the *New York Times*.[28] Melville Herskovitz, reviewing it for the *Nation*, called it "challenging" and "stimulating" but did not think the "applied anthropology" was of any interest to professionals.[29] Alfred Kroeber wrote to her privately, "[Y]ou have sharpened your technique, but been under the handicap of touching lightly on the culture in order to protect your husband."[30] His review in the *American Anthropologist,* however, was highly critical. Mead was now an established, if unorthodox, anthropologist and fair game for the full blast of peer criticism. Kroeber lumped her with the functionalists, whose approach he dismissed as being of only passing interest. But even comparison to Malinowski, the father of functionalist anthropology, he wrote, is "to Dr. Mead's disadvantage." Malinowski had given to anthropology "unusually saturated, detailed, accurate, well-integrated, and valuable" ethnographic information, Mead only "scraps." He again took a swipe at her professional relationship with her husband: "[I]s the providing of [ethnographic detail] always to be left to a Krämer [31] or a Fortune?" Mead's "near-genius," he wrote, was essentially aesthetic, but, he pointed out, "a piece of work need not be ethnographically unreliable because it is aesthetically effective." [32]

In Britain, as well, doubts began to be expressed about Mead's ability to do "real" anthropology. A review by Edith Clarke of the University of London was both restrained and damning. Mead was accused of empirical and theoretical naiveté and of conducting fieldwork too hastily and without adequate language skills. Internal contradictions in the book, such as Mead's contention that the Manus were virtually untouched by European encroachment, were politely but firmly exposed. Clarke noted that, "On her own showing European influence has profoundly modified native life." Mead's assessment of the "emptiness" of Manus children's play was likewise greeted with a mixture of incredulity and disdain.

> For my own part, my first reaction to the account of these efficient babes tumbling in and out of canoes, romping on the half-submerged islands, untrammeled by grown-ups, and bathing the live-long golden day in the waters of their lagoon was: "What a children's Paradise!" It brought back to me my own riotous childhood, sharing similar joys with little black hoydens in the river that turned the water-wheel of my grandfather's sugar estate. And I thought: maybe the English visitor might have said the same of our play as does Miss Mead of the games of the Manus children; whereas a deeper understanding and the sympathy which comes from sharing the people's lives might have made her think differently. [33]

The Australian C. W. Hart, less restrained, wrote a withering review for *Man,* querying whether or not Mead was "an anthropologist at all" and condemning the ethnographic section for "oversimplification and unjustifiable dogmatism." In a left-handed compliment to Fortune, he suggested that Fortune had not completed his promised general ethnography because the time in the field was not sufficient "to allow the more careful and judicial Mr. Fortune, trained in English methods of scientific research, to give an authoritative account of the culture." [34] Hart, like Clarke and others, was especially critical of Mead's superficial analyses of modern life: "The second section of the book is of no value to anthropology and one imagines of very little value to any other of the social sciences. The use of Mr. J. B. Priestley's novel *Angel Pavement* as an account of English inter-family conflict with which to compare her own account of such conflict in Manus is not without its significance, while the naiveté with which she assumes the identity of English and United States communal values is remarkable, to say the least." [35] This review, published, like the others, when Mead and Fortune were back in the field, prompted letters from Benedict and Fortune in defense of both Mead's and Fortune's anthropological credentials. The editor of *Man* issued a restrained rap on the knuckle to Hart for professional discourtesy but did not publish the rebuttals. [36]

The anthropological response to *Growing Up* horrified Mead. By now well used to her public status as girl prodigy, she was shocked at the implications of ignorance and incompetence that underpinned these reviews. In a private letter to Kroeber, she struggled to contain her outrage with a man who was able to wield his influence over both her and Fortune's access to funding and jobs in the United States. She thanked him for "all his kind words of commendation in the review" and told him: "[It] taught me how incredibly naïve I have been in my reactions to previous criticisms. . . . To discover that [my colleagues] thought me so lacking in method, so deficient in ethnological training as to be making flimsy generalizations without having done the kinship system, or understood the economic arrangements or the religious ideas, was a real revelation to me."

Although treading cautiously on other criticisms in the review, she also took him directly to task for his unprincipled and sexist reference to Fortune. In a sentence that implicitly contrasted Kroeber's churlishness with Reo's gentlemanly behavior, she pointed out that Fortune had "always shared honors so scrupulously and generously with me that it makes me very unhappy to have had such a comment appear in a review of my work." [37] Kroeber, it must be said, wrote an apologetic letter to Fortune, and relations were patched up although never fully repaired. Although based on a maturing ethnographic capability, *Growing Up in New Guinea* undermined Mead's, and by association Fortune's, professional status within the international anthropological community. In 1933 Benedict wrote to a mutual friend, "I'm worried about the lack of appreciation [Margaret and Reo's] work gets, on both sides of the Atlantic. They care so much for approval, and so much of it is withheld just because people are chagrined by being outdistanced, and find it easier to refuse to believe than to recognize that work can be done more quickly and thoroughly than [others] could do it in the field. . . . So they come out a little at the end of the horn, and the pity of it is that they want recognition so much."[38]

Mead's response to the anthropological criticism was to come out fighting. In early 1931, she and Fortune were granted funding for two years of research in Australia and New Guinea. But rather than heading straight back to the field, Mead deferred the onset of the trip for six months. In order to shore up her damaged professional reputation, she added yet another book to her already formidable workload. Fortune had originally been committed to writing a "complete ethnology of the Manus culture."[39] However, sometime in early 1930, the division of labor over the Manus material was renegotiated. Fortune now limited himself to Manus religion, promising a book on language in the future, while Mead took over the detailed interrelationships between kinship and economics. *Kinship in the Admiralty Islands* was written to demonstrate her facility with the "real" concerns of anthropology—kinship, economics, and material culture. Tired of the accusations that her fieldwork was inadequate, she also wrote a spirited defense of both her approach to culture and her ethnographic methodology, "More Comprehensive Field Methods,"[40] which she sent to the belly of the behemoth *American Anthropologist,* her "home" journal, but one that had been consistently antagonistic to her and Fortune's work. Trying to complete their commitments in time to leave in June 1931 for New Guinea, they set up a grueling schedule. She wrote her mother that they were "leading a rather peculiar life." She added, "We can't get into our apartment until December so we have a room and bath and are never there. Reo has an office at Columbia and I meet him for dinner and we both work there in the evenings. At eleven or thereabouts we walk over to Broadway for a glass of orangeade and so home. . . . I am writing my Indian woman book in the day time and working on Manus with Reo at night."[41]

Despite this all-out effort to improve her professional credibility, Mead knew where her strongest support came from. Sticking firmly to her vision of a publicly accessible, comparative anthropology, she consolidated her reputation among the educators and the educated public by continuing to place her work in popular and educational periodicals that were less cognizant of the details of anthropology and more open to her pedagogical approach. However, she avoided putting her ethnographic work into the major anthropological journals, publishing only one such article from her Manus fieldwork and that, not in the *American Anthropologist* for which she wrote many reviews, but in the British *Journal of the Royal Anthropological Institute.*[42]

Even in the field of popular writing, not all her attempts were immediately successful. In these works, she trod a delicate line between education and exotica.

The *Saturday Evening Post* invited her to write an "amusing" article comparing "Manus people and our own."[43] Despite possessing a very acerbic sense of humor, Mead was not apt to display it in her public pedagogy. She decided to use the occasion to compare the education of Manus and American boys. In an attempt to stave off criticism of inadequate knowledge of her own culture, she spent months finding the very few studies of the post-graduation careers of college men. The article was entitled "Stone Age Education—and Ours." Its premise was that Americans were creating unnecessary inefficiency and unhappiness by sending their young men to college rather than training them for business in their teenage years, when they were more pliant, just as the Manus were creating miserable adults by allowing their children to run free until marriage. She concluded her article:

> But is there any need for us to go on wasting the time of our youth in this way? The chief boast of the machine age over the stone age is self-consciousness. Where stone age man had to muddle along, dependent upon some chance invention, some accidental adjustment, to better his lot, modern man can stand aside and analyze his environment. The Manus have probably been wasting their young men's time for a thousand years. We, with our different rate of change, have made the same mistake for a couple of generations. It should take an even shorter time to evict this stone age anachronism from our twentieth century machinery.[44]

After months of negotiation over the content of the article, the *Post*'s editor was not impressed. His response was swift and final:

> I am awfully sorry to have to tell you that "Stone Age Education—And Ours" does not pan out as we had hoped it would. You have been a little broad in your indictment of our educational system, and have thus killed what pleasant humor there might have been in the article. Somehow we can't stomach such a sweeping blow at practically everything we stand for. . . . At any rate, we are regretfully sending back the manuscript and we cannot, with any conscience, suggest a revision, for the chances don't look too good. I am only sorry that we have put you to such an amount of work with no reward.[45]

Mead was later to publish this paper as "Growing Up in the South Seas" in *Forum: The Magazine of Controversy*, which must have seemed a more appropriate venue, and by 1932, as the Depression deepened, its chastising tone may have been more palatable.[46]

The nonacademic reviews of *Growing Up in New Guinea*, however, were, with a few exceptions, positive, if lacking the giddy excitement that characterized those of *Coming of Age in Samoa*. Most reviewers were charmed by Mead's account of the Manus as very like Americans, with their profit-oriented adults and spoiled children. Her argument that indulging children did not necessarily lead to new heights of creativity was particularly noted. The Progressive Education movement, like other liberal theories of the twenties, made a comfortable and reassuring target for commentators searching for answers to America's plight. The reviews, by focusing on the spoiled children of Manus and America, in fact deflected the message Mead was trying to get across. The complex problems of cultural conservatism she was trying to address got reduced to "spoiled children." Many reviewers also commented on the sexual prudery of the Manus. A number remarked that the book dispelled the myth of savage bliss and sexual freedom. The parallels drawn with American society did not stop reviewers from describing the Manus as "curious," "startling," "weird," and "strange," and some compared Mead's emerging corpus to *Gulliver's Travels*.[47] Many newspapers and magazines and even the American Library Association referred to it as a "travel book," prompting Ruth Benedict to request that the ALA reclassify it as social science, social psychology, or education.[48] Again, reviewers in the elite press were less impressed with the lessons she tried to draw for America, and advised her to stick to ethnography. But, unlike the spirited responses to *Coming of Age*, most reviews tended simply to summarize Mead's findings and urge readers to consider her "provocative" ideas. By comparison with reviewers of *Coming of Age*, however, no reviewer seemed to be particularly provoked. It is a dour book, offering much criticism of American society but little vision of the way forward.

Growing Up in New Guinea undoubtedly has the most complex intellectual genealogy of all Mead's early books. It is ostensibly a book on comparative "education"—or what would later come to be called socialization. Mead brought together a range of intellectual sources in part 2, which she entitled "Reflections on the Educational Problems of Today in the Light of Manus Experience." Mead was not particularly fastidious about citing her intellectual sources: in *Growing Up in New Guinea* she cites only two—Ruth Benedict's foundational article on personality and culture[49] and Robert and Helen Lynd's groundbreaking study of Muncie, Indiana, *Middletown*[50]—and these very briefly. But she makes extensive use of the debates that had been going on for twenty years about the state of "civilization" in the United States. In fact, she addresses her audience as if she and they share an understanding of the essential characteristics of American society. Those characteristics are precisely as interpreted by the New York cultural critics.

For its intellectual direction, the book draws directly on notable cultural critiques of the previous two decades. The frequent references to the Manus as Puritanical, for example, resonated with all the meanings that word had developed since Santayana published "The Genteel Tradition" in *Winds of Doctrine*.[51] One of the central parallels that Mead draws between Manus and America is that both societies are preoccupied with trade, materialism, and profit and have never developed artistic life. This argument was made most forcefully by Van Wyck Brooks in 1915 and repeated time and again over the next fifteen years. By the early 1930s, this characterization of American life was so taken for granted among the intellectual elite, who had of course invented it, and in the popular press, which had disseminated it, that not one reviewer questioned Mead's description of America or Manus or the necessary connection between them.

This is particularly telling because of the extremely contradictory way in which Mead again used the concept of repression. As Hale has noted, intellectuals who were psychoanalyzed between 1910 and 1930 tended to see repression as located in their parents' actions, or in society at large.[52] This interpretation dovetailed with the way cultural critics used psychoanalysis to explain the connection between the American economy, American culture (as way of life) and absence of culture (as artistic life). Thus, Mead in 1930 was able to argue, without contradiction from the psychoanalytic community, that children in Manus suffered no repression. In making this characterization, she not only ignored the standard Freudian meaning but also the more common meaning of societal constraint, having already documented the rigid taboos around excretion and sex, taboos with which Manus children were inculcated. In virtually the same breath, she was able to describe Manus adults as Puritans—with all that term's connotations of sexual repression. The message being conveyed was, however, that repression was not related, except incidentally, to sex or sexuality but to the economic system in which the Manus adult men were enmeshed. The "repression" of the women received barely a mention in the comparative part of the book.

This emphasis on the transition from boyhood to manhood permeates both part 2 of the book, and the popular articles. The Samoan child was female, and the Manus child was, by default, male. In the popular articles, it is the boy child who is described frolicking in the lagoon, punting his miniature canoe between the house posts, demanding care from his parents, and then, under the pressures of marriage, slipping sullenly into fishing and trading to pay for his bride. In the book itself, Mead devoted an entire chapter to the comparison of fathering of boys in America and Manus. She contrasted the warm, intimate care Manus men gave to their children with the distant, impersonal fathering she argued was characteristic of American men. In Manus, men were the primary caregivers of children past weaning. They carved their toddlers little canoes, taught them to punt both these and full-sized versions, indulged them with betel nuts, took their sides in conflicts with their mothers. Mead argued that the Manus boys and men had strong, highly individuated personalities because of this opportunity for close, loving identification between son and father. She cites the case of boys fostered at different ages by different types of men and argues that boys' personalities changed depending on the life stage and relative success of their fathers or foster fathers.

For her ethnography of fathering in America, Mead drew on Robert and Helen Lynd's *Middletown*, which had been published just as she returned from the field and which had gained much attention in the press. Almost certainly, she also drew on her own and her younger brother's relationships with their difficult, distant father. For Mead, the American father was "an unknown force hard to reckon with, . . . a recalcitrant breadwinner who sometimes refuses to dispense the desired amount of pocket money, . . . a usually indifferent member of the household who suddenly exercises a veto supported by superior strength and economic superiority."[53] This was the father, like Edward Mead, who had to be manipulated into allowing his daughter a college education, who withdrew funding for her master's degree, who mocked his musically gifted son and bullied him into an economics career, and who, consequently, was not told, until after the fact, of his children's marriages and divorces, and then not by them but by their long-suffering mother. This, obviously, was not a unique pattern of paternal functioning. The Lynds found that neither working-class nor business-class men in Middletown spent time with their children, although business-class men tended to feel that they should. Business-class men spent what leisure time they had at civic clubs, attending to the social relations that determined their access to credit. Their children listed "spending time with his children" most frequently in their list of "ten . . . desirable qualities in a father."[54]

By contrast with Manus boys, American boys had no opportunity to develop strong identifications with their fathers and to thus develop strongly individuated personalities: "[T]he degeneration of the father's role into that of a tired, often dreaded nightly visitor makes his son's happy identification with him impossible." American boys, she argued, were raised principally by mothers, nurses, and female teachers who "muffle [them] in feminine affection" and act as a "smoke-screen through which the father's image filters distorted, magnified, unreal." This, Mead argued, is a "precarious business in a heterosexual world": if he identifies himself with [his mother] it is at the risk of becoming an invert, or at best of making some fantastic and uncomfortable emotional adjustment." She saw problematic identification as particularly damaging in the case of successful men's sons, who, she argued, rather than building on their father's successes, were often "failures *because* their fathers were famous." America was wasting its youth; even more seriously, it was wasting the gains made by one generation through its failure to secure them in the next: "a strong man's sons should be strong, every gain made by an individual should be conserved for the next generation."[55] The end result was, she argued, a loss of vitality that was as much a loss to the society as it was to the individual. Given only "a dull generic idea of *manhood*," "[t]he American boy's conceptions of manhood are diluted, standardized, undifferentiated. . . . The contrast between what we might make of our boys and what we do make of them is like the contrast between a series of beautiful objects made by individual loving craftsmen, and a series of objects all turned out by a machine."[56]

Concern with individuation and standardization permeates both the book and the articles written from the Manus material. This longstanding theme in 1920s cultural critique was one of three that emerged out of the Stearns 1920 symposium on American civilization.[57] It was also one of the persistent themes of *Middletown*. The Lynds argued that it was access to credit that was repressing individuation in middle America, because banks and other financial institutions set standards not only of financial liquidity but of personal behavior.[58] However, they were unusual in their attribution of the source of standardization: cultural critics more commonly blamed it on "the machine," Taylorist work practices, and the advertising industry. Mead drew on these ideas to argue that age grading in American schools should be discarded or at least modified in favor of more attention to individual ability, such as Manus children received from their fathers.[59] In "Standardized America vs. the Romantic South Seas," she shifted her argument somewhat, pointing out that "homogenous" primitive societies were internally standardized: "[W]hile it is true . . . that one small group of people differ[s] from another small group of people, that [does] not result—as so many enemies of the machine age believe—in giving individuality to people who lived under this system. . . . From the standpoint of a man of Manus or a woman of Baluwan, life is infinitely, unbelievably more standardized than it is to the humblest inhabitant of Sioux City."[60]

Large-scale manufacture allowed "the common man . . . to build and externalize an individual taste."[61] She compared consumer choice to a mosaic in which although "each small block of color has a thousand exact counterparts, . . . the combination, the design is new and individual and worthy of attention."[62] The problem, she argued, was not with the machine age per se but with the organization of society that standardized human beings. This article, published as Mead returned to New Guinea in 1931, attracted a great deal of comment, with "almost all the book columns [making] special remarks about it" and many people discussing it.[63]

The most frequently cited passage in the reviews of *Growing Up* is one in which Mead develops the notion of the "art of living." This idea appears first in the introduction, and many reviewers quoted and commented on this passage in approving tones: "Like America, Manus has not yet turned from the primary business of making a living to the less immediate interest of the conduct of life as an art. . . . The dreamer who turns aside from fishing and trading and so makes a poor showing at the next feast is despised as a weakling. Artists they have none, but like Americans, they, richer than their neighbors, buy their neighbor's handiwork. To the arts of leisure, conversation, storytelling, music, dancing, friendship and lovemaking, they give scant recognition."[64]

In this oft-quoted passage, Mead clearly spoke to the concerns of reviewers and to the intellectuals and artists, many of whom saw themselves as alienated from and unappreciated in America. She echoed that genealogy of cultural critics who saw American culture as damaged by the irrevocable split between the pragmatics of business and the life of the mind and spirit. The cultivation of the art of living was, for Croly, the whole point, and the end to which the Progressive reorganization of business, politics, and social life was aimed. As the political aspirations of the Progressives had soured and intellectuals had turned to "culture" as a way of redeeming America, self-development and the integration of art into the personal and the personality grew. In the face of standardization, appreciation of "the finer" values served to distinguish the civilized from the machine-generated hoi polloi.

What Mead added to this modernist mix was an emphasis on tradition and respect for elders, values that had been repudiated by Bourne and other young American moderns. More than any of her other lessons, this one she built from comparisons between America and Manus on the one hand, and Samoa on the other. Perhaps one of the things that eventually turned Mead against the functionalism of Malinowski and Radcliffe-Brown was what she saw as the disjuncture between the Manus' admirable childrearing practices and their disagreeable adult culture. She saw no smooth fit between the lively intelligence and flexibility she observed among Manus children and the undignified, unhappy social order of the adults. By contrast, she argued that Samoan social life was superior: "[A]lthough the Manus system would appear to be a better one for training young people to be progressive flexible leaders in adult social life, actually the Manus social life is politically anarchical. The Samoan children, less well trained in appearance, inherit a social form so superior to the Manus, that adult social life is a far finer social product than is Manus."[65]

In another article, she wrote that "the Samoan contribution to the world gallery of human experiment is primarily a point of view, an attitude of mind, a grace of living, impossible to impale on the iron pin of the collector, almost impossible to preserve in films and records . . . a unique spirit of living."[66] This spirit or art of living was one in which finer values—discipline and dignity; respect for knowledge, the arts, and experience, and for one's elders; valuing the person, not his possessions—were the guiding principles. These she saw as giving a grace and gravitas to Samoan society that was sorely lacking in Manus and American life. More than that, she saw America as hostile to those whose temperament inclined them towards such values: "a type of personality which sets a premium upon the art of living is out of place in present day America."[67] The "meditative person," the person with "other world values," the individual bent on self-expression, were not valued by American society, which determined that "even a parson must be a go-getter and the premium is always to the energetic,"[68] another instance of standardization.[69]

By reading across these texts, it is possible to see what Mead apprehended as the links between these themes of masculinity, individuality, standardization, and the art of living. She repeatedly poses the question of how to preserve what is valuable in American culture while allowing for innovation and change. Unlike *Coming of Age in Samoa*, wherein America's heterogeneous "culture" is seen as providing options for change in the modern West, in *Growing Up in New Guinea*, "culture" is the dead hand. *Growing Up in New Guinea* was originally conceived as a refutation of progressive education theory, which assumed, on the basis of bowdlerized versions of psychoanalysis, that children can be the source of social change if they are freed to express their creativity. Manus children, she argued, although free and undisciplined, showed no signs of imaginative play or artistic creativity. The capacity for and content of imagination, she thus maintained, is no more natural than the strains and stresses of adolescence. Both are provided or set in place by culture or "tradition" as lived and practiced by adults. Generalizing, she argued that "[t]he inevitable fashion in which children of each society become the adults of that society would discourage any tendency to utopian dreams of reforms sprung from the schoolroom."[70] Change must come from adults; in order to change, society had to produce adults strong enough and individual enough to set new directions.

This argument was most clearly set out in an article for the *Thinker,* entitled "Are We Mature?" The prompt for the article was the publication of Floyd Dell's *Love in the Machine Age.* Dell argued that "the machine age" offered the possibility of overthrowing old patriarchal structures of organizing sexual relations. Unfortunately, he posited monogamous lifelong heterosexual marriage as the sign of both personal and social maturity, whereas prostitution, homosexuality, delayed marriage, and adultery were signs of arrested development and "the old patriarchal order."[71] Incensed, and no doubt personally insulted, Mead struck out at Dell, who saw himself as a rebel and creator of a new order. What any society takes for maturity, she argued, are simply those behaviors that correspond to its dominant values, thus putting Dell's pretensions to radicalism in their place. Adherence to those values is, for most people, a necessity, for "[w]ithout a chosen and cherished road for the feet of the majority of its people, a culture loses form." However, if a culture allows no venue for change, it will not advance: "[G]enerations would merely follow each other down the road of social maturity. For change we need immaturity—rejection of the beaten track."[72]

Although Mead's concern with the "deviant" has been read as a covert way of justifying or working out her love for women, that interpretation oversimplifies both her intentions and her ambitions. Mead saw America as a culture stuck on the beaten path. The 1920s gains in prosperity and freedom were in jeopardy, wasted by the spoiled, rambunctious, and undisciplined youthful country. In the face of crisis, leadership was badly needed, but the culture had not set in place the necessary conditions for the cultivation of strong, individualistic leaders. It is in this context that emphasis on boys and men in the Manus texts can be understood, for they were "the sex which has the greatest freedom to make permanent contributions."[73] To develop strong personalities, Mead argued, boys needed close and intimate association with a particular strong man. That opportunity was denied American boys at the cost of the whole society. Distant "generic" fathering led to a myriad of social and individual problems: either overemphasis on the peer group and lack of respect for experience, or over-identification with women, with its consequences of emotional maladjustment and inversion. Mead couches this threat as dangerous for the individual boy "in a heterosexual world." While this phrase signaled to the cognoscenti that homosexuality might be not so dangerous in another culture, it also played to wide societal fears of homosexuality as a threat to social order—the possibility that distant fathering was emasculating America. In any case, both the strengths of previous generations and the potential for change in the current one were jeopardized.

Although many reviewers picked up on the parallel between the spoiled children of Manus and America, almost none commented on her contrast between Manus and American fathering. Even as her analysis synthesizes some of the predominant social themes of her times, her solution—better, closer fathering—was peculiarly blind to the economic exigencies and fears that were preoccupying America. As a prescription for change, it offered little to grasp onto. For American men, who were watching jobs disappear daily, and with them, their ability to provide the necessities of life for their families, Mead's proselytizing on their further inadequacies offered neither a humorous distraction nor a practical solution. However, the links Mead made between Puritanism, repression, and the absence of art were so well established in American cultural critique that, by "finding" those same links in Manus, Mead secured her place in the ranks of the arbiters of American culture. Her account of spoiled Manus children turning into sullen debt-racked men was an uncannily precise affirmation of the latent Calvinism that underpinned American society, with its ongoing struggle between pleasure and discipline. As the country braced itself for another winter, it is not surprising that Mead's solution to America's ills—better fathering—received no mention at all.

Growing Up in New Guinea was, however, an oddly prescient text. Published a year later, when the cry for strong and innovative leadership was being trumpeted in the elite magazines and the newspapers alike, it would, one suspects, have galvanized public attention. As it is, the press picked up on the parallels between American and Manus spoiled children and between the economic obsessions of the two societies but paid little attention to the relationships Mead posed between fathering and leadership. Ironically, given recent controversies about her work, the response to *Growing Up in New Guinea* within anthropology was far more critical than was the response to *Coming of Age in Samoa*. Indeed, the book was virtually uniformly severely criticized in anthropological reviews. Paradoxically, its earnestness, it chastising tone, its iconoclastic position on the natural creativity of children, and, above all, its uncannily precise articulation of the concerns of intellectual and liberal middle-class America on the cusp of the Depression confirmed and consolidated Mead's position as a leading public intellectual. Her professional colleagues might be critical of her methodology, her ethnographic interpretations, or her understanding of modern society. However, there can be no doubt of Mead's ability to read her public and to reflect back to it, in the guise of scientific ethnography, its principle preoccupations.

5 "Every Woman Deviating from the Code"

Cultural Lag, Moral Contagion, and Social Disintegration

OF THE FOUR non-specialist ethnographies that Margaret Mead wrote between 1928 and 1935, the least well known is *The Changing Culture of an Indian Tribe*. There are a number of reasons for this. In the first place, the research was located in the American Midwest, well outside Mead's usual provenance of Oceania, an anomaly in her oeuvre. Perhaps more important is the fact that Mead herself never popularized this work. Unlike the three more famous monographs, *Coming of Age in Samoa, Growing Up in New Guinea,* and *Sex and Temperament in Three Primitive Societies, Changing Culture* inspired no spin-off articles in *Cosmopolitan* or the *Parents Magazine* that described the practices of the Antler Indians and drew moral or pedagogical lessons for (white, middle-class) American parents and educators, and, coincidentally, widened the book's readership. The "Antlers,"[1] therefore, occupy a curious space or lacuna in Mead's work, appearing, and then rarely, only in the comparative articles she was asked to write for academic collections on child psychology or for the *Encyclopedia of the Social Sciences*. This absence is not confined to Mead's own writings. Micaela di Leonardo omits this work in her analysis of Mead's anthropology between the wars.[2] George Stocking calls it "[o]ne of the earliest and most interesting studies" of acculturation done in this period but goes on to analyze others;[3] a film retrospective takes Mead directly from Manus to Arapesh with no mention of the intervening fieldwork in Nebraska.[4] Even the centennial retrospective of Mead's work in the Library of Congress failed to feature the work in Nebraska.[5] Many anthropologists are not aware that Mead did this research and wrote a book about it.[6] Of her four early research projects and their renderings in the form of monographs, the Antler work and *Changing Culture of an Indian Tribe* is the one with the least name recognition among professionals and public alike.

There is one immediate explanation for Mead's uncharacteristic reticence about the Antlers in the popular press, and that is that the research on their culture was undertaken covertly. The Antlers were, in reality, the Omaha, who, since the mid-1850s, had occupied a reservation in the vicinity of Macy, Nebraska. Mead presented herself to them simply as Mrs. Fortune, a wife "killing time in idle conversation or attendance at ceremonies"[7] while her husband did research on Omaha religious practices. She used Fortune's name, took no notes in public, and asked questions in a form of "gossipy curiosity." She justified this deception as necessary to protect individuals from the shame that would follow her reportage of the intimate details of their lives. Retrospectively, however, she acknowledged the loss of authenticity that results when the researcher does not declare herself.[8]

While the covert nature of the research may explain Mead's unwillingness to publish on the Omaha in the popular press, there is a more specific paradox involved in the position she herself took with regard to this work. The paradox is that this research, which arguably had much more immediate applicability and urgency for American policy makers and educators than did any of her other studies, did not stir Mead to pedagogical ends. In fact, she specifically disavowed any intention of "rendering immediate aid to government or suggesting social panaceas"; the study was undertaken "purely with a view to adding to our knowledge."[9] Unlike her research in Samoa, the Admiralty Islands, and New Guinea, the Omaha work died a quiet death. This attitude to a piece of research, understandable in other scholars, is strikingly out of character for Mead, who, from the beginning of her career, defined her mission as social pedagogy. As a self-appointed interpreter of the "primitive" to the modern, Mead was able to make (sometimes outlandish) recommendations about social change on the basis of taken-for-granted knowledge or even very questionable interpretations of evidence. In this book, she specifically disavowed any such motive.

The quiescent history of this research cannot, of course, be attributed solely to Mead's own actions or attitudes about the research and its subsequent publication. The book did not "grab" the public attention, the popular press, or even her professional colleagues' imaginations in the way that *Coming of Age in Samoa* had, nor indeed did it gain even the more circumspect attention that *Growing Up in New Guinea* had attracted and that *Sex and Temperament in Three Primitive Societies* would attract four years later. To write about *The Changing Culture of an Indian Tribe* in the context of the early years of the Depression in America, then, is a curious activity. It is, in fact, to write about an absence, a non-occurrence, a non-response, a repression, both by Mead herself and by the many intellectuals, journalists, and educators who seized on her other books and made them into best-sellers. The book tells a story that no one, not even Mead herself, wished to hear, a profoundly disturbing story of the shattered American dream. If Mead's books can be read as allegories about America, *The Changing Culture of an Indian Tribe* is perhaps the most allegorical, precisely because it disavows any intention to moralize or solve the problems it exposes, a disavowal that parallels policy and anthropological attitudes of the time. The conditions she exposed were not news to anthropologists. Lewis Merriam's 1928 report on the state of Native Americans had roundly condemned conditions on reservations.[10] Despite this, academic and museum-based anthropologists in America were still largely committed to "salvage" ethnography in the guise of historical reconstruction. Indeed, Mead herself became increasingly sympathetic with this historicist bent over the course of the Omaha research, feeling that it was the best that could be managed, given the state of native communities. However, in writing a book about that most potent and ambivalent figure, the "Indian," Mead inevitably also told a tale of America at large. The book participated in a long history of representations of the Indian as both the epitome of "America" and as its antithesis, and in the equally long denial of America's internal empire. The cultural tragedy Mead found in Omaha society was a painful and disrupting reminder of the failure of the American dream, a dream in which, Susan Scheckel suggests, "the ghost of the Indian as the object of genocidal violence has returned inevitably to haunt the nation and its narratives." [11]

The failure of that dream was being all too obviously lived out by Americans from across the social and ethnic spectrum in the early 1930s. The severity and relentlessness of the economic collapse went beyond the comprehension of even the most persistent critics of American culture and economy of the previous decades. Revolution and fascism hung in the air as threats or solutions to the problems that capitalism and democratic government seemed unable to solve. For two decades, intellectual life in the United States had been fueled by a critique of science, technology, and materialism and their dislocating and chaotic effects on individuals and communities. Faced with the collapse of that technological and economic infrastructure, intellectuals began to revive the Progressive vision of an integrated society, calling for a radical rethinking of American economics, culture and morals in order to shape a society which was not only prosperous, but also integrated and culturally unified. That dream of integration reached its fullest theoretical expression in functionalism just as the economy crumbled, giving anthropologists an influence in shaping the search for new social models. So-called primitive societies, portrayed as smoothly integrated mechanisms that met all of their members needs, fed into the desire for "wholeness," simplicity, self-sufficiency, and community in the face of the social disintegration all around.

In order to explicate this failed dream Mead drew again on an analytic model that had been circulating in American intellectual circles for more than a decade. This was her mentor William Fielding Ogburn's concept of cultural lag. Ogburn was a professor of sociology at Columbia University, where Mead took courses from him while a student at Barnard College. He enabled her to undertake graduate studies by employing her when her father refused further support. In his influential book, *Social Change with Respect to Culture and Original Nature* (published in 1922 when Mead was his student), Ogburn argued that customs, mores and mental habits (culture) did not change at the same rate as material conditions and technology did. When culture lags behind scientific and economic change, serious maladjustments occur, resulting in both individual problems (neurosis and psychosis) and also social problems, including crime, sex problems, and selfishness.[12] Cultural lag "quickly became an important part of the intellectual's vocabulary" and formed the basis of much subsequent intellectual social commentary.[13] Its most famous application was the Lynds' *Middletown*, the single most influential American social study of the interwar period. Five years later, Lewis Mumford

William Fielding Ogburn, photograph courtesy of the University of Chicago Library

would draw on the same model in writing *Technics and Civilization.*[14] As will be shown, the vocabulary of *Social Change* permeates Mead's book.

This chapter explicates the ways in which *The Changing Culture of an Indian Tribe* reflected "America" as the Depression held the country in an ever-tightening grip. The book presented the ugly alternative to modernism's romance with the primitive and provided a frightening account of the disintegration and degradation that followed the collapse of a "coherent" socioeconomic system. Ironically, the theoretical position Mead articulates reinforces that promise of the fully integrated life, locating it in a "primitive" Indian past. The Indian present, on the other hand, is the antithesis of that dream of integration. Chaotic and fragmented, it is most fully expressed in the figure of the Antler woman, whose disordered sexuality threatens the future of her people. The book marks a turning point in terms of Mead's ideas about the relative places of individuals and cultures, and she began from this point to posit culture as problematic and to put more emphasis on how individuals fare within the constraints of differing cultural forms.

In the spring of 1930, Mead was still riding the crest of her newfound celebrity. She was in high demand as a public speaker, commentator, and author for the popular press, commonly giving three, and often five, public speeches a month. Reo Fortune had just received his PhD from Columbia University, and the couple's principal worry was that there was no job in sight for him because universities and museums, responding to budget cuts, had begun to freeze positions and, indeed, to lay off staff. The spring of 1930 also saw an apparent revival of the stock market, bringing with it, for a few months at least, the hope that the depression of the winter was an aberration in the pattern of prosperity and growth that America had experienced since the end of the war. Financially, the couple was relatively secure. Mead's salary of $2,500 per annum was supplemented by $5,000 in royalties from *Coming of Age in Samoa* that had accumulated during their absence in Manus. In addition, Mead's popular articles, of which she wrote almost two dozen between late 1929 and late 1931, brought in intermittent, lump-sum payments, many of which were larger than a month's wages for the average worker in America. She had almost completed *Growing Up in New Guinea* and could expect a new stream of royalties in the fall. Although Fortune had no immediate prospects for employment, both he and Mead were committed field anthropologists who viewed their institutional positions primarily as enabling ethnographic research.

This was their situation when Mrs. Leonard Elmhirst's Committee[15] made an unsolicited grant of $750 to the American Museum of Natural History for a study of family life, in particular the life of women, in a contemporary American Indian tribe. Clark Wissler, chief ethnologist of the museum, and Mead's boss, was somewhat bemused by this windfall grant. However, in Margaret Mead he had the obvious candidate to do such a piece of research. Given Mead's high profile at the time, and Dorothy Elmhirst's connection to anthropology via her friendship with Elsie Parsons, it seems likely that the idea for the study was developed with Mead in mind. Mead, however, was extremely reluctant. Although she had almost finished *Growing Up in New Guinea,* she was anxious to get back to the South Pacific as soon as possible. Fortune was struggling to complete books on Dobu and on Manus before they departed. The prospect of three months in a culture in which they had no intrinsic interest and that imposed yet more writing obligations, was not welcome. To persuade Mead to accept the assignment, Ruth Benedict secured a Columbia University grant for Fortune to research visions, or rather their apparent absence, in the folk tales of the Omaha, thus filling a notable gap in the ethnography of the Plains tribes. Mead capitulated. The couple had not yet secured any funds for further fieldwork abroad, and writing obligations had to be balanced against the financial benefits of living in the field with all expenses covered. Furthermore, Wissler maintained a benevolent regime, under which Mead flourished, and Mead was always cognizant of her and Fortune's dependence on the goodwill of the "great men" who dominated anthropology at the time and who controlled access to research grants and jobs. And as she later wrote to Malinowski, "[I]t's the first job I've ever had to do that I didn't choose."[16] So, in June 1930, with the Depression deepening, Mead and Fortune bought an old car and drove west, to Macy, Nebraska.

Macy was the central township of the Omaha reservation, which had been established in 1854 along the Missouri River in northern Nebraska. This reservation was a final resting place, reached after a century of retreat westward from the Ohio River. European advances, smallpox epidemics, and warfare with the stronger Sioux meant that a much-reduced tribe of a little more than eleven hundred people was present when Alice Fletcher conducted the first tribal census there in 1883. The reason for the census was that the Omaha requested that their 300,000-acre reserve be divided into individually owned allotments, a request made in the hope that such entitlement would prevent a rumored further displacement to Oklahoma. Fletcher's scheme for distributing the land, embodied in the Omaha Allotment Act (1882) became the basis for the Dawes Severalty Act (1887), which made such breaking up of reservations standard policy. By the time the Omaha Act was passed, the buffalo, which had been the mainstay of the Omaha economy, had been hunted to the edge of extinction. Fletcher believed (and convinced the United States government) that the allocation of individual farms would enable the Omaha to learn to live like whites and be assimilated into "civilization."[17] Mead's brief was to study the effect of these changes on family life (which she interpreted as women's lives).

Unlike on other trips, Mead produced no bulletins during her summer in Nebraska. However, her letters to Ruth Benedict, Clark Wissler, Bronislaw Malinowski, and other colleagues indicate that this was not a happy time. In contrast to her bulletins and letters from her other research sites, the letters from Nebraska are uniformly grumpy and complaining. The weather was scorching, the people demoralized and difficult to work with: "You find a man whose father or uncle had a vision. You go to see him four times, driving eight or ten miles with an interpreter. The first time he isn't home, the second time he's drunk, the next time his wife is sick, and the fourth time . . . you start the interview with a five dollar bill and . . . [he] proceeds to lie steadily for four hours." [18] She described herself as "doomed to spend a few educational months among these most dilapidated American Indians from which our very souls recoil." [19] Furthermore, in comparison to Pacific research, undertaken in economies still largely based on fishing, gardening, gifting, and barter, work among the money-oriented Omaha was expensive, involving "endless contributions to feasts and . . . gasoline for everything is five miles from everything else." [20] The situation was a far cry from the more amiable working conditions she had enjoyed in Samoa and Manus.

Within a month of arriving, Mead summarized the situation in a letter to Franz Boas: "Here it is a case of the Indian, living on rents and payments, having developed a perfect leisure class psychology, paying his gambling debts, scrupulous in his play obligations, scornful of work and of the poor renter who rents his land and slaves away upon it, European peasantry style. Very little of the old life style is left, but solidarity of race and language are still absolutely untouched." [21]

However, that glib analysis quickly dissolved as the complexities and entrenched problems on the reservation became more apparent: "It's deadly work," she wrote to Malinowski, "everything so influenced and modified, that it's almost impossible to draw any conclusions at all." [22] Nevertheless, she gleaned an enormous amount of information in a very short time, and by mid-August she wrote to Wissler that they would wrap the work up in two or three more weeks. She included a two-page summary of her planned report (which, incidentally, was more innovative than the book turned out to be). Funding had come through for research in New Guinea, and she and Fortune were anxious to get back to New York so that the following spring they could return to what Mead was beginning to characterize as "real anthropology."

The Changing Culture of an Indian Tribe was written between September 1930 and April 1931. The book is extraordinary, as much for its delicate interpretations of change and continuities in Antler life as for its ruthless pronouncements on individual character, bureaucratic bungling, and corruption. In eschewing her usual comparative approach, Mead was forced into a more detailed consideration of the very complex, and often tragic, lives of the Antlers. There are moments of great pathos in the book, often beautifully expressed. At other points, the language used is jarring by today's more circumspect, less apparently judgmental, standards. However, Mead justified her use of "moralistic terminology," albeit in a footnote towards the end, by saying that it accorded with "Antler feelings." [23]

The book is structured like a "preachment yarn," a genre that was characteristic of many early Depression films. Also known variously as propaganda or Americanism films, these were films that, against the grain of the Hollywood tradition, tackled the difficult social issues of the day: exploitative class, gender, and race relations; poverty; and brutality. They were characterized by "two recurrent markers": the exculpatory preface, which gave "plausible deniability to polemical purpose," staking a claim for impartiality, and the Jazz Age prelude, "a first act, flashback, or expository montage" that carried the message "The mess we're in now came about because of the mess we made then." [24] Thomas Doherty argues that "[t]he preachment yarns of the Great Depression express the anguish of the dispossessed and fearful, but they have no idea how to alleviate the symptoms of what seems a terminal case." [25] The Changing Culture of an Indian Tribe has all the hallmarks of a preachment yarn: an exculpatory introduction; a historical tale of corruption, incompetence, and resources squandered; and, sadly, a solution that is no solution at all.

Exculpation in The Changing Culture of an Indian Tribe takes the form of claims to science. These begin in Clark Wissler's foreword, where he states that the study was undertaken "from the plane of scientific curiosity only and not with a view to reformatory or ameliorative developments," [26] a strange claim for a book by Mead. The introduction, written by Mead herself, is principally a methodological defense of the study of small-scale societies against the "the tendency to identify science with quantitative methods and to accept no social data without their probable error and standard deviation." [27] The ethnologist's job, Mead explained, was either to reconstruct historical social form (most American anthropology) or to determine the relationship between "original nature and social environment," an indication that Mead was moving beyond cultural determinism in thinking about the relationship between individuals and their cultures.[28] These terms echo Ogburn's: he laid out his first principles in Social Change as distinguishing between social heritage and original nature.[29] Mead designated these two ethnological tasks as "historical" and "sociological" or "social psychological." [30] Although an ethnologist cannot offer statistical significance as a defense of her findings, she can, Mead argued, offer the "homogeneity" of a "complete culture, and the interrelation and functioning of its parts."[31] However, the student of a "transitional primitive culture" is at a disadvantage: homogeneity and the smooth articulation of interacting parts have gone, but numbers are still too small to satisfy the sociologists' need for statistical significance. The paradigm for the ethnological method in such cases must be drawn then, not from the social sciences, but from medicine, specifically pathology and psychiatry. These disciplines present "each case in detail because of its power to illuminate our knowledge of . . . physiology . . . and of the human mind."[32] Mead took the medical paradigm seriously, using the language of infection, disease, and pathology throughout the book.

In the introduction Mead went on the offensive against her fellow anthropologists, criticizing American colleagues who had insisted that culture contact "preserve some shadow of the peaceful diffusion between cultures that are evenly matched,"[33] instead of facing the very real power imbalances that the Antler faced. She also disavowed British studies "immured from use by serious students in a wealth of invective against imperialistic policies or missionary influences."[34] This study, she was telling her readers, had a carefully considered methodology, was robustly situated in a medical paradigm, eschewed invective in the service of pure contribution to knowledge, and was realistic, objective, and balanced.

Mead's methodological defense of her study must be seen as preemptive in addition to exculpatory. The highly critical reviews of *Growing Up in New Guinea* were coming out as she wrote *Changing Culture*. In a disciplinary culture that emphasized language fluency and long periods of fieldwork over many years, her eight-month stint in Manus (shortened to five months, in the anthropological gossip mill) excited both private derision and public criticism. Her three months in Nebraska, with no attempt to learn the language, made this study even more vulnerable to such criticism. This derision seems to have been based in equal parts on professional jealousy and genuine skepticism. Her reported statement that she "saw and solved all problems"[35] in Manus was implicitly insulting to her fellow anthropologists who put years of work into single cultures.

Her confidence in her results, seen as arrogance by many of her peers, arose from her assumption of the homogeneity between individual and society in "primitive" cultures: she believed that knowing a few individuals well, or observing a limited number of events in detail, gave the anthropologist access to the whole culture. This assumption was the foundation of her emerging theory of the difference between temperament, personality, and individuality, which developed over the summer in Nebraska.[36] She articulated this first in a letter to Clark

Wissler. Wissler had written to Mead about Edward Sapir's new research. Sapir, Wissler wrote, was "keen to show that personality is wholly a resultant of economic and social forces operating at the time and place."[37] Mead advised him to caution Sapir against undertaking any psychoanalytic studies of personality among Native American tribes:

> I consider a homogenous culture the only ideal place to study personality because there the only differences which can occur are differences in temperament, as a homogenous culture does not permit the development of individuality. But individuality, differences in people due, not to temperament, except possibly as basic cause, but rather to diversity of experience and cultural content, can be ideally studied in a transition culture such as this one, where one of the chief medicine men was once a show at Coney Island, another old woman traveled through Canada as Alice Fletcher's companion, a third once worked in a printing office in Elizabeth New Jersey, and a fourth was an American sailor aboard a British Man of War, and yet all of them bring these diverse experiences back to a common point of reinterpretation—their own culture. Conversely, such a culture is a bad place to study true personality differences in because they are obscured by these differences in individuality.[38]

This three-tiered schema of temperament (biology), personality (culture), and individuality (individual experience) underpinned Mead's emerging conception of the proper scientific domain of anthropology. Again, she drew on Ogburn's formulation that original nature interacting with social heritage results in "behavior in culture."[39] This model implied a particular role for the discipline that differentiated it from other social sciences. For example, towards the end of August she wrote to Wissler, outlining her research report. "Do you think that will do?" she queried. "It seems to me about all the energy, time and money which the problem deserves. Its value is far more an empirical one than a scientific one because the value of anthropological studies, is, as I see it, in definite proportion to the homogeneity of the culture and the typicalness of any individual of his age and sex group."[40]

This position was articulated publicly for the first time in her field-defining article, "The Primitive Child," for *The Handbook of Child Psychology*, the standard psychological text for many years. In an oblique reference to her Omaha work, she began the article thus: "The primitive child is of interest to science chiefly as an excellent subject for experiments in social psychology. By the time that primitive children become problems for pedagogues and students of juvenile delinquency, they have ceased to be genuinely primitive—i.e., members of homogenous social groups which depend entirely upon their local oral tradition. The American Indian child or the South African child in school presents interesting opportunities for studying social change but is an inferior subject for the student of child psychology."[41]

Informally, she took this position even further, virtually dismissing American anthropology from the realm of proper anthropology. She wrote Malinowski that she was "beginning to understand why the American school has historically stressed history rather than function." She cited the reasons: "a. because you can't do function decently, and b. because all function is obscured by the hodge podge of traits borrowed from hither and yon."[42] After she returned to New York, she was publicly dismissive of American anthropology in an interview that undoubtedly raised the stakes in her uneasy relationship with the "big men," such as Sapir, Kroeber, and Lowie, of American anthropology. "Fieldwork," she is reported as saying, "makes heavy demands on health and tact. You must eat anything, sleep anywhere, fraternize with all types of unwashed, like people as people, and forget pruderies. There isn't any fieldwork left in the United States, so one has to go to Africa, South America, the Pacific Islands or Siberia."[43]

Her growing conviction that her work among the Omaha was not anthropology propelled Mead to seek an explanation of the state of the Antlers in their recent history, following the more usual American model of anthropological enquiry. She exposes the sorry saga of Antler–American interaction, which had led to the contemporary situation, in part 1 of the book, entitled "General Background." This consists of a section called "Retrospective Sketch" and then gives more detailed accounts of both historical and contemporary Antler economics, politics, social organization, religion, and education. She draws extensively on research done in the last quarter of the nineteenth century by the Episcopalian missionary James Dorsey under the auspices of the Bureau of Ethnology of the Smithsonian Institution, and by Alice Fletcher and Francis La Flesche. Dorsey worked as a missionary with the Omaha in the 1870s and thereafter made several more field trips to Nebraska, in addition to corresponding with Omaha leaders and hosting them during their trips to Washington. Fletcher and La Flesche were an unlikely pair: she was the daughter of a prominent New York lawyer, who became interested in Native American culture under the tutelage of Frederic Putnam, the director of the Peabody Museum; he was the son of an influential Omaha chief who earned a law degree and was eventually appointed to the Bureau of Ethnology. They formed a working relationship in the early 1880s, when Fletcher was appointed to implement the allotment scheme.[44] Fletcher informally adopted La Flesche, and their collaboration, which lasted until her death in 1923, provided most of what anthropologists know of the old cultures of the Southern Plains.[45]

Mead used their material to construct a history of Antler society in three phases: a traditional phase, in which the culture was stable, "whole," and functionally integrated; a post-allotment phase, during which Antler culture was "attenuated," a shadow of its former complexity but still coherent and in a state of "slender equilibrium"; and, finally, its current state of disintegration. This is a historiography that implicitly posits plenty and stability, followed by attrition and wasted resources, and finally chaos and degradation. This account ignored the 150 years of known history that had seen the Omaha displaced from the east to the northwest of the Missouri River and decimated by smallpox and intertribal warfare. In this, Mead was following a pattern set in her earlier books, that of minimizing the effect of Europeans on so-called traditional social forms. Indeed, she argued that "[t]he additional complication, present in so many tribes, of a change, not only of economic base, but also to a completely strange locality, is therefore not present in their case. . . . The invasion of the white man was gradual, and unaccompanied by bloodshed."[46]

Instead, Mead described an unchanging, functional, traditional social organization that, for men, centered on the buffalo hunt and raid-style warfare, followed by feasting and the gifting of stolen or captured horses (a European introduction). These prestigious activities enabled men to attain rank, participate in secret societies, and have their wives, daughters, or nieces tattooed—the ultimate marks of high status. Although women were excluded from all these activities, excepting that they served as the final markers of their fathers' or husbands' status, they contributed to the subsistence through gardening maize, gathering wild foods, and processing buffalo hides, which were used to make clothing and shelter. However, they had no special ceremonies or societies of their own; they participated in the ritual and prestige activities only as wives or daughters, leading Mead to conclude that traditional Antler culture was, in effect, a man's culture.

Mead dated the first major changes in Antler culture from the decline of the buffalo and the establishment of missions in the second half of the nineteenth century, and culminating in the Omaha Allotment Act (1882). The Antler, she found, viewed this period with nostalgia. Women's work changed very little, except for the fact that in winter they occupied frame houses rather than tipis. Men took to the "cattle convention" of "quick-shooting, hard-drinking [and] gambling."[47] However, the decline of the buffalo and curtailment of raiding soon resulted in the disappearance of the traditional avenues to male power and prestige. Secret societies waned; farming, seen as "women's work," could not sustain the complex social system of chiefdoms that rested on the buffalo hunt, horse capture, and conspicuous prestation. Soon, white farmers, hungry for land, displaced the cattle ranchers, and the practice of leasing land commenced. According to Mead, two thirds of Antler men abandoned any attempts to farm, and "ceased to make any further economic struggle,"[48] living instead off the proceeds of leases and their wives' subsistence gardening and gathering.

The third phase commenced with the end of a twenty-five-year moratorium on the sale of Antler landholdings. This coincided with a new influx of white farmers. The practice of leasing increased and, more seriously, the Antlers began to sell land and live off the proceeds. By the beginning of the Depression, white-owned or -leased farms abutted Antler ones throughout the 145 square miles of the reserve. However, although they patronized the same picture theatres, rodeos, and shops and often attended the same schools, the white and Antler communities seldom interacted. They never socialized together or attended the same dances, and they rarely intermarried. Despite the "influence" and "modification" introduced by contact with white society, the Antlers, Mead concluded, had a curious disconnection from their white neighbors and the dominant white culture. In August she wrote to Wissler: "My present judgment on these people is that they are a completely primitive people who have adjusted to their white neighbors in the same way that they would adjust to sharks, crocodiles, hurricanes and man eating tigers. They have definite ways of treating this phenomenon of white invasion, but they do not mingle with it in thought or feeling."[49]

However one might fault Mead's early historiography, her analysis of the problems faced by the Antlers, both men and women, is both acute and heart-rending. She was no fool, and faced with the enormous problems of trying to make sense of this human disaster, she unflinchingly drew together the complex issues that contributed to it. She described how an education system that fitted them with no useful skills and that undermined their gendered social order, in combination with a land-allocation system totally unsuited to their socioeconomic organization and values, and a corrupt and inept government bureaucracy interacted with traditions of sharing and "kin solidarity," female modesty and male predation. The current generation of Antler adults had been educated principally in large, multi-tribal, coeducational boarding schools where they were taught industrial trades and skills, few of which could be used on the reservation. However, Antlers of both sexes were able to acquire large sums of money by selling land. This money was regarded as outside the bounds of traditional kinship obligations. It was usually expended on conspicuous individual consumption—large cars, drinking, gambling, restaurant meals, and fancy "American" clothes. All other sources of income, whether from rents, crop sales, pensions or various kinds of windfalls, were "subject to the demands of relatives."[50] Any relative could requisition savings or accumulated food, clothing, or bedding. The Antler who wished to "get ahead" through thrift or hard work was said to have "gone white," and faced both the opprobrium of other Antlers and rejection by the none-too-friendly white community. In a society in which the traditional routes to male prestige had disappeared or lost meaning, the pressure to capitalize land through sale, and live in a chiefly fashion, was immense. The net result was an increasing number of people dependent on a steadily diminishing economic base, a situation exacerbated by the depression in farm prices and consequent loss of what income there had been from crop sales or casual labor on white farms.

Mead regarded her book, which she originally titled *The Reservation Woman*, as a study of the lives of girls and women. However, less than a third of the text actually focuses on women, which prompted Columbia University Press to unilaterally change its title after Mead had left for New Guinea. Nevertheless, it is in describing the particularly poignant paradoxes of these women's lives that Mead's talents are most clearly demonstrated. Her analysis of the changes in the lives of Antler women since the Allotment Act is predicated on a slippage in the meanings she gives to "culture." She moves between using the term to denote the ceremonial and institutional aspects of Antler society, as above, and using the term to indicate all the practices and meaning-making systems of the society. The first meaning, however, is the one on which she hangs her analysis, and in using this definition, she makes the argument that culture, not only Antler culture but culture in general, is gendered.[51]

A woman from another culture can enter a primitive society and, as soon as she can speak a few words, can find a hundred points of interest to discuss with native women. It may be months before a man can establish a similar rapport because the white male investigator has first to get by heart the peculiar cultural preoccupations which distinguish one culture from another and which are of so much more importance to the men than are the routine affairs of domesticity. For this very reason, the breakdown of culture is almost always of more vital concern to the men than to the women. The old religion, the old social values, the old braveries, and the old vanities may be taken away from the men, leaving them empty-brained and idle-handed.[52]

Traditionally, she argued, Antler women had lived in the shadow of their fathers and husbands. Those few women who had membership in secret societies did so by virtue of their fathers' accomplishments; they "held" rather than owned or exercised ritual privileges. Women had no specific societies, no religious ceremonies, and, although their food production, through foraging, agriculture, and meat processing, was "the least perishable, the most dependable, the foods which kept people from starvation,"[53] it was accorded no prestige. All religious and political ceremonies centered on and were controlled by men. Women played only a minor, "generic" role in Antler culture. Traditional Antler culture, she argues, was the province of men. She argued, therefore, that the decline of hunting and the ritual societies per se had little effect on women's lives. They continued to forage for berries and grow maize, albeit while living in scattered frame houses rather than clustered tipis or earth lodges.

The most important change in the lives of women, she argued, was the introduction of government schooling, especially coeducational boarding schools, which radically undermined Antler gendered behavior. Before the introduction of formal schooling, girls were cultivated into "an extreme state of bashfulness, fearfulness [and] inhibition"[54] and were constantly chaperoned. Women were expected to be both chaste and modest. Unchaperoned women were regarded as fair prey for any man, and women who were suspected of sexual impropriety were subject to strong, and often violent, sanctions. In the new educational institutions, boys and girls, who would have been isolated from each other or at least

Omaha women at a powwow in the late 1920s, photograph courtesy of Nebraska State Historical Society

closely chaperoned in earlier times, learned an easy familiarity that, Mead suggested, broke down the girls' traditional shyness and modesty. However, it did not modify the belief, held by both men and women, that any female not immediately protected by a brother, husband, or father, was fair game for any unrelated men. Thus, once out of school, Antler women, even after marriage, were seldom left alone. Reading between the lines, it is apparent that young Antler women played a dangerous game, exercising their newfound boldness at the risk of retribution from their families or rape by men who regarded them as fair prey if they were found alone. The scattered frame houses on individual allotments did not allow for the easy gathering of kin and tribe for processing food, playing games, and conducting ceremonies, nor did they offer protection for women left with only children for company. So, houses were often empty for long periods when married women attended their husbands in town, visited other relatives, or participated in hand games, thus undermining the vital contribution that women made to subsistence through gathering, gardening, and food processing.

There was a strong belief that women were more fragile than men, less able to cope with emotional trauma: "Women were believed to be made of frailer, more brittle psychic material than men. . . . Grief of any sort which would merely bow a man's head in temporary mourning, might completely disorder a woman's life."[55] This belief had persisted into contemporary times. The common manifestation of this state, Mead argues, was promiscuous sexual behavior. Poverty, disease, alcoholism, elevated child mortality, and other accompaniments of disadvantage meant that many women lived lives that were tragic and violent. Mead recounts, as examples, the histories of several women who, after the death of children, or house fires, walked away from their families and became involved in a series of sexual relationships. This increasingly common pattern of sexual "delinquency" had, Mead argued, a cumulative effect. Mothers with a history of sexual promiscuity, although welcomed back into the family fold, forfeited moral authority with regard to their daughters. Thus, when the daughters began to show signs of "delinquency," the mothers did not command the necessary respect to rein them in. Mead deployed her pathology paradigm to argue that this sexual promiscuity or delinquency spread not only through the generations but also through propinquity, suggesting that "every delinquent girl is a plague spot, a source of infection to the other girls."[56]

The coincidence of formal education's breaking down the moral code; Antlers' increasing emulation of the "white way," for the most part as evidenced in Hollywood movies; and the traumas of poverty, disease, and social disorientation meant that most women had at one time or another "strayed" sexually. Yet, this change in practice, Mead argued, did not result in any slackening of the moral attitudes towards such transgressions: "with every woman deviating from the code being disapproved of by men and women alike and feeling herself a sinful person, nevertheless the majority deviate." This paradoxical relationship between dearly held values, virtually universal transgression, and similarly universal disapprobation led Mead to categorize the "Antlers" as a "maladjusted society in which all are sinners and everyone points the finger of scorn."[57]

Despite this desolate picture, Mead insisted it was the women who still had a sense of themselves as "Indian" in positive terms. Whereas men had allowed their "culture" to atrophy, women were revealed as the bearers and sustainers of what would today be called Antler identity. Women's confidence in their "Indian-ness," she argued, was grounded in the continuity of the domestic routines of childcare, cooking, and household organization, "which bind mother to daughter and both to the grandmother." These traditions, "taught by one generation to the next, bind . . . the group together in a set of positive habits which distinguish them from other peoples and give to them a sense of security and meaningfulness which their husbands and brothers lack."[58] In a passage that celebrates the solidarity of womanhood across the generations and that demonstrates Mead's craft as a writer, she describes the women dancing after a hand game: "If one watches the feet, which move so slowly, in perfect time to the drum beats, while the voices follow a different rhythm with their song, one sees moccasins, worn shoes, and high-heeled slippers, purple and red and green; one sees old cotton and woolen stockings in the style of fifty years ago, and the latest black-and-white silk fad, all moving in perfect accord to the drums, and over the whole group rest the shawls. From old women to smallest toddler the women are one, their differences in generation and outlook forgotten in the dance."[59]

This strong sense of identity was accompanied by what Mead saw as a strong cultural conservatism. She argued that despite the fact women now owned property and met most subsistence needs and thus potentially could wield economic power, they remained "[c]onservatively rooted in old habits of thought"[60] that left them prey to the more dissipated practices of their menfolk. One particularly disturbing example of this was a pattern whereby women would apply to sell their land in order to pay for treatment for tuberculosis, only to see the men spend the money instead on cars, "American clothing," and restaurant meals. This practice was so common that Mead reported that the "particular conjunction of wealth and tuberculosis is not an accidental one."[61] This conservatism also made women reluctant to leave the reservation for life in the cities, and it was this, Mead believed, that condemned the Antler to a continuing downward spiral.

The Changing Culture of an Indian Tribe was published, after months of delay, in mid-1932, as the Depression worsened beyond the ability of governments to control it or intellectuals to accommodate its magnitude. In July 1932, President Hoover ordered the military to disperse the Bonus Army, thousands of veterans who had marched on Washington to petition Congress to pay them immediately service bonuses that were due to them in 1945. The newsreels of soldiers burning the shanty homes of unemployed men and their families in the shadow of the Capitol building horrified the nation, despite the administration's attempt to cast the army as revolutionaries and radicals. That summer, revolution hung in the air.

Publication was delayed as the publisher waited to see if the economy would improve.[62] When it did finally come out, the book received far less publicity than had *Growing Up in New Guinea* and *Coming of Age in Samoa*. Rather than publishing it with Morrow, Mead had chosen Columbia University Press. It therefore did not benefit from the same publicity machine that Morrow put to work for its authors. However, despite being published by an academic press, it is written, like Mead's other work, to be accessible. It has few of the technical aspects of formal ethnographies, and it addresses its readers in a tone similar to that used in her other books—as educated and informed readers rather than specifically professional ones. This tone of address reflects the fact that Mead did not see this work as "anthropology" but rather as a cross between a scientific report and a book aimed at the educated public.

Most of the reviews held in her archives are written by anthropologists. However, they were published in range of venues: academic journals, elite magazines, and newspapers. Unlike those of *Growing Up in New Guinea*, the reviews of *Changing Culture* were very positive. The balance of pedagogy and ethnography in the book was more in keeping with standard anthropological works, the topic sufficiently new, and the findings sufficiently sobering to stave off the usual criticisms of her work. Furthermore, Mead did not overextend her material as she had in past work. Alfred Tozzer called it "a successful and a pioneer work in the American field," pointing out that it was "far better organized, presented, and documented than William Pitt-Rivers's *Clash of Culture and the Contact of Races,* which attempts to cover the same subject in Polynesia."[63] C. Daryl Forde's review in *Man* was restrained and for the most part descriptive. It acknowledged Mead's vivid style and the importance of studying "these extreme examples of diffusion and culture change" (thus reiterating the standard anthropological gloss of empire that Mead had criticized in her introduction).[64] Alexander Goldenweiser reviewed it twice: once for the *Nation* and once for *American Anthropologist.* He called it "a signal contribution" and suggested that the work was so significant that it would lead to further such studies of "acculturation," which it did. In the conclusions to both reviews, he wrote of the emotional effect it had had on him. For the *Nation*, he wrote, "It is difficult to read the pages of Dr. Mead's book without experiencing a sense of shame. In this, perhaps, lies one of its merits." [65] In *American Anthropologist*, he reported a more curious response: "When pondering one's state of mind as the result of reading this study, one is inclined to compare oneself to a spectator of a tragedy and say with Aristotle: my emotions were purified even though the tale was sad." [66]

One of the notable features of all these reviews is the way in which they, in different ways, elide the issues raised for the Antlers themselves. In this, they parallel Mead's own couching of the work in terms of its contribution to science rather than its exposure of the destructive effects of America's internal empire or its potential for solving some of the problems the Antlers faced. For Forde, the condition of the Antlers is a result of "diffusion" and "culture contact," very mild synonyms for the historical processes of displacement, disease, and depopulation to which the Omaha had been subject. Mead's former professor, Clare Howard, couched most of her review in a silly reflection on Mead's "romantic" career. For Howard, the book was "as fascinating as a novel by Jane Austen." She added, "It feeds our curiosity about human beings." [67] Goldenweiser's two reviews are, at the end, more concerned with his emotional response than with the Antlers' social conditions, as if the book were the equivalent of a Greek tragedy structured for the edification of its readership. Only Ruth Benedict's review for the *New York Herald Tribune* seems cognizant of the scale of the human suffering represented in Mead's book. She describes the Antler situation as "a cultural shipwreck," "devastating," a "tragedy of life," and "a problem the complexity of which we have barely imagined." However, even Benedict accepts Mead's analysis that the problem, if there is one, is a problem of "maladjustment" of the smaller society to the needs and institutions of the larger. Benedict's repeated references to the Antler's "unfittedness" for American citizenship and their childlike relationship to land and money has the unfortunate effect of reinforcing paternalistic and racist attitudes already well entrenched in America, although no doubt Benedict herself would have been horrified at that interpretation. [68]

Thus praised, and having recouped Mead's reputation as a serious anthropologist (ironically, because she didn't consider it to be anthropology), *The Changing Culture of an Indian Tribe* passed into oblivion, not to be reissued until 1966. Yet, no less than its predecessors, the book was a creature of its times. Published at the depth of the Depression, it reflected the country's mood of hopelessness and despair. It articulated that despair through a theoretical framework that has come to be identified with anthropology—functionalism. This is Mead's most explicitly functionalist book, and it is this theoretical frame that articulated the book most directly to the intellectual problematic of the day and that most inexorably anchored the sense of hopelessness. And it was the way in which gender ramified with functionalism that secured both the framework itself and the message that this was a society in disorder.

What Mead hated most about the Omaha work was the impossibility of making sense of what she deemed a "broken culture."[69] This term, which echoes through Mead's work on the Omaha, reveals how committed Mead was, by this time, to the idea of human societies as self-contained, functional wholes. Images of chaos and disorder permeate both her informal and formal writing on the Omaha. Terms like "hodge podge" and "hither and yon" are sprinkled through her communications to colleagues. She writes of "cultural disintegration, lack of coherence" and describes the change wrought on native culture by white intrusion as "meaningless and random." In the conclusion, she uses the house as a metaphor for culture. The structure of a house may change over time but will always bear some relation to the activities of the people who inhabit it. A culture that has been overrun by a dominant one, she argues, is like a house being demolished by a wrecker. The order of demolition bears no relation to the structure of the inhabitants' lives.[70]

During that summer in Nebraska, this confrontation with the Omaha crystallized Mead's commitment to functionalism. Thus, although disgruntled, her letters from Macy are distinguished by an emphasis, relatively new to her, on theory. While in Nebraska, she continued her correspondence with Malinowski, writing to him about the relationship between the Oedipus complex and the structure of kinship, the effect of prolonged nursing on the mother–child bond, and the effect on the child of a nurturing father.[71] Although she was clearly delighted with his interest in her work, ultimately his neo-Freudian approach didn't capture her imagination, and her letters soon became descriptive rather than analytic. However, his functionalist framework made more and more sense to her as the Omaha work proceeded. Malinowski's views, developed in a fieldwork situation approximating her own formative ones, accorded more readily with Mead's than did the historical reconstructionist project that dominated American anthropology at the time.

However, there was also an earlier, and more indigenous, lineage to Mead's functionalism, one that, it might be argued, predisposed her toward the formal theory when it arrived in America from Britain's shores.[72] The underlying analytic concept of *The Changing Culture of an Indian Tribe* is "cultural lag," a temporal disjuncture between the "culture" of the Antlers and their material and social conditions. As early as 1922, Ogburn had clearly outlined a functionalist vision of society, describing culture as involving "correlation and interdependence of parts," and cultural lag as being "a problem that occurs when there is a rapid change in a culture of interdependent parts and when the rates of change in the parts are unequal."[73] Ogburn gave a name to the problem that American cultural critics had been grappling with for two decades—incoherence, dissolution of community, and disjunctions among the American economy, culture, and values. For Croly "the promise of American life" lay in the possibility of creating a true community, moral and cultural, economic and political, in which individuals and groups interact harmoniously, and each individual "should find some particular function."[74] Brooks argued that America would not come of age until it gave away self-aggrandizing materialistic individualism in favor of organic integration between person and society. For Brooks, this involved the creation of a national culture that did not reject the technical and material achievements of the United States but developed from them and within them a culture of self-fulfillment and inventiveness "through literature, the arts, mechanics, or industry itself."[75] The material base was in place; the task was to create from it an organic national culture based on good workmanship, cooperation, and community. Ogburn's "cultural lag" gave a name to America's current condition—a highly developed technology that had not given rise to an equally developed culture, a condition that he argued gave rise to forms of maladjustment, including "nervousness and insanity" and "social problems."[76] Ogburn held out the promise that this incoherence was not endemic to modernity but was a matter that could be rectified by the creation of a culture more appropriate to the technology, or by bringing technology into the service of culture.

Ironically, by the time Ogburn coined the term, the cultural tide had turned. Artists and cultural critics of the 1920s abandoned the Progressive ideals of an integrated society in favor of a more individual salvation. However, the inward turn of the 1920s was more a disillusionment with the practicability of the Progressive and post-Progressive ideals than with its ultimate vision of an integrated society. The Progressive solutions might lie in scientific management and rationalized bureaucracy, wedded to an elevation of art and culture, whereas the 1920s artist or cultural critic was more likely to enjoin the individual to increase his self-knowledge and aesthetic awareness to build a coherent society through individual enlightenment. But these differing solutions were posed as answers to the same problem—the chaos and alienation of modern life.

The romance with the notion of the holistic, organic society persisted through the 1920s, safely located, however, in the primitive and the rural (which were indeed often conflated).[77] Thus, anthropology became the haven of functionalism and its vision of an integrated life. The anthropological vision of discrete societies, untouched by history, in which "[p]arts of the culture . . . reinforced and articulated with each other in a smoothly functioning whole"[78] neatly encapsulated the Progressive dream of an integrated society, albeit in the metaphor of the machine. It also provided an illusory alternative to modernity's fragmentation. It is no accident that the so-called golden age of American anthropology[79] and the rise of anthropological functionalism coincide with the inward, individualist turn of cultural criticism. It was this "primitivist holism" that Mead evoked so effectively in *Coming of Age in Samoa,* where the individual was said to be wholly "at one" with the society.

In the 1930s, many intellectuals returned to the ideal of a functionally integrated society as they searched for a way out of the crisis around them. The collapse of the economic system that had sustained prosperity for so long revivified the analysis that an entirely new order, cultural and moral, in addition to economic, was needed. For those, like Samuel Schmallhausen,[80] the new social order would produce a new kind of person—healthier, integrated, at peace. In a series of articles for the *New Republic* in 1930, subsequently published in a book entitled *Individualism Old and New,* John Dewey re-invoked cultural lag to argue for the necessity of creating a new set of values, a new individualism, commensurate with the technical and economic capacity of modern America.[81] Lewis Mumford's classic study of the transition from feudalism to industrialism, *Technics and Civilization,* attempts to find a balance between technological development and social integration.[82] Mumford and Dewey were in search of new models, in which technology served the values of "a new [integrated] individualism, consonant with the realities of the present age."[83] For Dewey, that necessarily involved accepting and embracing, rather than blaming, science and technology, and disseminating scientific ways of thinking through all levels of society.

Other writers, however, continued to see science and technology as false gods and, inspired by anthropologists, they went in search of "organic" communities. Robert Redfield's *Tepoztlan,* for example, was influential in sending many to Mexico.[84] Stuart Chase wrote a bucolic celebration of Mexican peasant life, published in 1931 as a series of articles in the *New Republic* and subsequently in a book entitled *Mexico: A Study of Two Americas.*[85] Peasant life, he argued, was integrated, self-sufficient, craft-based, and satisfying in a way that the life of "Middletowners," working to a clock, producing goods they did not consume, consuming goods they did not produce, could never be. Mexico, Chase argued, in a vein uncannily similar to Mead's evocation of Samoa, was a place where "there is no progress, . . . there is no visible material decay." He continued, "Such equilibrium causes a Nordic philosopher acute katzenjammer, but that only proves him an indifferent philosopher." [86] The dream of a society that was whole, integrated, orderly, and functional, in which individual and community were one, reentered the scene with a new and more radical urgency.

If *Coming of Age in Samoa* had represented the dream of an integrated society in its ultimate form, *The Changing Culture of an Indian Tribe* was a dark nightmare. Its treatment of the concerns of the time—the disjunction between individual and society, the lag between cultural values and current realities, and the chaos that results when the economic base of a society collapses—locates the book firmly within the intellectual debates of the early 1930s. The Omaha's "broken culture" was a frightening reflection of the breakdown of American civil society in the early Depression years, when revolution and fascism were being touted in both the intellectual and popular media. Its focus on Native Americans both secured this frightening message and rendered it deniable. From the moment that a group of irate men dressed in war paint and native costume dumped a cargo of tea into Boston Harbor in a conjunction of street (or ship) theatre and civil disobedience, the "Indian" has stood in some sense as the personification of America.[87] Yet this representational strategy has always been haunted by ambivalence, for the American nation was built on the violent exclusion of indigenous peoples from those very rights that the American state was established to protect—the accumulation of property, the right to political representation, the pursuit of happiness. As Michaels, Scheckel, and Deloria, among others, have shown, "Indians" commonly stand as "real" Americans or, at least, as the ancestors of "real" Americans in texts that range from public policy debates to Klan polemics to the novels of Faulkner, Cather, Fitzgerald, and Hemingway.[88] The wasteful and self-destructive society that Mead depicted in *The Changing Culture of an Indian Tribe* could not help but feed into two competing discourses on Native Americans: one, which saw them as a debased race rightfully dying out in the advance of civilization; and another, which saw them as a metaphor or proxy for American society at large. It reflected America's constant anxiety, which seemed to be being realized in the 1930s, that "the nation was in a state of decline." [89]

The focus on women exacerbated the potential for ambivalent identification. The move towards more-conservative views on women during the 1930s, especially on women and work, has been well documented. Unemployed women were ignored, even in New Deal legislation; fiction valorized mothers and wives who supported their men, and demonized those who took "men's jobs."[90] The inability of men to support their families was a major source of strife and anguish within families. In Antler society, Mead portrayed an inverted, perverted gender order. Men were wastrels who exploited their wives' illness and wasted their wealth. Women were the economic mainstays of their families, supporting them with gardening and gathering. Further, they also were the guardians of culture, which both Mead and her readers knew was properly men's realm. The promiscuity of the women secured this analysis, women's disordered sexuality being a longstanding trope for social disorder in general. What made Mead's portrait of the Antlers more horrifying was her conclusion that the women's promiscuity, reinforced by their cultural conservatism, would lead only to further moral decay and disorder.

In *Coming of Age in Samoa* and *Growing Up in New Guinea,* Mead was able to draw conclusions about directions for societal change, if only changes in attitude. Committed as she was to the vision of stable, homogenous primitive societies, the Omaha work left her with nothing but individual moral character to draw on. Mead believed that the only way out of the current situation for the Omaha lay in assimilation, the "gradual amalgamation of the Antler into the white population through scattered residence and absorption into various industrial pursuits."[91] However, she saw no reason to hope that this could be accomplished, insofar as the conservative attitudes of the women and their cumulative moral decline prevented it. The women refused to leave the reservation and their extended families so their husbands could work in the cities, and thus they effectively blocked assimilation. Yet, she argued that conflict between an affect "left over" from traditional culture and the changed sexual behaviors on the reservation "promise[d] to produce, with each decade, women of less moral fiber, less willingness to struggle, with fewer reliable habits."[92] Mead's solution, assimilation into urban industrial society and abandonment of reservation life with its ties of kinship and "race solidarity," is an indicator of her impotence when faced with complex cultural disaster, an impossible solution proposed without regard for the Depression ravaging America and hitting hardest those, like the Omaha, who had no skills and who were, at the best of times, marginal to mainstream society. It also reflected Mead's increasingly objectified concept of culture as something that could mined for its good bits but also as something that, once broken, could and should be left behind.

6 "Maladjustment of a Worse Order"

*Temperament, Psychosexual Misidentification, and the
Refuge of Private Life*

IN THE AUTUMN issue of the 1931 volume of *Oceania*, the Notes and News section contained the following announcements:

> Dr. Margaret Mead (Mrs. Fortune) and Dr. R. F. Fortune have arrived in New Guinea. They will carry out field work inland of Wiwiak until about the middle of 1932, after which they propose to undertake research among an Australian tribe.
>
> Mr. Gregory Bateson arrived in Sydney on December 17th, and after a short stay in Brisbane is proceeding to New Guinea to continue his study of the culture of the tribes of the middle Sepik region.[1]

Two years later, Notes and News carried another announcement regarding the same principals.

> Dr. Margaret Mead has returned to America, and Mr. Gregory Bateson to Cambridge, England. Dr. Reo Fortune is remaining for some time in Sydney. All three gave lectures to the Anthropological Society.[2]

For those very few in the know, these re-orderings signaled a shift in personal alliances that still stands as the great anthropological ménage à trois—a triangle that formed on the Sepik River and that was to be played out over the next three years in locations around the globe. It was in fact, not a ménage à trois, but a de facto "ménage à quatre." For that meeting of the "theoretically starved" Mead and Fortune with the "methodologically floundering" Bateson was also when Ruth Benedict, a past lover and a lifelong love of Mead, sent draft chapters of *Patterns of Culture* for comment and critique. An unprecedented number of anthropological classics came out of this four-month period on the Sepik River. In addition to Benedict's best-selling book, Mead's *Sex and Temperament in Three Primitive Societies* and Bateson's *Naven*[3] were products of the intense discussions among the three anthropologists. Fortune's *Sorcerers of Dobu*, published while they were in the field, became a classic, at least in part because Benedict used Fortune's material in *Patterns of Culture*. As George Stocking wryly comments, "If the history of anthropology were to be made into a television, one of its 'great moments' would surely be set on the Sepik River early in 1933."[4]

The impact of this historic encounter has only recently been reconsidered in the light of newly released letters. Jane Howard drew almost exclusively, and uncritically, on Mead's own account in *Blackberry Winter*,[5] as did David Lipset,

Mundugumor woman holding child away from her body, Sepik River 1932; photograph courtesy of the Institute of Intercultural Studies and the Library of Congress (Manuscript Division 152)

Bateson's biographer.[6] Hilary Lapsley gave it more detail but underplayed the significance in terms of Mead's theorization of her work.[7] In her joint biography of Benedict and Mead, Lois Banner treats the incident extensively, emphasizing the psychosexual dynamics among the three principals.[8] But still the most interesting take on the topic is James Boon's 1985 article entitled "Mead's Mediations," which, more self-consciously, uses only what Mead "found fitting to publicize, to commit to public print, to reveal to a readership."[9] Boon's sly, seriously comic, and determinedly indeterminate article cleverly deconstructs Mead's story but ends with more seriously indeterminate questions about the direction of the discipline and the persona of the woman who managed always to place herself in the center. Boon disingenuously declares himself to be "unconcerned with Mead's private side," all the while engaging in some playful psychoanalyzing. However, I would argue that of all her early books, *Sex and Temperament*, based on the theoretical framework developed in this period, is the most personal, the one that is most marked by the demons that had been stalking Mead for years and that pounced on her at the Sepik River in 1933.

Sex and Temperament in Three Primitive Societies also marks a turn in Mead's theoretical position. Certainly since Samoa, and explicitly in her correspondence during the summer of 1930, Mead had begun to distinguish temperament from personality. Although there are hints of this distinction in her earlier work, it is in *Sex and Temperament* that she first (I hesitate to say fully) articulates it and makes an attempt at theorizing it. In *Blackberry Winter,*[10] published forty years later, she makes clear that she still feels that the three anthropologists had discovered a universal truth about the relationship between sex and temperament, not sex and personality, on the Sepik. The significance of this is that, for Mead, temperament was innate and not cultural.

Sex and Temperament in Three Primitive Societies is a plea for a change in cultural values to enable all members of society to develop their individual potential. As such, it has a much more complex relationship to the intellectual and popular climate than did her previous monographs. In one sense, it participated in a larger shift in the meanings of American selfhood that occurred over the course of the 1920s and 1930s. Read in this way, the book is an endpoint in a significant change in Mead's theorization—a move from cultural determinism to what might be called "temperamentalism"—the idea that basic human temperaments exist, that they shape cultures, and that they are in some ways intractable to cultural pressures and forces. This shift in Mead's theorization of the relationship between self and culture maps onto those versions of selfhood identified by Taylor as "the shape of a life [as] simply the result of . . . happenings as they accumulate" or "this shape as something already latent, which emerges through what comes to pass,"[11] and which I have termed eventuation and actualization. *Coming of Age in Samoa* is a tale of the self as eventuation, *Sex and Temperament* as actualization.

This change in Mead's stance is not, however, simply a matter of idiosyncratic theorization, or vacillation between two repeating themes in Western conceptions of selfhood. It contributed to, participated in, and emerged through a more general change in notions of selfhood and American nationhood, in intellectual culture at least, in the second to fourth decades of the twentieth century. Walter Benn Michaels traces the change neatly over the course of the 1920s. He argues that the change was part and parcel of the way in which American modernism was intrinsically nativist, and in some sense, natalist. By the end of the Great War, Randolph Bourne and Waldo Frank saw "America" and "American" as something that was achieved, and argued that cultural diversity was the strength that would enable America to lead the way to a new, cosmopolitan world order.[12] By the end of the 1920s, Michaels finds a distinct move away from the Bourne–Frank position. In a wide range of discourses, from high literature to policy and legislative documents, "American" had become something familial, inherited, almost racial. American culture was something that "Americans" had, something distinctively "ours," which others might envy or wish to emulate but could never "own." This is a version of culture that is separable from the activities, values, and actions of individuals: culture as a commodity form, equivalent, able to be owned, capable of being broken up into its components. The emerging discipline of anthropology, of course, made a fundamental contribution to this change through its development of the concept of "culture" as distinctive, equivalent, and analyzable ways of life. More specifically, the Boasian emphasis on cultural traits reinforced the idea that "culture" or "cultures" were partible. Read in this way, *Sex and Temperament* participates in and indeed contributes to the consolidation of the idea of culture as a commodity form, separate and separable from the individuals who bear it, and to the underlying notion that "culture" is underpinned by inherited or innate characteristics of individuals. Mead's emphasis on the intractability of temperament thus parallels larger changes taking place in American thought.

Read differently, however, *Sex and Temperament in Three Primitive Societies,* with its emphasis on the need for a culture that accommodates and indeed supports a wide range of temperaments, sits somewhat uncomfortably in the intellectual corpus of the mid-1930s. Intellectual self-identification underwent a rapid and radical shift in the early 1930s, a shift that could be characterized in terms of a move from alienation to collectivism. Intellectual leaders, including Robert Lynd, and even the inimitable John Dewey, recast their work. Novelists and critics such as Harold Stearns[13] and Malcolm Cowley, who had spent the 1920s either living abroad or wishing they did, downplayed their position that the artist or intellectual in America was an alienated hero with few options other than to retreat into spiritualism or to escape to the more tolerant climes of Paris. Perhaps the most influential recanting of the 1920s is Cowley's much-quoted memoir, *Exile's Return*, written in a tone that is simultaneously elegiac and cynical. Of this "lost generation," Cowley retrospectively wrote: "The sense of uneasiness and isolation that oppressed American writers was not the result of a purely geographical process and could not be cured by retracing their steps. . . . Their real exile was from society itself, from any society to which they could honestly contribute and from which they could draw the strength that lies in shared convictions."[14]

For many intellectuals and artists, the Depression prompted an about-face from this perceived exile. Shocked by the severity and intransigence of the economic crisis, many critical intellectuals of New York embraced socialism as the only system that could cure the ills the country faced. However, it was a socialism highly inflected by the psychology of self-development that had become such a major feature of popular and intellectual culture over the previous two decades. The holistic, integrative ideal of prewar critical thought reappeared: there was a broad consensus that economic reorganization along socialist lines, involving redistribution of goods and power, was neither sufficiently ambitious nor an end in itself. Personal spiritual and cultural development and integration into community became once again the goals of radical thought. The revolution that America needed, many intellectuals argued, was a total revolution, one that, in addition to being economically stable and equitable, would "introduce a new social order as a prelude to the creation of a new, healthier human being."[15]

This shift in intellectual stance was accompanied by a change in the iconic group that constituted "real America." Over the course of the 1930s, "America" came to be signified neither by the Puritanism of the East Coast's middle class nor by the stultifying Babbittry of the Midwest but by "the people." Given the socialist predilections of these early Depression intellectuals, it is not surprising that "the people" were initially the urban working class. However, the urban working class was demoralized and difficult to organize. Moreover, large segments of the urban poor were ethnically distinctive, holding on to "old world" cultures, rather than living an "authentic American" way of life. So, soon the focus shifted to the country, to the "Okies," the farmers, the sharecroppers. Writers such as Edmund Wilson, Stuart Chase, and Sherwood Anderson were but a few of the many New York intellectuals who, driven by the need to see and understand, took to the road to chronicle the "real" American people and their folkways. Richard Pells maintains that in the face of the social and economic catastrophe all around, they were driven by a need to gather facts, to describe simply and accurately.[16] It seems likely that their need to identify with the mass of working class and rural Americans on the move made this traveling engagement seem more authentic by allowing them to partake in that movement around and across the country. This movement gave rise to what are widely acknowledged to be the two greatest pieces of American writing of the decade: John Steinbeck's *Grapes of Wrath*[17] and James Agee's *Let Us Now Praise Famous Men*.[18]

The desire for a distinctive American culture, which impelled much of the writing of the mid-1930s, was, of course, not new. What was new was the shift in the meaning of culture. When Van Wyck Brooks called for a new "middle" way between highbrow and lowbrow culture in 1915, he had not completely distinguished between the meanings of culture as "art" or "the marker of civilization" and culture as "way of life." During the 1920s, both anthropologists and other intellectuals tended to use civilization and culture interchangeably, as Mead herself did, for example, in *Coming of Age in Samoa*. In the 1930s, by contrast, "culture" emerged as the conceptual alternative to a "civilization" that had gone from being nonexistent (as per Harold Stearns's famous collection) to being the source of contemporary ills. This move to culture was given impetus, of course, by the increasing number of anthropological studies published in the 1920s and early 1930s and by the discovery of the Southwest, and then Mexico, by the literati. By the 1930s, the two meanings of "culture" had finally come apart, impelled at least as much by anthropological writings and debates as by nativist modernism and populist racism.

Mead's work was a central contributor to the developing sense of a distinctively American culture. American culture emerged in her work through the stencil of other peoples' lifeways. All her writing was propelled by the drive to relativize the behaviors, beliefs, and practices of her, largely American, readers, by showing them how other people acted and thought. However, it is not Mead's many works but her friend Ruth Benedict's *Patterns of Culture* that has been identified as the landmark text that gave both credence to the idea of cultural relativism and comfort to those trying to argue for social change in the middle of the Depression.[19] *Sex and Temperament* is the complement of Benedict's more successful book in two significant ways. First, it makes explicit Benedict's more circumspect argument that there is a universal continuum of innate human temperaments. Second, it makes a different, and more liberal, argument with regard to deviance. If Benedict's emphasis is ultimately on culture, Mead's is ultimately on the individual. Benedict focused on the need for cultural integration, tapping into (and reflecting back) the twenty-year yearning of American intellectuals for a homogenous and organically unified society. She holds firmly to the view of "extreme types," such as shaman, as sick individuals. Mead, by contrast, argues for social and cultural change to enable all men and women to attain their potential.

Ultimately, Mead's position is less practical, more utopian, than Benedict's. The source of this difference lies in their personal histories and the accommodations they had or had not reached with their own lives in the mid-1930s. Benedict, who had been plagued by depression and feelings of meaninglessness all her life, had settled down with a young woman. Her letters to Margaret during the period repeatedly proclaim her to be at peace and happier than she had ever been, with "no devils and more drive" than ever before.[20] Having finally overcome her despair, she could look back on her sense of alienation with a degree of distance and resolution. "I don't write verses anymore," she wrote to Mead, "but in my present mood I can well do without them. I wonder how you'll like me when you get home, as a quite cheerful and easily pleased matron."[21] Mead, the commonsense pragmatist, had a more recent, and arguably more severe, experience of mental disturbance to contend with. Like a good anthropologist, she looked for the explanation in culture.

The dynamics on the Sepik in the autumn of 1933 and their effect on Mead's work must be understood in terms of pressures that had been building up since she and Fortune reunited in France in the summer of 1926 and that had been exacerbated during their two years in New York, some of which have been alluded to in chapter 3. It had been an extraordinary time for Mead. In a period of two years, she had become a national figure in the United States and was developing an international reputation. She had a permanent (or as permanent as could be in 1931) position as the assistant curator of ethnology at the American Museum of Natural History in New York. Fortune, on the other hand, was in some sense both jobless and homeless. He had a New Zealand master's degree, a Cambridge diploma in anthropology, and a PhD from Columbia. Like Mead, he had written four books, but they had not resulted in the professional recognition that Mead had attained, and indeed publication of these was repeatedly delayed due to the economic situation. He faced a shrinking job market in both the United States and the United Kingdom, and his chosen discipline, anthropology, was only marginally institutionalized in his own country. Born on a dairy farm in rural New Zealand, albeit to a father, at any rate, who valued education, he lacked the social, cultural, and economic capital that Bateson took for granted and that Mead found so attractive. Many writers, including Mead, have commented on Fortune's sense of alienation and, by implication, his de-masculinization, in Mead's New York milieu. This was a situation that had been anticipated by at least one of Fortune's friends, who wrote to the couple in late 1929 that he was "very curious to know" how Fortune was "getting on in New York," adding, "I hope he is not too scornful of it."[22]

There is, however, another side to the story of this doomed marriage of rival egos. The anthropological savaging of *Growing Up in New Guinea* in both the United States and Britain had repercussions for both Mead and Fortune. The professional culture allowed Alfred Kroeber and C. W. Hart to take swipes at the couple's relationship in the principle disciplinary journals in the United States and the United Kingdom. This suggests that they were the subject of considerable informal gossip as well. Although Fortune may have been personally dislocated and publicly outshone, his reputation among his anthropological peers on two continents was being tarnished through his association with Mead. When criticisms of her competence and expertise impelled Mead to demonstrate her scholarly skills by writing *Kinship in the Admiralty Islands*, she could do so by only poaching what was to have been Fortune's piece of the Admiralties action. This was not the only instance of such boundary crossing. Mead's comparative articles regularly used his Dobu work, and their joint field research, as exemplars. The difficult, and reluctantly undertaken, period of fieldwork in Nebraska in 1930 had added unanticipated writing obligations and further delayed their return to the field, exacerbating Reo's sense of social and financial dependence. The professional tensions and jealousies, one may assume, ran both ways.

Underpinning those tensions was a fundamental difference in values around sexuality. The commitments involved in their decision to marry had come at a considerable cost. As early as the summer of 1926, Mead and Fortune had had major disagreements over her relationship with Benedict. Mead foreswore other sexual relationships in order to marry Fortune, although she had come close to calling off the marriage on the brink of her departure for Manus because of her doubts about her willingness or ability to honor this commitment. But the relationship with Benedict remained one of deep devotion, which could barely be encompassed within the notions of friendship. Her letters to Benedict often express deep love and explore the range and depth that Benedict brought to Mead's sense of her own life. Although Fortune liked and admired Benedict, he had stern notions of fidelity and, above all, loyalty and friendship, and he could not accept or understand Mead's desire and ability to love both widely and deeply. The two years in New York, in almost daily contact with Mead's former lovers, must have proved a constant strain. All this came to a head on the Sepik in the austral summer of 1933.

Mead and Fortune departed New York for their third major field trip in three years at the end of August 1931. They left behind family, friends, and country—

all in a spiraling economic crisis. Letters from Mead's family and from Benedict chronicle the wider economic and social mayhem and the toll it was taking on intimates and acquaintances. Having secured fellowship funding, independent of Mead's salary, the two anthropologists were determined to weather the Depression by remaining in the field as long as possible.[23] They stopped briefly in New Zealand to visit Reo's family and arrived in Sydney in early October.

In Sydney their relative prestige shifted due to Reo's United Kingdom and New Zealand connections. Of Fortune's fellow New Zealander Raymond Firth, Mead wrote, "[He] is trying to be Brown and Malinowski both at once; he looks down his nose and says when will some real anthropology be done in America."[24] Obviously miffed, she complained to Wissler: "The banner of Malinowski is waving in these parts a little noisily and pompously; to have been trained under Malinowski [as, of course, Fortune had been] is equivalent to having received the Holy Ghost from a member of the Apostolic succession."[25] After six weeks in Sydney arranging their affairs and seeking advice about field sites, they sailed for New Guinea. Mead worked on *Kinship in the Admiralty Islands* while they were at sea. She wrote her mother, "I have been trying to get Reo to read my kinship system which he is most unwilling to do."[26] Landing at Rabaul, they traveled along the coast to Karawop, staying with a couple named Cobb, who had a plantation and labor-recruiting station. In order to secure enough men to carry both their goods and Mead, who had injured her ankle, up into the highland plains, Reo blackmailed the local villagers by threatening that he would reveal their secrets to the government agent. In the mountaintop village of Aliatoa, the carriers revolted and refused to go further, so, with characteristic practicality, Margaret and Reo once again ordered a house to be built and began work.

In a bulletin home, Margaret wrote that they were settled in "a delightful climate." In the letter she wrote: "These natives—they have no name and we haven't decided what to call them yet . . . are a most amiable, gentle courteous people. . . . [They] lack most of the necessary ways of making themselves comfortable . . . but they also have not invented very many ways of making themselves miserable."[27] Despite these pleasant working conditions, she was plagued by ill health, both mental and physical, a state that was to continue for the next two years. Her injured foot would not heal, and after being carried up the mountain she was unable to leave the village for seven months. Although her surviving letters and field bulletins are chirpy and humorous, and she frequently comments on their good health, she later remembered the period as one in which she became depressed, feeling that "everything ahead looked pallid and uninviting."[28]

Mead stayed in the (often empty) village; she was miserable but, characteristically, got on with her work. Reo made forays into the interior, leaving her alone for days at a time.[29] He also had to repeatedly traipse down the mountain to Karawop for supplies and mail—a two-day trip each way. Close to the end of their seven-month stay, Mead wrote her mother, "Reo got back here four days ago and tomorrow he has to set off for Wiwiak to try to arrange for transportation up the Sepik. . . . Poor Reo is so tired of being a 'transport officer'—he hasn't been able to settle down to his own work for two weeks running in the last three months."[30] He had a bout of serious illness that Mead could neither diagnose nor treat, and recovered his health only slowly. News came that Bateson, who was Fortune's contemporary at Cambridge, had been appointed to a prestigious fellow's position, for which Reo had also applied. Meanwhile, the couple waited with bated breath for a published copy and reviews of *Sorcerers of Dobu*, with its as yet unseen introduction by Malinowski. Although the reviews were generally good, Malinowksi credited himself and Mead with inventing the "case study method" that was "a special merit of Dr. Fortune's book."[31] It was at this time that they also got news of Hart's excoriating review of the English edition of *Growing Up in New Guinea* in *Man*.[32]

Finally, by the end of August, Margaret's foot had healed sufficiently that she could travel down the mountain. She and Fortune spent a month at the Cobbs' plantation at Karawop, arranging to have themselves and their goods transported up the Sepik. By October 4, they had settled with the Mundugumor on the Yuet River. They spent two and half months with this "violent," "irascible," and "charming" people, who "go in for cannibalism, headhunting, infanticide, incest, avoidance and joking relationships, adultery, and biting lice in half with their teeth." From separation and pleasant work conditions they were precipitated into close quarters, their discomfort exacerbated by extreme heat. "The mosquitoes . . . are the most amazing determined, starving crew imaginable; . . . most of them never had a full meal and are fighting for just one before they die." They spent most of their waking time in a "horribly small," wire-mesh room 9 by 9 by 10 feet in dimensions, "climbing over each other all the time."[33] They both had recurrent bouts of malaria. By Mead's account, Fortune climbed mountains to walk his sickness out, abandoning her to her fevers. Her letters home "seemed a wee bit homesick and forlorn, with Reo away, but always brave."[34] As we will see, Fortune, whose own story is missing in the many re-tellings, and who burned most of his personal papers shortly before he died, gave a different account of Mead's illness. Perhaps still smarting from Mead's appropriation of Manus kinship, Fortune evidently "insisted that he would work alone on the kinship system." Mead later wrote that she discovered that he had "missed a clue," "a contradiction of good scientific practice."[35] However, whatever the problems she and Fortune had, Mead wrote her mother on October 25 that she was "comfortably married for good." In the same letter, she added that "[t]he four servants have at last produced a loaf of bread which is edible, that is a triumph. . . . Bateson is coming and Reo is pleased with the idea of having bread for him." [36]

They continued to be desperately worried about their future, both personal and professional. Margaret wrote Benedict,

I have as inferior job as I can have and have one at all, and if I ask to have it improved, I'll probably be fired. Anyway I won't dare raise the issue as long as Reo has nothing. And who will find him anything? Not Papa Franz. And likely Brown won't have the power, if he has the inclination. In some way we seem to have managed very badly, Reo because he has been flung about so from one place to another, and I, I don't know quite why. . . . But without academic prestige, no matter how good work one does, no one will pay any attention. . . . [W]hat is the use of being in a subject where people are so stupid, stupid, stupid? [37]

Their concern over their career prospects was especially poignant because they had once again reopened discussion about whether or not to have children. They felt that unless Fortune could secure a job, they could not possibly consider Mead's leaving the museum to look after a child.

Bateson, working just upriver, had his own history of illness and depression. He had spent three years (1927–1930) in New Guinea working first with the Baining then the Sulka and finally the Iatmul peoples. He came away feeling that his fieldwork was a failure. He was bored, malarial, and acutely aware of being deceived by his informants, and briefly considered suicide. He viewed fieldwork diffidently; felt that it involved "poking [his] nose into the affairs of other races." [38] He returned to Cambridge in 1930, but found it, too, distasteful and withdrew to a farm where he worked for a year writing a largely descriptive master's thesis, which was significant for its explication of his fieldwork difficulties. In 1932 he returned to New Guinea to work again among the Iatmul. And once again he alternated periods of intense activity with periods of "shames and depressions." [39] He was lonely and wanted a fieldwork partner, sex unspecified. He had a number of affairs, including one with the wife of a Rabaul solicitor who followed him up the Sepik, but she became ill and had to leave, a tidbit reported to Mead in a gossipy letter from Fluff Cobb.[40] He then became involved with "a warm, tough, little pagan of about 38–40 [who had] been in the territory for 15 years or so," and who was "a licensed engineer and lived on boats." [41] When he finally met up with Mead and Fortune for a Christmas at the district officer's house in December 1932, he had become engaged to yet another young woman, who was expected to join him in the field.

The initial meeting, as described by Mead in *Blackberry Winter*, has all the hallmarks of a romantic epic—with Mead as damsel in distress, Fortune as heartless villain, and Bateson as tender prince.[42] However, the competitive dynamics were not, at least in the beginning, that straightforward. Initially, it was Mead who was excluded: "We picked Gregory Bateson up in the afternoon and slept that night in his village, or rather I slept and he and Reo talked." Mead's exclusion continued the next day in even more trying circumstances: "[T]he battle raged in the pinnace cabin as to whether we three were to talk anthropology or whether Mr. Thomas [a "young, incredibly earnest and awfully loquacious patrol officer"], fortified with a year of Radcliffe-Brown's lectures as a cadet, was to talk it. Reo and Gregory took to the baking roof in despair, while I listened sympathetically to Mr. Thomas and steadily made vows about teaching anthropology to otherwise reasonably harmless people."[43]

However, from Mead's point of view, it was love virtually at first sight. On December 26, she began a long letter to Benedict chronicling the first weeks of the affair: "It's Bateson, of course. Nothing that I had heard had prepared me for him. . . . You've no idea how moving six feet four of vulnerable beauty is." Within a few days, Bateson took them out in his canoe looking for a "people" to study. The emotional drama escalated immediately. Fortune, up until then abstemious, got drunk for the first time, at least in Mead's experience of him. He woke in the middle of the night and saw Mead and Bateson talking and sharing a cigarette, and sensed the intimacy that had grown up so quickly between them. The next day, with Reo still drunk and angry, they continued their trip with "some pretty violent scenes along the way."[44] Despite the emotional tension, they were able to persist until they found a group of people suitable for their research—the Tchambuli (Chambri) on the shores of Lake Chambri. In a bulletin that masks all the emotional drama that was consuming them, Margaret reported that she was enchanted with the setting, calling the black, lotus-covered lake and its environs "far the most beautiful in which we have ever been." They bought a motorized canoe, and her foot had mended to the point where she could walk everywhere: she felt as if "let out of gaol."[45]

In order to be close to them, Bateson also "changed people," moving to Aibom, also on Lake Chambri, virtually next door. Margaret waxed and waned in her relationships with the two men over the next two months. In March, Gregory came to stay in their camp for two weeks, playing chess at night with Reo while Margaret wrote feverish, contradictory, and self-justifying letters to Benedict. The emotional dramas escalated. Reo continued to drink heavily, "the most fiendish amount of whiskey and gin and what not," attacked a recruiter, hallucinated.[46] He and Mead alternated raking over the past and trying desperately to work out some accommodation for their future.[47] Mead begged him to try living her "culture" of open, heterogeneous sexual relationships and wrote to Benedict that Reo had finally realized that "the fighting I've done over Gregory was a fight in the light of all my sense of deprivation about you."[48]

With the exception of Benedict, the world was presented with the picture of a happy meeting of anthropological minds. Bateson wrote to Malinowski: "[The] Fortunes have . . . administered an accurate kick in the pants so now I am starting off on a new regime." In this regime, "[t]he wretched informants get hurried and chivvied & bounced about & their feelings are never spared. So they become hypnotized & the information just drips out of them." He intended, he said, to introduce this "reign of terror."[49] However, the emotional triangle played havoc with the fieldwork. In early March, Mead again wrote to Benedict: "We continue to be so swamped with events (culture and personal (our own)) that we have hardly made a start on learning the language. . . . Gregory has been in Aibom ten days—coming for dinner and usually staying the night and leaving after breakfast."[50] She repeatedly apologized to Benedict for their failure to address the draft of *Patterns of Culture* she had sent for comment.

Throughout this period, all three were repeatedly feverish, and Mead was severely stung by a scorpion, rendering her incapacitated for two weeks. According to Jean Houston, Mead became pregnant but miscarried when Fortune knocked her down. Despite Mead's later assertions that he did not want children (belied by contemporary correspondence), Fortune accused Bateson of "eating" their baby.[51] Mead later wrote Benedict that they had expected that Reo would shoot them and then himself.[52] She called this period on the Sepik "the closest I have ever come to madness"; Bateson is reported to have commented, "All three of us were pretty well psychotic."[53] Fortune, silent on almost all other counts, wrote an (again partial) account of the madness, in an apologetic letter to Malinowski almost five years later:

About past history I owe you some apology for my disturbance in mind when I was in London. I can tell you a little of it some day perhaps—I had come from nursing an alienist's job in my then wife on the Sepik River complicated by Bateson—and the mess made worse by him deliberately. Meanwhile there were hot baths for Mead every half hour under the obsession that she was dying, incitements by her to shoot the various natives who pressed in on us, typescripts by her of new racial "theories"—about Jesus Christ & Henry Ford not discovering the four psychological races that were going to revolutionise medicine, education, etc.—division of our meagre stock of medicines into appropriate medicines for each race by her—in short a dangerous madness. I have kept the typescripts. Bateson egged it on to make me sicker and it became so terrifying that I feared for her mind's permanent condition.[54]

Mead also kept one of these typescripts, and it is a mad document indeed.[55] It is titled "Summary of Statement of the Problem of Personality and Culture." By M. Mead and R. Fortune. Fortune's name is crossed out, and "I have nothing to do with this RFF" is written in the margin. This text purports to have solved the problem of the relation between personality and culture. It begins with a "summary" of the current "suppositions" of science and psychology about the relation between sex and gender, focusing particularly on the explanations of physiological or biological "freaks"—"individuals who conspicuously differed from the types which were assumed." All current biological and psychological explanations, the text asserts, were wrong. A new theory is proposed that will explain the ontology of "mixed types"; that is, those people whose gendered behavior is at odds with their biological sex, and of "all diseases which can be cured by suggestions, . . . of group hysteria, of glandular unbalance, . . . of the failure of many individuals of both sexes to mate, of the susceptibility of people to different foods, . . . of inability to write, of inability to spell, the inability to comprehend the work of a given group of poets, novelists or philosophers, and many other problems."

The theory is as follows: "There are two types of human beings: each of these types includes males and females. . . . One type is characterized by the psychology, physiology, etc. of the type usually called maternal, the other of the paternal." There were three variables that went into constituting these types: physiological gender, physical type, and temperament, and it is temperament with which Mead was most concerned. She wrote:

The perfect male [M] temperament, found in either males or females, is expressed in the individual who goes out and chooses his mates, his friends, his associates, etc., and having chosen them, cherishes them and guards them jealously from all aggressors of the same temperament. The perfect female [F] temperament, remembering that this temperament is also found almost equally in each gender, is that which responds to every call and cherishes each thing to which it responds, and is ultimately most completely possessed by a member of the male tempera-

Gregory Bateson, Margaret Mead, and Reo Fortune, Sydney, July 1933; photograph courtesy of the Institute of Inter-cultural Studies and the Library of Congress (Manuscript Division 139a)

ment group to whom is then given the most complete and watchful cherishing attention.

Whether a child has an M or F temperament is said to depend on whether both parents are active or passive during intercourse. Bizarre attributions of health problems, "perversions," psychological problems, incest, and even body odors depend on whether an individual is an F female, F male, M female, or M male.

The conclusion is devoted to explaining how this discovery was made. This finding was possible only when

> [t]he combination was reached of three people, equally strong and equally gifted met [men] who were a MALE IN M and a female in f, in combination with either a woman in M or a male in F, all born of twinning stocks. When that occurred the perfect mating and the perfect brother and sisterhood within the group M or F asserted itself, the situation which has been described as mediumistic [re]sulted and understanding could be reached.[56]

This is possible, the document asserts, because when twins are conceived by "women in M," one twin is absorbed into the placenta, leaving the remaining one with a lifelong sense of loss, which drives it to seek completion. It is apparent that Mead saw herself, Fortune, and Bateson as this fortuitous combination. Her attribution of co-authorship to Fortune and the noting of "perfect mating" suggest that the marriage was still intact at the time the document was written. More significant for their futures was the "perfect brother and sisterhood," herself and Bateson, each the other's "lost twin."

This document was a more extreme version of a general theory of innate temperaments or races that the anthropologists developed. Based on the four directions (north, south, east, and west, known as the "four squares"), they assigned temperament types, responses, innate sadism or masochism, and theories of "best marriage partner" to the four "squares." Fortune became increasingly isolated by the growing assertions of identity and complementarity between Mead and Bateson (M female and F male, according to one of the schema they had developed; warm, gentle "southerners," rather than cold, jealous "northerners," like Reo, according to another). He later wrote that he "did some quick surgery & got well away."[57] For whatever reason, to preserve sanity, as per Fortune, or because they had a "major idea," as per Bateson and Mead, they decamped from the Sepik, traveling to Sydney together. Margaret immediately cabled Boas that they had made a most important discovery and wrote to Ruth Benedict in ecstatic, almost manic, tones,

"[W]e are frightfully excited, personally, scientifically and every other way—and so will you be when you hear about it." She also hinted that significant changes were afoot: "[A]ll my letters become completely invalid before I send them. . . . As soon as life becomes a little clearer, I'll write you a fuller account."[58]

On the boat, Reo began an affair with a woman (whom Mead nicknamed Mira) he had known previously, who was traveling with her two daughters. In Sydney, all six of them moved into three apartments in the same building. But the ménage à trois continued to be everyone's principle preoccupation. Bateson and Fortune had regular lunches and chess games together. Each in turn would decide that the only way to resolve the situation was for one to leave, but each time the others refused to allow it. Mead continued to be torn between them, while clearly recognizing the strength of the bond between Bateson and Fortune, a love that she felt was being played out through her.[59] The situation came to a head one night when Mead returned to the apartment she shared with Fortune, in tears, but telling him that "her business was none of [his]" (in what Fortune later described as Samoan invective). Fortune, by his own account, hit her and told her to get out. He sent a note to Bateson informing him as much.[60] Margaret decided to return by herself to New York, keeping her plans a secret from Fortune, abetted by Bateson and Carolyn Tennant, a budding anthropologist in the Sydney department. She had a "civilized," "surface" lunch with Reo and went directly to the ship, leaving a letter for him telling him of her departure.[61]

As it became clear that Mead was intent on leaving Fortune, Benedict became concerned about the damage that the breakup of this second marriage could entail. She wrote urgently to Mead "to take all kinds of precautions" to protect her professional standing. She advised Margaret to keep the matter a secret from the Sydney anthropologists and to "c[o]me back without Reo, a deserted wife, more or less, and without joining Gregory . . . get a divorce at Reo's request."[62] Thus, a plan began to be formed to put the onus for the breakup on Fortune in order to protect Mead's career, a plan that his short affair with Mira helped cement.

It took Mead almost a year after leaving the field to come to grips with writing *Sex and Temperament in Three Primitive Societies*. She returned to New York in early September in a highly disturbed state. In a letter to Bateson, Benedict described her as in "a strange turmoil . . . as if in leaving one world behind . . . and leaping into an old familiar one something had happened to her sense of reality." Her sense of reality was surely compromised by her taking Ruth's advice to keep her separation from Fortune a secret even from her own family. She went back to their shared apartment, put Reo's name on the door and on the phone account, and arranged with Benedict and Tennant, her only Sydney confidant, for money to be conveyed to him, disguised as a research grant and a loan repayment. Emotionally, she vacillated between defending Fortune from the ill treatment he had received from the American academic community and agonizing about right and wrong, all of which was tied up with her allegiance to the "square" schema worked out on the Sepik. Ruth tried to keep up with the "square" categories in order to be able to communicate with her emotionally labile friend but confessed that Margaret "shifted the boundaries bewilderingly." Loyally, she wrote Bateson that she would be better able to use this new schema when "the alignments stay put for a week, or when I am taking part too in working at them." [63]

Although confusion reigned inwardly for a long time, outwardly things had begun to improve in the country. Franklin Delano Roosevelt had taken office in January and had immediately begun his hundred days of reform, beginning with a bank holiday that stabilized the banking system. He followed that with a number of major legislative initiatives that cut federal spending, regulated farming, took the United States off the gold standard, provided direct federal grants to states for relief, established the Civilian Conservation Corps to provide employment for men outside the major cities, and established the Home Owners Loan Corporation, which would refinance the loans of one out of five mortgaged homes in the country. While the efficacy of many of Roosevelt's early initiatives continues to be the subject of debate, there is little doubt that he gave hope to the nation. He began his first radio-broadcast fireside chats the first week of his presidency; within the week, half a million Americans had written to him. Although the U.S. economy continued to wobble precariously for the next four years, he was seen directly as rescuing people's savings, homes, and dignity. Moreover, one of his first moves as president was to repeal Prohibition. Beer and wine flowed freely, bars and pretzel factories reopened, organized crime lost a major source of revenue, and working men and women began to believe in the possibility of their own lives. [64]

Professionally, there were new possibilities opening up as private foundations, especially the Rockefeller Foundation, began to pour money into anthropological research. Mead was accumulating more kudos, giving her access to these funds. In October she was appointed a fellow of the American Academy of Science, and in March 1934 she was invited to participate in the exclusive, Rockefeller-funded, month-long Hanover Conference on Human Relations, along with such notables as Robert and Helen Lynd, Erich Fromm, Laurence Frank,[65] and John Dollard. This balanced out her disappointment at not being named as one of the top hundred scientists in the United States, and a more serious disappointment at being turned down for a Guggenheim fellowship so that she could write her book in the United Kingdom. The honorarium from Rockefeller was sufficient to fund her to

England at the end of August 1934 to attend the International Congress of Anthropological and Ethnological Sciences, and, not incidentally, to live with Bateson for at least a short while.

Mead identified the Hanover Conference on Human Relations as formative in her conception of the book. However, the form of the book and much of the analysis recapitulates her earlier work—a general introduction, followed by an ethnographic description, with a final section that examines the implications of her findings for American society. It seems likely that her emphasis on the development of trust, in her description of childhood among the Arapesh, comes from Fromm's consolidation of his theories of the importance of trust, presented at the conference. Mead later reported that John Dollard converted her to Freudianism at Hanover, but there is little evidence of Freudian analysis, except perhaps her reference to "specific drives" in the conclusion.[66] The notion of identification on which she builds her theory of deviance is not much more clearly developed in *Sex and Temperament* than it was in *Growing Up in New Guinea*.

Sex and Temperament is organized around clear stereotypes of masculine and feminine behavior. The book purports to demonstrate that qualities the modern West assigns to one sex are assigned to either both sexes or to the opposite sex in the three cultures she studied. Initially, Mead had believed that there was marked gender differentiation in Arapesh culture: "[T]he emphasis upon sex difference begins in the cradle, baby girls are decked out in earrings and necklaces, while a boy wears no ornament until almost grown. Little girls of four and five strut and flirt."[67] However, she later changed her mind, arguing that the Arapesh, both men and women, were maternal; the Mundugumor, both men and women, were said to be not paternal but violent, aggressive, harsh, and "positively sexed," "a personality type that we in our culture would find only in a violent and undisciplined male."[68] The Tchambuli she presents as a reversal of American culture, with "dominant, impersonal, managing" females and "less responsible and emotionally dependent" males. The last chapter in each of the three ethnographic sections is devoted to "deviants" in each of the three societies: aggressive men and women in Arapesh, gentle ones in Mundugumor, and submissive women and dominating men in Tchambuli. *Sex and Temperament* is ostensibly focused on the management of heterosexual relations in these three societies. However, its principle concern is the same problem that is the focus of the Tchambuli document: the explanation of deviants or "mixed types," those people whose temperaments are at odds with the cultural expectations appropriate to their physiological sex.

As she did in *Coming of Age in Samoa* and *Growing Up in New Guinea*, Mead devoted the final section of *Sex and Temperament* (part 4) to the implications of her findings for American society. This section is distinctive in terms of Mead's early work in that, for the first time, she sets out an explicit theory of the ontogenesis of cultural formations, and a theory of psychosexual development. Despite professing the "preponderant importance of cultural conditioning"[69] in the development of personality, she maintains that cultures take their form from variations in individual temperament, an idea Benedict had expressed in terms of culture as "personality writ large." Anthropological reviewers were to take Mead to task for the vagueness of her notion of "temperament,"[70] but she does set out her assumptions about this vexed category and acknowledge their limitations given the contemporary state of knowledge. First, she asserts the "over-riding importance" of culture in shaping personality. However, she also asserts that the same range of temperaments occurs among human beings in all societies. She argues that it therefore follows that there must be some innate pre-cultural differences among human beings: "[I]f human nature were completely homogenous material, lacking specific drives and characterized by no important constitutional differences between individuals, then individuals who display personality traits so antithetical to social pressure should not reappear in societies of such differing emphases."[71] This leads her to assume that "there are definite temperamental differences between human beings which if not entirely hereditary at least are established on a hereditary base very soon after birth," adding parenthetically, "[f]urther than that we cannot at present narrow the matter."[72] Given this range of innate human temperaments, the more "definite and integrated" a culture, the more likely it is that it will be uncongenial to some of its members, with at times devastating results. "To the extent that a culture is integrated and definite in its goals, uncompromising in its moral and spiritual preferences, to that very extent it condemns some of its members—members by birth only—to live alien to it, in perplexity at the best, at the worst in a rebellion that may turn to madness."[73] Mead's indictment of "integrated" cultures shows how far she had moved from the days of her Samoan and Omaha fieldwork.

Although the argument, as built on the ethnographic material, is made to apply to anyone whose temperament puts them at odds with their society, it is psychosexual deviance that Mead is most at pains to explain. Chapter 18 of Part Four, "The Deviant," is principally a treatise on the origins of homosexuality, or inversion and the costs to individuals of a rigid cultural categorization of personalities according to sex. Mead's textual relation to "the homosexual," or "the invert," is slippery and inconsistent. In setting out her argument, Mead is at pains to exclude from consideration the "congenital invert," the "practicing homosexual,"[74] and the "physiologically inadequate"[75] from her analysis. She says that she is concerned only with "those individuals whose adjustment to life is conditioned by their temperamental affinity for a type of behavior which is regarded as unnatural for their own sex and natural for the opposite sex."[76] She theorizes that such temperamental affinities cause children to identify with opposite-sex parents. This kind of psychosexual misidentification, Mead argues, can occur only in societies where different personalities are assigned to the two sexes. Although other cultures, such as the Arapesh and the Mundugumor, which expect no differentiation in the personalities of men and women, have people who deviate from their norms, they cannot have psychosexual deviance. However, in societies such as America, where distinct personalities are mandated for each sex, a girl innately averse to demonstrative behavior, for example, may identify with her father, who has a like aversion. The difference is that his aversion is deemed appropriate for his sex, whereas hers is not. The result may be Mead's hypothetical woman who ends up "wearing mannish attire, following a male occupation, and unable to find happiness in marriage."[77] Such a person, for temperamental reasons quite divorced from any innate sex-linked behaviors, is thus made to feel "sex-disenfranchised."

Mead's attitude towards psychosexual misidentification, and indeed to inversion, is at best ambivalent. On the one hand, she downplays its significance, linking homosexuality with vegetarianism as "merely" an "elaborated idiosyncrasy of behaviour."[78] On the other hand, in a number of places, she clearly indicates that the crossing of such boundaries is dangerous. For example, if a child is attracted to activities culturally associated with the opposite sex, "the occupational choice or hobby throws him more with [that sex and] he may come in time to take on much of [its] socially sex-limited behaviour."[79] The cost of maintaining sex-specific personalities, she tells her readers, is "maladjustment of a worse order."[80] Her solution to this problem is to eliminate the requirement for sex-specific personalities. Although this appears a laudable goal and was indeed seen so by most reviewers, Mead also holds out the promise that such change will see the elimination of homosexuality. Repeatedly, she tells her readers that there can be no psychosexual misidentification where there is no definite assignment of distinct personalities to the two sexes. Sliding between two categories that she purports to keep apart, she tells her readers, there is "no homosexuality among either the Arapesh or the Mundugumor."[81]

Mead concludes the chapter with a discussion of the problems that occur for even those "normally"–identified individuals in such a society. She argues that it is not only those who have misidentified who suffer because of Americans' attribution of specific sex-linked personalities. Her examples seem drawn from very close to hand. She discusses the dominating male who encounters a woman "who is naturally as dominating as he is himself, or even a woman who . . . is able to outdistance him in some special skill or type of work," asserting that, as a result, "a doubt of his own manhood is set up in his mind."[82] She considers the cross-cultural marriage, in which expectations of the two sexes differ and which leaves an individual doubting "the completeness of his or her possession of a really masculine or a really feminine nature."[83] Needless to say, both of these could refer to her relationship with Fortune and may explain why he was so outraged at the book. Her description of the woman-identified woman, who attaches herself to a dominating female could be a description of her devoted friend Marie Eichelberger, who struggled for years to hold her romantic feelings for Mead at bay.[84]

The book was written in a six-month period at the end of 1934, during which Mead moved from New York to Hanover, and thence to England and Ireland to be with Bateson. She also met Fortune in England and broke finally with him. Although destitute, he refused to accept money from her and was rescued by Malinowski and Raymond Firth. His "beggarly" position was especially humiliating because it was played out in the context of an international anthropology conference. He left England, spent the next thirteen years in a kind of exile, and finally got his first permanent job (at Cambridge) only after the war. In *Blackberry Winter,* Mead wrote that her decision to leave Fortune for Bateson, and to try to have a child, came from her distaste for the Mundugumors' approach to child life. As in her account of her first marriage breakdown, Mead contended that it was not the man who was at stake but his potential for fatherhood. That, along with Fortune's apparent inability or unwillingness to have children, comprised the reasons that were circulated through the anthropological community to explain his "desertion" of her. Fortune was well aware of Mead's characterization of the reasons for the split and was bitterly ironic about the accusations of infertility.[85] Apparently, he was, however, not aware of the extent to which Bateson, who continued to correspond with him, often under instruction from Benedict, was complicit in the picture of the marriage breakup and dissemination of the news through their professional community. It is tempting to see *Sex and Temperament* as simply yet another brick in the façade that Mead, Benedict, and Bateson built in order to protect Mead's career.

However, that position overlooks the extent to which Mead needed to reconstruct her sense of self after her shattering experiences on the Sepik. In the book, Mead clearly identifies the inability to "find happiness in marriage" as the cost of psychosexual misidentification, whereas marriage and, particularly, the care of children are presented as the private solace of those who cannot conform to their culture's expectations in other ways.[86] The maddened, embittered breakdown of her second marriage, again after only five years, must have undermined Mead's sense of herself on a number of levels, not the least as the purveyor of scientific knowledge into social good. She told family and colleagues about the divorce only after she had married Bateson in Singapore on the way to Bali in 1936, with funding secured for two years of fieldwork and enough distance between herself and the scholarly community to guarantee that gossip would have stilled by the time she returned to New York. Uncharacteristically, she left it to Bateson to inform Fortune of the marriage.[87] In rejecting Fortune and, retrospectively at least, justifying this as choosing motherhood, Mead can be seen as reining in her persona, re-securing respectability, or asserting her safe deviance, not as a "congenital invert" or "faithless wife" or "madwoman," but as a career woman interested in children.[88]

Sex and Temperament has been and continues to be read in many ways. Contemporary accounts read it as feminist, providing evidence that limitations on women were cultural, rather than innate. Di Leonardo reads the conclusion, at least, as antifeminist.[89] Lipset regards it as prescient in foregrounding of "actions, voices and dispositions of both women and men, almost a half century prior to the emergence of a feminist anthropology, . . . not to mention long before the recognition of polyphony and dialogism in culture."[90] There is certainly a case to be made that it can be read as homophobic, or at least hypocritical. However, it is more faithful to the text to read it as confused, reflecting Mead's own confusion about her sexual relationships. On the one hand, she holds out the promise of the end of homosexuality and redeems her persona through a resort to what would now be called "family values." On the other hand, she clearly calls for the creation of a society that is more tolerant, flexible, and supportive of a wide variety of temperaments, including, or perhaps especially, those perceived as sexually deviant.

Anthropological reviews of the book were mixed, with Linton[91] and Benedict[92] (not surprisingly) reviewing it positively for newspapers; Richard Thurnwald gave it an excoriating, if familiar, review in *American Anthropologist*,[93] to which Mead wrote a detailed reply.[94] By this time, the professional reviews were predictable, those who favored Mead or her comparative and apparently culturalist approach reviewing it positively, while others attacked her lack of rigor. The popular press's response to *Sex and Temperament in Three Primitive Societies* was similar in tone to that which had greeted *Coming of Age in Samoa*, particularly in its humor. If Mead needed any indication that sexual themes were more likely to maintain her public profile, the contrast between the reviews of *Growing Up in New Guinea* or *The Changing Culture of an Indian Tribe* and those of *Sex and Temperament* would have served. Whereas the former tended to get sober, even if positive, reviews, there was an explosion of witty, humorous, and overwhelmingly positive reviews of *Sex and Temperament*. Again, her work was compared to the great tales of travel to mythical lands—*Gulliver's Travels, Erewhon,* and *Alice in Wonderland*.[95] The apparent reversal of roles among the Tchambuli, especially, tickled the fancy of reviewers. The most common response of (female) reviewers was, as might be expected, humorous and gleeful. If reviewers took any serious message from the book, it was the call to a more tolerant and flexible society. Not surprisingly, reviewers tended to ignore Mead's conclusions about psychosexual identification, and its implications for understandings of homosexuality, and to emphasize instead the heterosexual role reversals found in the three New Guinea societies.

Two quotes are found in many of the reviews. The first is her argument that "human nature is almost unbelievably malleable, responding accurately and contrastingly to contrasting cultural conditions"; the second, her call for "a less arbitrary social fabric, in which each diverse human gift will find a fitting place" and in which no individual will be forced by artificial distinctions, such as that of sex, "into an ill-fitting mold."[96] These two quotes speak to two contradictory impulses of the Depression-era intellectual—the need to "fit in," to lose oneself in the integrated collectivity, and the need to "be oneself," to stand out against the conforming pressures, a conflict exacerbated by intellectuals' and artists' felt need to "do something" in the face of the social devastation they were witnessing.[97] *Sex and Temperament in Three Primitive Societies* thus captures one of the central paradoxes of American popular and intellectual culture in the mid-1930s: how firmly ordinary Americans held fast to the myth of individual autonomy and responsibility in the face of the economic crisis. Levine's analysis of a wide range of media and genres from the period shows that this theme recapitulated through radio shows, books, and films, including gangster films and Frank Capra comedies.[98] Charles Hearn demonstrates that popular novels and short stories continued to be based on these notions while either escalating their possibilities through escapist fantasy or "scaling down" the goals to the nonmaterial ends of "peace of mind, love, family, harmony and respect."[99]

This trenchant individualism may, paradoxically, help explain what Walter Susman[100] has termed the "turn to culture" in the mid-1930s. The need to develop a distinctive American culture consonant with its technological resources had been a central issue in American intellectual life since early in the century. Yet, what "culture" meant in these early debates was not entirely clear. When Brooks argued for a middle way between an emasculated, foreign-generated "high" culture and mere money-grubbing materialism, he slid unselfconsciously between culture as a way of life, and culture as art and intellectual life, although undoubt-edly his emphasis was on the latter. Even for Bourne, culture was to be "continu-ous with the rest of one's life"—a definition still a long way from the Boasian view that culture was indeed one's whole way of life.[101] Yet, by the end of the 1920s, the latter, anthropological, notion of culture was widely accepted by intellectuals and the public alike.

Numerous scholars since Susman have commented on and tracked the impor-tance of the search to describe and define American culture (as lifeways) in the 1930s. One of the most interesting and politically detailed is Browder's account of the way local and state authorities supported culturalist or folkways projects while refusing to fund critical or socialist-inspired ones, such as *The Living Newspapers.* In this, they were abetted by a rift within the intellectual and artistic communities between those committed to a communist or socialist vision of society and those who had committed to celebrating the American folk.[102] Many intellectuals and artists who had spent the 1920s in flight from "Americanism" spent the early thir-ties committed to its downfall and the late thirties to its celebration.

The demise of radical socialist or Marxist-inspired critique and the "turn to culture" in the 1930s had a number of underlying "causes," not the least being the refusal of state and local authorities to fund projects critical of existing class rela-tions.[103] A major underlying contributor to the "turn to culture," however, derives from a fundamental affinity between intellectual and popular values of the era and the notion of "culture" itself, as they had been articulated to the public, especially through Mead's popular writings. One of the principle differences between the concept of "class," which underpins socialist thought, and the concept of culture as it developed in the United States in the first part of the twentieth century is the fundamentally different property relationships these two ideas embody. "Class" always assumes an "other," an enemy. Class is not something "we" "own"; it is something imposed on "us"—by the bosses, the capitalists, the government, the owners. Radical and left thought is aimed at the elimination of class. The "I" who theorizes "class" is not responsible for its survival but is committed to its demise. "Class" demands loyalty to an abstract entity that, if socialist theory is right and radical action is successful, will disappear. Class is a fundamentally negative idea.

In the early twentieth century, in American intellectual life, culture was assumed to be a positive, perhaps the most positive, value. It was something in need of development, certainly; but when developed, it would lift the population above the morass of the bare struggle for existence or the petty values of material-ism. But perhaps even more significantly, culture is "ours." By the beginning of the 1930s, intellectuals understood culture as something that "we" own, something that may enrich us or limit us, but that always belongs to us, as "their" culture belongs to "them." Culture is something we can all have; it is not a zero-sum game, in which, in order for some to win, others must lose. In this form, as something own-able and available to all, it accorded almost perfectly with the American dream of equal opportunity, and abundance for everyone.

There was a further dimension of this newly emerged notion of culture that also accorded with American popular ideals. Culture, as developed by the Boasian school of anthropology, and promulgated to a wide range of intellectuals and critics through the works of Parsons, Sapir, Mead, and Benedict, was made up of "traits" that, taken together, made the whole. Although in her ethnographic work Mead herself apparently increasingly emphasized the "wholeness" of "primitive" cultures, when she assessed the relevance of her findings to "Western civilization" she routinely suggested that traits or parts of other cultures could be appropriated to American (or British) culture to good effect. This objectification of "bits" of culture has the effect of distancing "culture" from the individuals who are its carriers, a distancing that had been given theoretical force by a variety of anthropological theorists. Kroeber, for example, had theorized culture as the "superorganic,"[104] whereas Sapir saw it not as a whole but only as "those general attitudes, views of life, and specific manifestations of civilization that give a particular people its distinctive place in the world."[105] The point here is not that Kroeber or Sapir were right or wrong but that the anthropological enterprise itself participated in the objectification of culture—and acted both to separate it from the individuals who embodied it and to render it partible. The implications of this are many, but one important implication is that this vision of culture leaves the autonomous individual intact. If culture is "ours," rather than "us," as Mead's earlier formulations might have it, then we retain a core that is indisputably and uniquely individual— "I," rather than "we." The individual remains, at core, outside culture.

The potent theme of both *Sex and Temperament in Three Primitive Societies* and of Benedict's *Patterns of Culture* was the struggle between the individual and the culture that shapes and constrains, but that, significantly, does not determine him or her. Both of these books gave a kind of lip service to Boas's brand of cultural determinism, all the while preserving the central character of the alienated individual, the hero of early-twentieth-century cultural critique. This is culture with a hook, culture that, as much as it is "ours," acts to repress and frustrate us. This "culture" is sufficiently vague and non-located that it can be seen as the source of our difficulties. We may own it, but we may not always be able to control it. It can be seen as "the system," an impersonal force that, because we can break it down to its components, may be amenable to change. Because it is made up of values, attitudes, behaviors, and rituals, we can frame change without hurting anyone or challenging fundamental property relations. In this sense, the "turn to culture" was a continuation or a logical extension of the self-image of the American intelligentsia that had been developing since the first decade of the twentieth century.

By framing this alienation from one's culture around sexuality, Mead drew on the most intensified attribute of the self. By the mid-1930s, psychology and psychoanalysis had been so widely popularized that the idea that sexuality is, in Foucault's terms, "the truth of self" had wide currency, at least among the middle class. The loosening of sexual mores in the 1920s had been rolled back by the mid-thirties. The introduction of the Production Code in 1930, and the establishment of the Hays Office in July 1934 [106] to police it, signaled an official end to the more liberal sexual mores of the previous decade. Yet, the alienated "deviant" who forms the subject of Mead's work sits at the center of a complex network of explicit debates and subterranean meanings circulating through America in the mid-1930s. The deviant, as the central character in *Sex and Temperament,* reaffirmed three core values: First, it asserted the intransigent core of the individual. No matter how much Mead and other anthropologists affirmed the infinite malleability of humans, the book in fact is about those individuals who are not malleable, who cannot be shaped by their culture, who stand outside it and suffer the consequences. This deviant spoke to the heart of artists, writers, and intellectuals, and indeed, to a wider range of people, who although without a public voice to express it, felt themselves alien in their own society. Second, it reinforced the conservative values of marriage and children as central to the well-lived life and as the solace of those who felt they did not belong in the wider society. Third, it called for cultural, rather than individual change, as a solution to the problems it identified, reinforcing the idea that the good society must provide for all the temperamental types it encompassed. It thus spoke to both deeply held, but also deeply contradictory, ideas and sentiments. It is, in the end, an optimistic, liberal book, in all senses of the word, one that rests on individual autonomy, family values, and social change for the better—a new deal.

7 On Creating a Usable Culture

THE INITIAL IMPULSE for this book came, as it usually does in academic life, from a previous piece of research. While researching a New Zealand government inquiry into "Moral Delinquency in the Young," I came across the following statement by Professor W. G. Minn, chair of social science at the Victoria University of Wellington. Professor Minn, called to give expert testimony, told the committee that

> we know [teenage sexual behavior] crops up over and over again, a lot of the children grow out of [it] any way—[the behavior being investigated] does seem so terribly organised. It seems to be almost something like a Samoan Youth Club. It does not fit it with our particular culture. I am not criticising the Samoans. They grow up. It is a different way of living and in the end it turns out all right. But our own particular culture has not been built up in that way. Our cultures have been built up on the fact that by and large people avoid too much sex play too early and that is our particular pattern.[1]

Thus, Margaret Mead and her Samoan "children" were brought to bear, as I now understand she would have intended them to be, on the "delinquents" of 1950s New Zealand. The quote piqued my interest, working as I do in a university with a substantial population of young Samoan students whose youth clubs did not seem to fit Minn's description. When an opportunity came to include a small case study in a larger application for a postdoctoral fellow, I decided that the popularization of Mead's ideas on Samoa would be an interesting offshoot. It would enable me to work, in a different context, on my longstanding interest in the relationship between academic ideas and popular culture. Once I got into Mead's archive in the Library of Congress, however, as is commonly the fate of academics who venture into its many meters of documents, Mead took over. As all worthwhile research does, this work took me into entirely unknown territory—first, American popular culture. Then, as I tried to make sense of Mead's themes and ideas, into the fascinating world of the New York Little Renaissance, the Lyrical Left, the debates on

American culture, and the emergence of American modernism, an intellectually exciting and sociopolitically tumultuous period of American history.

The book that has resulted attempts to track three facets of Mead's early popular work. The first is the change in her valuation of culture. I use the word "valuation" deliberately, for it became apparent that, over the course of these ten years, Mead came more and more to see culture as oppressive. This was her view of culture not only in the complex society to which she belonged, but in all but one of the indigenous societies in which she worked in the years covered by this book. At the end of this period, in an attempt to come to terms with her growing sense of culture as thwarting human potential, she had developed a theory of biological determinism so perilously close to a racial argument that she was persuaded not to publish it because it might be seen as giving comfort to those aligned to the rising tide of Nazism. The second facet of Mead's work—and this is a constant rather than a change—is the way that she uses sex (or sexual identity or gender identity) to express the essence of the individual's relationship to culture. In this, Mead was influenced by a trend that Foucault articulated in the 1970s—that in modernity, sex became the "truth of self." In so assiduously using this trope, Mead both participated in and contributed to its consolidation. Her work thus demonstrates again that modernity is not only gendered, but sexed, and Mead's popular writings were a major contributor to this sexing.

The third facet is the range of resources that Mead drew upon in creating her pedagogical ethnographies for the American public. The books weave together her personal experiences and struggles, the socioeconomic issues of the times, and what was by the mid-1920s a widespread "understanding" of the challenges facing Americans in creating a modern culture. I have argued that these "understandings" have their origins in what has been variously called the Lyrical Left, the cultural radicals, the Young Americans, or the cultural critics. If I have been guilty of overemphasizing the influence of these writers, it is because their definitions of the problems of American culture seem to leap from Mead's pages and also because they have been under-recognized in histories of anthropology. In the balance of this chapter, I attempt to spell out how these three aspects of her work interacted to get her to the point she reached in 1935, and then beyond.

Mead was not unlike Van Wyck Brooks in organizing her work around opposites. All her work explicitly contrasts "homogenous" and "heterogeneous" societies. The idea of a homogenous society seems odd to us now, but the term did not originate with Mead. Bourne used it in 1914 to describe the national cultures of Europe. Mead, however, used the term specifically to characterize societies that were untouched by European contact. The fact that every one of the indigenous societies with which she worked had had contact with Europeans and undergone significant change due to European colonialism only means that Mead chose to ignore evidence that didn't fit her schema, not that her schema wasn't a powerful organizing force in her (and others') work. Homogenous societies were, in this schema, in balance, unchanging, and stable, and offered little opportunity for individual variation or for the development for reflective thought. Probably the best expressions of what she meant by homogeneity are outlined in *Coming of Age in Samoa* and *The Changing Culture of an Indian Tribe* and are discussed in chapters 3 and 5. Heterogeneous societies, on the other hand, are characterized by change and, perhaps more importantly, conflicting values and thus choice. Mead's work was impelled by her belief that heterogeneous societies, especially the United States, needed sound bases for choice under conditions of change. By showing how things were done differently in other cultures, Mead hoped to give Americans the tools and knowledge they needed to make rational choices. She believed implicitly that American culture, and the indigenous cultures in the United States, needed to change for many reasons: adolescent storm and stress, the challenges posed by changing times, inefficient use of human potential, and, finally, alienation and the right of all individuals to live in cultures that allow them to develop to their potential and to attain happiness and belonging.

An implicit, but related, dichotomy in Mead's work is between integration and its Others. The difference between integration and disintegration is, of course, the basis for *The Changing Culture of an Indian Tribe.* In that book, Mead recounts a slide from an integrated, stable, unchanging culture to a disintegrated, maladjusted one. The term "maladjusted" gives us a clue: Antler society had not responded positively to change. Instead, it was a cauldron of violence and disease and increasingly undermined by its (particularly its women's) ever-weakening moral fiber. However, integration has another Other, never specifically named by Mead but spelled out in the conclusions to *Sex and Temperament.* It could be glossed as flexibility and openness to human variety, describing a culture that enables all its members to reach their potential.

The term "integration" has an interesting history in the debates on American culture, which we have seen through the palimpsest of Mead's work. For Progressives like Herbert Croly and the other editors at the *New Republic,* an integration of the social, political, economic, and cultural was key to a new future for America. Brooks echoed this sentiment, although he placed more emphasis on the arts and culture as integrative mechanisms than on the bureaucratization and professionalization espoused by the Progressives. Integration was also the key to the *New Republic* Progressives' attitude towards the immigrant communities that were such a source of contention throughout this period. They advocated and supported programs of Americanization that would educate the immigrants out of their particularities and render them true Americans. This position provoked angry disagreement between the *New Republic* stalwarts and Bourne and Frank. By 1936 Mead had come to espouse a position close to the latter twos' advocacy of a "loose, free country [with] no constraining national purpose . . . [to] hold people to a line."[2] Her argument that "[t]o the extent that a culture is integrated and definite in its goals, uncompromising in its moral and spiritual preferences, to that very extent it condemns some of its members—members by birth only—to live alien to it, in perplexity at the best, at the worst in a rebellion that may turn to madness"[3] is more Bournian than it is Progressive.

Yet another opposition that underpins Mead's work is more implicit—that is the opposition between tradition, on the one hand, and choice, change, and risk, on the other. Despite her bucolic renderings of Samoa, this is a contrast that inheres in all her work over this period. Even in her work on Samoa, the society that throughout her life she rendered most positively, she understood that "the ever-yielding, ever-accommodating social structure [that] remained much the same, generation after generation"[4] and that gave rise to a graceful spirit of living was not a possibility for modern America. In her later books, she came more and more to see tradition as repressive and oppressive, preventing societies from capitalizing on their strengths, and creating a great deal of individual human unhappiness.

Underpinning all these dualisms is an implicit balancing of individual and culture. Over the course of the ten years covered by this book, that balance tipped in favor of the individual, as Mead increasingly came to see culture as inimitable to individual and societal development. How did Mead, the student of Franz Boas and Ruth Benedict, come to this position? How did she move from "event" to "essence" in her account of the relationship between individuals and their cultures? And how did she arrive in 1933 at a quasi-racial classification of human types, one to which she was to adhere privately for many years? We could, perhaps, accept Walter Benn Michaels's[5] account that such biologism was an intrinsic aspect of American modernism and that Mead merely participated in a trend that was evident over a wide range of discourses and texts during this period. However, I think we can track the trajectory of Mead's thought more closely, beginning with the oppositions detailed above and linking them in the first place to Mead's use of the trope of sex, and in the second to the growth of functionalism.

The two most recent biographies of Mead—in fact, joint biographies of her relationship with Ruth Benedict—have focused on the ways in which Mead's sexual relationships and struggles over her sexual identity shaped her life and work.[6] Although both are rich and admirable works of scholarship, I believe that we make a mistake if we pursue too far the idea that it is personal identity, particularly sexual identity, that shapes a scholar's life and work, and indeed the relationship between two scholars. We fall too easily into accepting what Foucault has demonstrated in one of the most persistent and powerful myths of modernity—that sex is the "truth of self." Mead came of age in the time and place where that idea passed most potently into vernacular culture. Thus, her work cannot simply be seen as a working out of her own sexuality, although that was certainly a part of it. It was clearly situated in a socio-cultural context where the trope of sexuality was being deployed across a wider and wider set of discourses. In deploying those tropes, Mead was operating much closer to popular culture than to the more official discourses of psychology or psychoanalysis. Her use of the terms "repression" and "identification" were in no sense different from the way these terms were deployed in mass-circulation newspapers and magazines. Even *Sex and Temperament,* written while she was in regular conversation with John Dollard, Eric Fromm, and Karen Horney, shows little disciplined understanding of psychoanalytic theory of any ilk. I think it is fair to say that even as her ethnographic accounts were anchored (if sometimes on a long chain) in an increasingly professionalized anthropology, her bridge to her public was via a widely understood trope of sex and repression—one that bore little resemblance to Freud's usage.

It is tempting to wonder if she would have ended up in a different place theoretically if she had taken psychoanalytic theory more seriously, particularly if she had worked, as Malinowski tried to do, with a serious understanding or definition of the unconscious.[7] As it was, she had no way of thinking about or accounting for unruly behavior, no theory of desire (somewhat of an irony, given the extent to which she was both a victim of and intent on satisfying her own desires). She had no nuanced theory for understanding the genesis of variations in individual behavior. This lack was exacerbated by her over-determined view of culture. Fundamentally, Mead believed in the existence, both in the present and in the past, of homogenous, integrated, smoothly functioning cultures not subject to internal processes of change, that is, cultures without history. The emphasis in her dominant intellectual influences—Boasian culturalism, British functionalism, and the cultural critics—on cultures (whether for good or for bad) as functional, homogenous wholes rendered it difficult for her to believe otherwise. Without theories that could account for either individual variation or endogenous change, she could resort only to that which she understood to be outside both culture and history—that is, biology.

Perhaps fortunately for her and for us, Mead's turn to temperament went largely unnoticed, coming as it did as the rise of National Socialism made any recourse to such biological explanations as Mead had developed on the Sepik unpalatable in the circles in which she moved. *Sex and Temperament* was read, even by the popular press, as making the case for variability in gender roles and not for its more challenging assertions about psychosexual misidentification. Mead disappeared to Bali shortly after the book's appearance, returning to have a child and then to be absorbed into the government's war effort. Her theory of temperament was not to be her principal legacy. Her legacy was much more in keeping with the goal she had set for herself early in her career: to use her knowledge of other peoples to help modern Americans to make informed choices about their lives. In doing this, she carried on the important tradition of both Franz Boas and of the Young American cultural critics: to advance a cosmopolitan ethos.

In his 1985 preface to his classic essay "Ethnic diversity, Cosmopolitanism and the Emergence of the American Liberal Intelligentsia," David H. Hollinger identifies Margaret Mead as an exemplary cosmopolitan. He writes, "Not every citizen could be expected to become as multitudinous as Margaret Mead or Lionel Trilling, but all Americans needed to be protected from the hated ethnocentrism of the long-dominant Anglo-Saxons. Cultural pluralism was understood as a potential brake on this uniquely threatening variety of provincialism."[8] The essay itself, originally published in *American Quarterly* in 1975, begins with Randolph Bourne, who Hollinger points out, "expressed the hope that ethnic diversity would enable the United States to develop a style of life and thought more fulfilling than that of the single, national cultures of Europe and America."[9] This book, it is to be hoped, draws the line between Bourne, the obscure "prophet" of a cosmopolitan America, and Mead, its best-known public intellectual.

If Van Wyck Brooks saw his life's work as the creation of a usable past for American writers, then Mead just as surely saw hers as the creation of usable Others for American parents and educators. Sometimes, in reading back and forth between her books and the writings of the young cultural critics, I am tempted to believe that she saw herself as the standard bearer for the ideals of those young men in an age of increasing massification of popular culture on the one hand, and cynicism and disillusionment of intellectual and literary culture on the other. Never one to be put off a large task, she took it on herself to relay their messages through the vehicles of her "natives." We don't in fact know how self-conscious Mead was in her evocation of these themes or how much they were simply the air she breathed—the taken-for-granted issues and terms that defined the debate on American life. What we do know is that she had an ability to take her ethnographic experiences and tailor them to these ongoing debates with increasing sophistication over the ten years covered by this study.

Hollinger also argues that "[f]ull-blown cosmopolitanism was understood to be a realistic ideal primarily for intellectuals."[10] In this sense, Mead was not, consciously at least, exemplary. Although she has (justifiably) been accused of ignoring the vast socioeconomic inequalities and racial hierarchies that underpin American society, she was, by her own lights, committed to proselytizing a version of cosmopolitanism to a wide, public audience. She began with newspapers, radio talks, and public education programs and moved with the development of mass media into pulp magazines and television talk shows, none of these the preferred media of "the intelligentsia" to which Hollinger refers.

The central idea underlying this cosmopolitan impulse was, of course, culture, arguably the most privileged concept—if it can even be called anything as defined as a concept—of Americanist–modernist thought in the first four decades of the twentieth century. For the Young American critics, culture was both the unquestioned sphere that made life meaningful and enjoyable and the cure for all that ailed their country. This book, therefore, tackles two tasks. The first is to contribute to the ongoing scholarship on the origins and development of the idea of culture. The second is to provide a small case study of how culture is made—that is how ideas, notions, perceptions, and the relations between them emerge in the interplay among intellectual avant-gardists, popular media, and intellectual populists on the one hand, and the desires, fears, behaviors, and aspirations of a vast range of ordinary people on the other. The process by which these somehow come together and change not only the way we think but also the way we act in relation to ourselves and others is culture in the making.

Documenting the history of "culture" has largely been the work of cultural and literary historians. Some of those have undertaken literary biographies of the principals involved, some comparative studies, some histories of the little magazines through which the ideas were broadcast. However, although these works can trace the development and changes in ideas among the select few, they do little to address the issue of how such ideas found their way into the wider vernacular or popular culture. On the other hand, anthropologists, with a few exceptions, have taken little interest in how "their" concept came to be so ubiquitous that calls have recently gone out for its eradication. All four of the most recent excurses into the "turn to culture" and its relation to modernism and anthropology, Michaels's *Our America*, Hegeman's *Patterns for America*, Manganaro's *Culture 1922*, and Castle's *Modernism and the Celtic Revival*, are written by literary scholars.[11] Michaels more or less ignores anthropology's contribution to the spread of the idea of culture, whereas the other three, which use anthropological material extensively, have been largely ignored by the discipline. But perhaps more importantly, the latter three work within a narrow definition of modernism, focusing on canonical writers, such as Joyce, Eliot, and Yeats, and paying little attention to the broader ways in which the idea of culture became vernacular. Recent biographies of key cultural critics are likely to cite Boas as an influence on their developing ideas, especially those of Bourne. However, anthropologists have, on the whole, ignored the cultural critics' role in shaping anthropology. Mead's biographers invariably cite Boas and Benedict as her principal influences. This book demonstrates that she (and incidentally, I would add, minimally, Ruth Benedict and Elsie Parsons) has an intellectual genealogy outside anthropology. Although the Boasian influence was direct, it was also indirect: the ways in which Mead expressed her cosmopolitanism often seem to have more to do with Bourne, Brooks, and Croly than with Boas himself. Nevertheless, methodologically she was clearly Boasian. From him she took the assumption that cultures are composed of identifiable and separable traits and that these can be isolated, compared, and transferred to other cultures.

Although influenced by the cultural critics, she differed from them in significant ways. For example, Bourne saw the future for America as coming out of a mingling of peoples with different but dearly held national cultures or Beloved Communities: each contributing to the mix, each changing in relation to and in conversation with the others. For Mead, other peoples' cultures were a supermarket from which Americans could, and should, pick and choose. When she wrote *Coming of Age in Samoa,* the point of cosmopolitanism for Mead was to ensure that individuals could make informed, rational choices. For Bourne, it was to create a new, dynamic America that would lead the world towards a life "in which all can participate [in] the good life of personality lived in the environment of the Beloved Community." [12] By the time she published *Sex and Temperament in Three Primitive Societies,* Mead's goal, although less elegantly stated, was closer to Bourne's. Her view of culture had also moved closer to his, and perhaps further away from that of his friend Van Wyck Brooks. Although Bourne had a deep appreciation of (most) national traditions, he saw the (apparent) absence of such tradition in the United States as providing opportunity for the future. Brooks, though sharing Bourne's view that there was no usable tradition in the United States, spent most of the rest of his life trying to create what he called "a usable past." Mead was ambivalent about "tradition." In these ten years, the only tradition she really endorsed was that of Samoa. Of the societies she lived and worked in, only Samoa, it seemed to her, had developed a grace or art of living, and respect for wisdom and for the past. In each of the other cultures, Manus, Omaha,

Notes

Chapter 1: Introduction

1. Martha Banta, *Imaging American Women: Ideas and Ideals in Cultural History* (New York: Columbia University Press, 1987); C. Barry Chabot, *Writers for the Nation: American Literary Modernism* (Tuscaloosa: University of Alabama Press, 1997); Susan Hegeman, *Patterns for America: Modernism and the Concept of Culture* (Princeton University Press, 1999); David A. Hollinger, *In the American Province: Studies in the History and Historiography of Ideas* (Bloomington: Indiana University Press, 1985); James Hoopes, *Van Wyck Brooks: In Search of American Culture* (Amherst: University of Massachusetts Press, 1977); Rob Kroes, ed., *Highbrow Meets Lowbrow: American Culture as an Intellectual Concern* (Amsterdam: Free University Press, 1988); Walter Susman, *Culture as History: The Transformation of American Society in the Twentieth Century* (New York: Pantheon Books, 1984); Arthur F. Wertheim, *The New York Little Renaissance: Iconoclasm, Modernism and Nationalism in American Culture, 1908–1917* (New York University Press, 1976).

2. The full quote, which expresses succinctly the expatriate American position in the 1920s, is "The United States is just now the oldest country in the world, there is always an oldest country and she is it, it is she who is the mother of twentieth century civilization. . . . And so it is a country the right age to have been born in and the wrong age to live in." Gertrude Stein, "Why I Do Not Live in America," in *How Writing is Written: Volume II of the Previously Uncollected Writings of Gertrude Stein*, ed. Robert Bartlett Haas (1928; repr., Los Angeles: Black Sparrow, 1974), 51.

3. "Gender" is, of course, an anachronistic term in this period. However, there is no doubt that Mead's work, especially *Sex and Temperament in Three Primitive Societies*, laid the foundation for the development of the notion of gender as the cultural meanings assigned to biological sex.

4. Nina Miller, *Making Love Modern: The Intimate Public Worlds of New York's Literary Women* (New York: Oxford University Press, 1999), 98.

5. Eric Caplan, *Mind Games: American Culture and the Birth of Psychotherapy* (Berkeley: University of California Press, 1998).

6. To the various works of Foucault, one could add John Chynoweth Burnham,

Psychoanalysis and American Medicine, 1894–1918: Medicine, Society and Culture (New York: International Universities Press, 1967); Adele Heller and Lois Rudnick, *1915, The Cultural Moment: The New Politics, the New Woman, the New Psychology, the New Art and the New Theatre in America* (New Brunswick, NJ: Rutgers University Press, 1991); Julian Henriques et al., eds., *Changing the Subject: Psychology, Social Regulation and Subjectivity* (New York: Methuen, 1984); Judith Ryan, *The Vanishing Subject: Early Psychology and Literary Modernism* (University of Chicago Press, 1991).

7. Desley Deacon, *Elsie Clews Parsons: Inventing Modern Life* (University of Chicago Press, 1997).

8. Micaela di Leonardo, *Exotics at Home: Anthropologies, Others, American Modernities* (University of Chicago Press, 1998), 20.

9. Mark Manganaro, ed., *Modernist Anthropology: From Fieldwork to Text* (Princeton University Press, 1990).

10. Mark Manganaro, *Culture 1922: The Emergence of a Concept* (Princeton University Press, 2002), 13.

11. Hegeman, *Patterns for America*, 4.

12. Hoopes, *Van Wyck Brooks*, 118.

13. Her first two academic papers derived from her master's thesis and were cautionary notes on the growing literature on race and intelligence testing—the "race" she was referring to in this case being Italian immigrants: Margaret Mead, "The Methodology of Racial Testing: Its Significance for Sociology," *American Journal of Sociology* 31, no. 5 (1926); Margaret Mead, "Group Intelligence Tests and Linguistic Disability among Italian Children," *School and Society* 25, no. 642 (1927).

14. Margaret Mead, "The Need for Teaching Anthropology in Normal Schools and Teachers' Colleges," *School and Society* 26, no. 667 (1927): 467–468.

15. Margaret Mead, Letter to William Fielding Ogburn, April 27, 1927, in *To Cherish the Life of the World: Selected Letters of Margaret Mead*, ed. Margaret M. Caffrey and Patricia A. Francis, 243–244 (New York: Basic Books, 2006).

16. This fact sat uneasily with her liberal-minded and socially active family. In a letter written to her when she was in New Guinea, her aunt Fanny observed, not innocently: "By the way I must tell you a remark your grandmother made when your last bulletin arrived. She said—'Well, if they are going to be away so much I don't see how they can do the people in that village any good.' 'I said—Mother, do you really think that Margaret went to New Guinea to try to do some good to the people there?' 'Why of course I did'—says your grandmother. Sometimes I cannot tell whether such remarks are this sign of failing mentality or whether, in this case she has always thought that was your object." Fanny Fogg MacMaster, Letter to Margaret Mead, December 1, 1932, Box A4, file 6, Margaret Mead Papers.

17. James Clifford, "Introduction," in *Writing Culture: The Poetics and Politics of Ethnography*, ed. James Clifford and George Marcus (Berkeley: University of California Press, 1986), 5.

18. James Clifford, *The Predicament of Culture: Twentieth Century Ethnography, Literature and Art* (Cambridge, MA: Harvard University Press, 1988); James Clifford and George Marcus, eds., *Writing Culture: The Poetics and Politics of Ethnography* (Berkeley: University of California Press, 1986); Clifford Geertz, *Works and Lives: The Anthropologist as Author* (Stanford University Press, 1988).

19. For references, see Nancy C. Lutkehaus, "Margaret Mead and the 'Rustling-of-the-Wind-in-the-Palm-Trees School of Ethnographic Writing,'" in *Women Writing Culture*, ed. Ruth Behar (Berkeley: University of California Press, 1995).

20. Lutkehaus, "Margaret Mead and the 'Rustling'."

21. David Schneider, "The Coming of a Sage to Samoa," *Natural History* 4, no. 6 (1983), cited in Ray McDermott, "A Century of Margaret Mead," *Teachers College Record* 103, no. 5 (2001): 853. See also Roy Rappaport, "Desecrating the Holy Women," *American Scholar* 55 (1986).

22. Charles Taylor, *Sources of the Self: The Making of Modern Identity* (Cambridge University Press, 1989), 288.

23. Taylor, *Sources of the Self*, 289.

24. Benedict Anderson, *Imagined Communities: Reflections on the Origin and Spread of Nationalism*, 2nd ed. (London: Verso, 1991).

25. Robert J. C. Young, *Colonial Desire: Hybridity in Theory, Culture and Race* (London: Routledge, 1995), 50–54.

26. Young, *Colonial Desire*, 53.

27. Walter Benn Michaels, *Our America: Nativism, Modernism, and Pluralism* (Durham, NC: Duke University Press, 1995), 16.

28. Michaels, *Our America*, 139.

29. Edward Sapir, "Culture, Genuine and Spurious," *American Journal of Sociology* 29 (1924).

30. Terence Hays's analysis of use of case studies in introductory anthropology textbooks demonstrates that "Margaret Mead's ethnography [of Samoa] accounts for the vast majority of . . . citations" related to Polynesia. He goes on to argue that "a cursory examination of the most frequently cited societies of Oceania . . . is studded with 'classics,' including the Tiwi's curious marriage system; the Tasmanians' extinction; the Trobriand Island kula ring; Arapesh, Mudugumor, and Tchambuli alleged [*sic*] variations on sex roles; the postwar 'cargo cults' of Manus; Siuai as the locus classicus of the 'big man' concept; Samoans' 'stress-free adolescence.'" Of these seven classics, Mead authored three. Her work was not, of course, conveyed to college students solely through anthropology. She was frequently cited in psychology and sociology texts and collections as well. Terence E. Hays, "The 'Tiny Islands'": A Comparative Impact on the Larger Discipline?" in *American Anthropology in Micronesia: An Assessment*, ed. Robert C. Kiste and Mac Marshall, 506–508 (Honolulu: University of Hawai'i Press, 1999).

31. Ruth Fulton Benedict, *Patterns of Culture* (New York: Columbia University Press, 1934).

32. Ann Laura Stoler, *Race and the Education of Desire: Foucault's History of Sexuality and the Colonial Order of Things* (Durham, NC: Duke University Press, 1996).

33. Anne McClintock, *Imperial Leather: Race, Gender, and Sexuality in the Colonial Contest* (London: Routledge, 1995).

34. "Race suicide" was a term used by the opponents of birth control, and those anxious about declining British birth rates, to suggest that by limiting births (British, middle-class) women were intent on destroying the "British race."

35. Ann Douglas, *The Feminization of American Culture* (New York: Knopf, 1977).

36. Van Wyck Brooks is a good example. In *America's Coming of Age,* his criticisms of the literary "greats" such as Hawthorne and Poe are laden with feminized terms. They are "hysterical," "passive," "have no ideas," and so on. In the rather startling concluding paragraph, he writes, "When the women of America have gathered together all the culture in the world there is—who knows?—perhaps the dry old Yankee stalk will begin to stir and send forth shoots and burst into a storm of blossoms." Van Wyck Brooks, *America's Coming of Age* (New York: B. W. Huebsch, 1915). This and all subsequent citations from Van Wyck Brooks, "America's Coming of Age," in *Van Wyck Brooks: The Early Years,* 2nd ed., ed. Claire Sprague (Boston: Northeastern University Press, 1993), 158.

37. George Santayana, "The Genteel Tradition in American Philosophy" (address to the Philosophical Union of the University of California, Berkeley, 1911). All citations from George Santayana, *Winds of Doctrine, and Platonism and the Spiritual Life* (Gloucester, MA: P. Smith, 1971).

38. Andreas Huyssen, *After the Great Divide: Modernism, Mass Culture, Postmodernism* (Bloomington: Indiana University Press, 1986), 47.

39. See Andrew P. Lyons and Harriet Lyons, *Irregular Connections: A History of Anthropology and Sexuality* (Lincoln: University of Nebraska Press, 2004), for a survey of anthropology's engagements with sexuality.

40. Margaret Mead, *Coming of Age in Samoa: A Psychological Study of Primitive Youth for Western Civilization* (New York: William Morrow, 1928). All subsequent citations from Mead, *Coming of Age in Samoa* (New York: Morrow Quill Paperbacks, 1961).

41. Margaret Mead, *Growing Up in New Guinea: A Comparative Study of Primitive Education* (New York: William Morrow, 1930). All subsequent citations from Mead, *Growing Up in New Guinea* (New York: Perennial (Harper Collins), 2001).

42. Margaret Mead, *The Changing Culture of an Indian Tribe* (New York: Columbia University Press, 1932), 6.

43. Margaret Mead, *Sex and Temperament in Three Primitive Societies* (New York: William Morrow, 1935). All subsequent citations from Mead, *Sex and Temperament,* (New York: William Morrow, 1961).

44. During her fifty-year career she published more than thirteen hundred books and articles.

45. Mead's marriage to Bateson, years of work in Bali, and subsequent absorption into the war effort meant that the spin-off articles that came out of her work of this period virtually ceased. She was not to systematically engage in writing for the popular press again until the 1960s, when she was contracted to produce a regular column for *Redbook.*

46. Joan Gordan, ed. *Margaret Mead: The Complete Bibliography, 1925–1975* (The Hague: Mouton, 1976).

47. Margaret Mead, *An Inquiry into the Question of Cultural Stability in Polynesia* (New York: Columbia University Press, 1928); Margaret Mead, *Social Organization of Manu'a* (Honolulu: Bernice P. Bishop Museum, 1930); Margaret Mead, *Kinship in the Admiralty Islands* (New York: American Museum of Natural History, 1934).

48. Carolyn Steedman, *Strange Dislocations: Childhood and the Idea of Human Interiority, 1780–1930* (London: Virago, 1995).

49. Marina Warner, *Six Myths of Our Time: Little Angels, Little Monsters, Beautiful Beasts, and More* (New York: Vintage Books, 1995).

50. Steedman, *Strange Dislocations*, 18.

51. Frederick Jackson Turner's famous thesis that American society was shaped by frontier conditions revolutionized American historiography, and Frontier Mentality became a byword for outdated mindsets among young moderns. Frederick Jackson Turner, "The Significance of the Frontier in American History" (address to the American Historical Association, July 12, 1893), www.uta.fi/FAST/US2/REF/turner.html (accessed December 14, 2006).

52. Herbert Croly, *The Promise of American Life* (New York: Houghton Mifflin, 1909). This and all subsequent citations from Herbert Croly, *The Promise of American Life*, ed. Arthur M. Schlesinger (Cambridge, MA: The Belknap Press of Harvard University Press, 1965), 414.

53. Miller, *Making Love Modern.*

Chapter 2: The Problem of American Culture

1. For an account of this visit, see Saul Rosenzweig, *The Historic Expedition to America (1909): Freud, Jung, and Hall the King-maker, with G. Stanley Hall as Host and William James as Guest,* 2nd rev. ed. (St. Louis: Rana House, 1994).

2. Herbert Croly, *The Promise of American Life,* ed. Arthur M. Schlesinger (1909; repr., Cambridge, MA: The Belknap Press of Harvard University Press, 1965).

3. Franz Boas, *The Mind of Primitive Man* (New York: Columbia University Press, 1911).

4. George Santayana, *Winds of Doctrine, and Platonism and the Spiritual Life* (Gloucester, MA: P. Smith, 1971).

5. Randolph Bourne, *Youth and Life* (Boston: Houghton Mifflin, 1913).

6. Sandford Gifford, "The American Reception of Psychoanalysis," in *1915, The Cultural Moment: The New Politics, the New Woman, the New Psychology, the New Art and the New Theatre in America*, ed. Adele Heller and Lois Rudnick (New Brunswick, NJ: Rutgers University Press, 1991).

7. Philip Cushman, *Constructing the Self, Constructing America* (Reading, MA: Addison-Wesley, 1995), 71.

8. Cited in John Burnham, "The New Psychology," in *1915, The Cultural Moment*, ed. Heller and Rudnick, 124.

9. Burnham, "The New Psychology," 120.

10. Edwin Bissell Holt, *The Freudian Wish and Its Place in Ethics* (New York: Henry Holt, 1915); James Putnam, *Human Motives* (Boston: Little, Brown, 1915).

11. Nathan G. Hale, *Freud and the Americans: The Beginnings of Psychoanalysis in the United States, 1876–1917* (New York: Oxford University Press, 1971), 76.

12. Malcolm Cowley, *Exile's Return: A Literary Odyssey of the 1920s* (New York: Viking, 1934). This and all subsequent citations from Malcolm Cowley, *Exile's Return: A Literary Odyssey of the 1920s* (1934; repr., London: The Bodley Head, 1951), 61–62.

13. Arthur M. Schlesinger, "Introduction," in Herbert Croly, *The Promise of American Life*, ed. Arthur M. Schlesinger (Cambridge, MA: The Belknap Press of Harvard University Press, 1965), iii.

14. Thomas Bender, *New York Intellect* (Baltimore: Johns Hopkins University Press, 1987), 222.

15. Croly, *Promise of American Life*, 12.

16. Croly, *Promise of American Life*, 22.

17. Croly, *Promise of American Life*, 21.

18. Croly, *Promise of American Life*, 21.

19. Croly, *Promise of American Life*, 414.

20. Dorothy Whitney Straight was the daughter of William C. Whitney. Her first husband was Willard Straight, with whom she founded the *New Republic*. After Willard's death, she married the innovative British agricultural economist Leonard Elmhirst. In 1925 they purchased Dartington Hall in Devon, where they set up a model community dedicated to experimentation and innovation in education, art, sustainable land use, architecture, and social responsibility. She headed a committee of women who sponsored Mead's work among the Omaha in 1930. See chapter 4.

21. F. L. Mott, *A History of American Magazines: Vol. 5 Sketches of 21 Magazines, 1905–1930* (Cambridge, MA: The Belknap Press of Harvard University Press, 1957).

22. Santayana, *Winds of Doctrine, and Platonism and the Spiritual Life*, 188. Santayana argued that while the American Will occupied the skyscraper, the American Intellect, "predominantly the American woman," occupied the colonial mansion. The essay, largely a tribute to William James, argues that James offers something not only to the hungry intellect but also the "normal, practical masculine American." The final paragraph is an assertion of masculine intellectuality: "By their mind, its scope, qual-

ity and temper, we estimate men, for by the mind only do we exist as men." See also footnote 36, chapter 1, this volume.

23. Bourne, *Youth and Life*.

24. Cited in C. Barry Chabot, *Writers for the Nation: American Literary Modernism* (Tuscaloosa: University of Alabama Press, 1997), 15n159.

25. Edward Abrahams, *The Lyrical Left: Randolph Bourne, Alfred Stieglitz and the Origins of Cultural Radicalism in America* (Charlottesville: University Press of Virginia, 1986), 46–49.

26. Leslie J. Vaughan, *Randolph Bourne and the Politics of Cultural Radicalism* (Lawrence: University of Kansas Press, 1997), 224–235.

27. Waldo David Frank, *Our America* (New York: Boni and Liveright, 1919), 217.

28. Randolph Bourne, "Trans-National America," *Atlantic Monthly* 118 (1916). Subsequent citations from Randolph Bourne, "Trans-National America," in *The American Intellectual Tradition: A Sourcebook*, ed. David A. Hollinger and Charles Capper (Oxford University Press, 1997).

29. Randolph Bourne, "Twilight of the Idols," *Seven Arts* 2 (October 1917); Randolph Bourne, "The War and the Intellectuals," *Seven Arts* 2 (June 1917).

30. Mary Esteve, "Shipwreck and Autonomy: Rawls, Reisman, and Oppen in the 1960s," *Yale Journal of Criticism* 18, no. 2 (2005): 338.

31. Bruce Clayton, *Forgotten Prophet: The Life of Randolph Bourne* (Baton Rouge: Louisiana State University Press, 1984), 190.

32. Bourne, "Trans-National America," 175.

33. Bourne, "Trans-National America," 178.

34. Bourne, "Trans-National America," 175.

35. Bourne, "Trans-National America," 174.

36. Abrahams, *Lyrical Left*, 46.

37. James Hoopes suggests that Brooks was likely influenced by Santayana's ideas but that, equally, "The Genteel Tradition" contains definite echoes of *The Wine of the Puritans*. James Hoopes, *Van Wyck Brooks: In Search of American Culture* (Amherst: University of Massachusetts Press, 1977), 62.

38. Van Wyck Brooks, *The Wine of the Puritans* (London: Sisley's, 1908). All citations from *Van Wyck Brooks: The Early Years*, 2nd ed., ed. Claire Sprague (Boston: Northeastern University Press, 1993).

39. Van Wyck Brooks, "America's Coming of Age," in Sprague, *Van Wyck Brooks*.

40. Brooks, "America's Coming of Age," 83.

41. Cited in Brooks, *Wine of the Puritans*, 8.

42. Van Wyck Brooks, "On Creating a Usable Past," *Dial* (1918), reprinted in Sprague, *Van Wyck Brooks*, 226. All subsequent citations from Sprague, *Van Wyck Brooks*.

43. Brooks, "America's Coming of Age," 95.

44. Casey Nelson Blake, *Beloved Community: The Cultural Criticism of Randolph*

Bourne, Van Wyck Brooks, Waldo Frank, and Lewis Mumford (Chapel Hill: University of North Carolina Press, 1990), 131.

45. Randolph Bourne, "The Cult of the Best," *New Republic* 5 (January 15, 1916).

46. Abrahams, *Lyrical Left*, 48.

47. Bourne, "Cult of the Best."

48. William Wasserstrom, "Preface," in *Van Wyck Brooks: The Critic and His Critics*, ed. William Wasserstrom (Port Washington, NY: Kennikat, 1979), ix.

49. Ezra Pound, "Provincialism the Enemy," *New Age* 22 (1917), cited in David A. Hollinger, *In the American Province: Studies in the History and Historiography of Ideas* (Bloomington: Indiana University Press, 1985), 60.

50. Hollinger, *In the American Province*, 59.

51. Nina Miller, *Making Love Modern: The Intimate Public Worlds of New York's Literary Women* (New York: Oxford University Press, 1999), 101.

52. Miller, *Making Love Modern*, 129.

53. James Burkhart Gilbert, *Writers and Partisans: A History of Literary Radicalism in America* (New York: Wiley, 1968).

54. Abrahams, *Lyrical Left*, 3.

55. Adele Heller and Lois Rudnick, *1915, The Cultural Moment: The New Politics, the New Woman, the New Psychology, the New Art and the New Theatre in America* (New Brunswick, NJ: Rutgers University Press, 1991); Arthur F. Wertheim, *The New York Little Renaissance: Iconoclasm, Modernism and Nationalism in American Culture, 1908–1917* (New York University Press, 1976).

56. Susan Hegeman, *Patterns for America: Modernism and the Concept of Culture* (Princeton University Press, 1999), 54–55.

57. Abrahams, *Lyrical Left*, 23. For more elegies to Bourne, see Eric J. Sandeen, "Bourne Again: The Correspondence between Randolph Bourne and Elsie Clews Parsons," *American Literary History* 1, no. 3 (1989).

58. John Dos Passos, *1919* (New York: Harcourt & Brace, 1932), 105–106.

59. Margaret Mead, Letter to family and friends, September 20, 1925, Box N4, file 1, Margaret Mead Papers. Rather than write many individual letters, Mead wrote what she called "bulletins," which were sent to family and friends and gave general news of her activities. Her mother retyped them and circulated them to family. These bulletins are the basis of *Letters From the Field*. Margaret Mead, *Letters from the Field, 1925–1965* (New York: Harper & Row, 1977).

60. Margaret Mead, Letter to Ruth Fulton Benedict, September 8, 1924, AAW Copy 2, B/B61 Boas Papers.

61. Margaret Mead, Letter to Ruth Fulton Benedict, August 30, 1924, Addition III, Box S3, file 2, Margaret Mead Papers.

62. Mead to Benedict, August 30, 1924.

63. Bourne was fired from the *New Republic* for his antiwar sentiments and subsequently lost his job when *Seven Arts* folded due to its antiwar position. He found it

increasingly difficult to publish even his non-war-related writing. He died of influenza, possibly exacerbated by malnutrition and lack of heating. For the best biographies of Bourne see Clayton, *Forgotten Prophet;* Vaughan, *Randolph Bourne and the Politics of Cultural Radicalism.*

64. Iris Dorreboom, *The Challenge of Our Time: Woodrow Wilson, Herbert Croly, Randolph Bourne and the Making of Modern America* (Amsterdam: Rodoipi, 1991), 206.

65. Paul R. Gorman, *Left Intellectuals and Popular Culture in Twentieth-Century America* (Chapel Hill: University of North Carolina Press, 1996), 73.

66. Reproduction of September 1917 frontispiece in Gorman, *Left Intellectuals and Popular Culture,* 66.

67. Gorman, *Left Intellectuals and Popular Culture,* 72.

68. Cited in Gorham Munson, *The Awakening Twenties: A Memoir–History of a Literary Period* (Baton Rouge: Louisiana University Press, 1985), 100.

69. Waldo David Frank, *Our America* (New York: Boni & Liveright, 1919).

70. Munson, *Awakening Twenties,* 54.

71. It is unclear whether this quote, cited in Munson, is from Bourne or from Scofield Thayer. Munson, *Awakening Twenties,* 103.

72. Harold E. Stearns, ed., *Civilization in the United States: An Inquiry by Thirty Americans* (New York: Harcourt, Brace, 1922).

73. Stearns, apparently disillusioned, shortly after this left for Europe, where he became a racing editor in Paris and was immortalized as Harvey Stone in Ernest Hemingway's *The Sun Also Rises* (New York: Scribner, 1926).

74. Joan Shelley Rubin, *The Making of Middlebrow Culture* (Chapel Hill: University of North Carolina Press, 1992), 31.

75. Munson, *Awakening Twenties.*

76. Sinclair Lewis, *Main Street* (New York: Alfred Knopf, 1920). Subsequent citations are from Sinclair Lewis, *Main Street* (New York: Harcourt, Brace & World, 1948).

77. Francis Scott Fitzgerald, *This Side of Paradise* (New York: Scribner, 1920). Subsequent citations from Francis Scott Fitzgerald, *This Side of Paradise,* ed. James L. W. West (Cambridge University Press, 1995).

78. Rubin, *Making of Middlebrow Culture.*

79. George Amos Dorsey, *Why We Behave Like Human Beings* (New York: Harper & Brothers, 1925).

80. Susan Porter Benson, "Living on the Margin: Working-Class Marriages and Familial Survival Strategies in the United States, 1919–1941," in *The Sex of Things: Gender and Consumption in Historical Perspective,* ed. Victoria de Grazia and Ellen Furlough (Los Angeles: University of California Press, 1996).

81. Robert S. Lynd and Helen Merrell Lynd, *Middletown: A Study in Contemporary American Culture* (New York: Harcourt, Brace, 1929).

82. Utah, Virginia, and Ohio, for example, all entertained bills to regulate skirt length and décolletage. Frederick Lewis Allen, *Only Yesterday: An Informal History of the 1920s* (New York: Harper & Row 1964), 77.

83. Hilary Lapsley, *Margaret Mead & Ruth Benedict: The Kinship of Women* (Amherst: University of Massachusetts Press, 1999).

84. Margaret Mead, "Group Intelligence Tests and Linguistic Disability among Italian Children," *School and Society* 25, no. 642 (1927), 467.

85. Franz Boas, "New Evidence in Regard to the Instability of Human Types," *Proceedings of the National Academy of Sciences of the United States of America* 2, no. 12 (1916).

86. Michael Silverstein, "Boasian Cosmographic: Anthropology and the Sociocentric Component of Mind," in *Significant Others: Interpersonal and Professional Commitments in Anthropology*, ed. Richard Handler (Madison: University of Wisconsin Press, 2004).

87. Reo Franklin Fortune, *Sorcerers of Dobu* (London: G. Routledge & Sons, 1932).

88. Margaret Mead, "Introduction," in *Margaret Mead: The Complete Bibliography 1925–1975*, ed. Joan Gordan (The Hague: Mouton, 1976), 18.

89. Among Mead's own detailing of her work and intellectual development, see Margaret Mead, "Margaret Mead," in *A History of Psychology in Autobiography*, ed. Gardner Lindzey (New York: Prentice-Hall, 1974); Margaret Mead, *Blackberry Winter: My Earlier Years* (New York: William Morrow, 1975). The most notable biographies are Lois Banner, *Intertwined Lives: Margaret Mead, Ruth Benedict and Their Circle* (New York: Knopf, 2003); Jane Howard, *Margaret Mead: A Life* (New York: Simon & Schuster, 1984); Lapsley, *Margaret Mead & Ruth Benedict.*

90. Margaret Mead, Letter to Reo Franklin Fortune, June 19, 1934. In *To Cherish the Life of the World: Selected Letters of Margaret Mead*, ed. Margaret M. Caffrey and Patricia A. Francis, 98–100 (New York: Basic Books, 2006). For the depth of her relationship with Ogburn, see also letters to him in the same volume, 243–244, 259–261, 271–273.

91. Mead, *Blackberry Winter: My Earlier Years.*

92. Mead, "Margaret Mead," 301.

93. Howard, *Margaret Mead: A Life,* 25.

Chapter 3: The "Jungle Flapper": Civilization, Repression, and the Homogenous Society

1. "Scientist Goes on Jungle Flapper Hunt," *New York Sun Times,* November 8, 1925, clipping, Box L3, file 1, Margaret Mead Papers.

2. Micaela di Leonardo, *Exotics at Home: Anthropologies, Others, American Modernities* (University of Chicago Press, 1998), 18.

3. In using this word, I am aware of Steedman's point that the "layering" of meanings is a symptom of the very process that she describes: "[I]t seems that in the late twentieth century we really cannot help reaching for that 'proper' depth nor . . . can we help believing that it is already there to be found." Carolyn Steedman, *Strange Dislocations: Childhood and the Idea of Human Interiority, 1780–1930* (London: Virago, 1995), 15.

4. Lawrence W. Levine, *The Unpredictable Past: Explorations in American Cultural History* (New York: Oxford University Press, 1993), 191.

5. According to Yellis, "[T]he term 'flapper' originated in England as a description of girls of the awkward age, the mid-teens. The awkwardness was meant literally, and a girl who flapped had not yet reached mature, dignified womanhood." The characteristic dress, of long, straight lines with little or no waist, was designed to cover this awkwardness. It was in America, however, that the term came to signal a generation of young women. Kenneth Yellis, "Prosperity's Child: Some Thoughts on the Flapper," *American Quarterly* 21 (1969): 49.

6. Frederick Lewis Allen, *Only Yesterday: An Informal History of the 1920s* (New York: Harper & Row, 1964), 73–101.

7. Yellis, "Prosperity's Child," 44–45.

8. Caroll Smith-Rosenberg, "The New Woman as Androgyne: Social Disorder and Gender Crisis, 1870–1936," in *Disorderly Conduct: Visions of Gender in Victorian America* (New York: Oxford University Press, 1985).

9. John D'Emilio and Estelle Freedman, *Intimate Matters: A History of Sexuality in America,* 2nd ed. (New York: Harper & Row, 1997), 188–194.

10. Smith-Rosenberg, "New Woman as Androgyne," 247–252.

11. The Depression would finalize this trend by demonizing working women and elevating the supportive martyr–mother or –girlfriend to mythic status. See, Laura Hapke, *Daughters of the Great Depression: Women, Work and Fiction in the American 1930s* (Athens: University of Georgia Press, 1995). It would be another thirty years before the possibilities that the New Woman had held out would again emerge at the forefront of the social agenda.

12. Levine, *Unpredictable Past,* 201.

13. Allen, *Only Yesterday,* 82.

14. Sinclair Lewis, *Main Street* (1920; repr., New York: Harcourt, Brace & World, 1948), 1.

15. Francis Scott Fitzgerald, *This Side of Paradise,* ed. James L. W. West (1920; repr., Cambridge University Press, 1995), 61.

16. Fitzgerald, *This Side of Paradise,* 183.

17. Franz Boas, Letter to Margaret Mead, July 14, 1925, Box B2, file 3, Margaret Mead Papers.

18. Derek Freeman, *Margaret Mead and Samoa: The Making and Unmaking of an Anthropological Myth* (Cambridge, MA: Harvard University Press, 1983); Jane Howard,

Margaret Mead: A Life (New York: Simon & Schuster, 1984); Hilary Lapsley, *Margaret Mead & Ruth Benedict: The Kinship of Women* (Amherst: University of Massachusetts Press, 1999).

19. Franz Boas, Letter to Ruth Fulton Benedict, July 16, 1925, AAW Copy 2, B/B61 Boas papers.

20. Ruth Fulton Benedict, Letter to Franz Boas, June 26, 1925, Film 1263, Reel 15, B/B61 Boas Papers.

21. Boas to Mead, July 14, 1925.

22. Mead later wrote of having "a room in the hotel . . . that had been the scene of Somerset Maugham's story and play, *Rain* which [she] had seen performed in New York." Margaret Mead, *Blackberry Winter: My Earlier Years* (New York: William Morrow, 1975), 158. The play *Rain,* based on Maugham's short story "Miss Thompson," was written by John Colton and Clemence Randolph (1922) and was staged discontinuously from September 1922 until March 1926. "John Colton," *Internet Broadway Database,* www.ibdb.com/person.asp?ID=6793 (accessed November 13, 2006).

23. Margaret Mead, Letter to family and friends, August 1925, Box N4, file 4, Margaret Mead Papers.

24. All quotes in this paragraph from Margaret Mead, Letter to family and friends, October 31, 1925, Box N4, file 1, Margaret Mead Papers.

25. Margaret Mead, Letter to Franz Boas, January 16, 1926, Film 1263, Reel 15, B/B61, Boas papers.

26. Margaret Mead, Letter to family and friends, December 11, 1925, Box N4, file 1, Margaret Mead Papers.

27. Margaret Mead, Letter to Franz Boas, December 13, 1925, Box N1, file 1, Margaret Mead Papers.

28. Margaret Mead, Letter to Franz Boas, January 5, 1925, Box N1, file 1, Margaret Mead Papers. The date of this letter is wrong. It was actually written on January 5, 1926.

29. Margaret Mead, Letter to Franz Boas, January 16, 1926, Film 1263, Reel 15, B/B61 Boas Papers. This little-girlish behavior in relation to older men was a ploy Mead would repeat, at least at times self-consciously, in her dealings with Ogburn, Radcliffe-Brown, and Malinowski.

30. Franz Boas, Letter to Margaret Mead, February 15, 1926, Box N1, file 1, Margaret Mead Papers.

31. Margaret Mead, Letter to Franz Boas, March 14, 1926, Film 1263, Reel 15, B/B61 Boas Papers.

32. Margaret Mead, Letter to family and friends, February 9, 1926, Box N4, file 1, Margaret Mead Papers.

33. Margaret Mead, Letter to E. S. C. Handy, December 21, 1926, Box I4, file 16, Margaret Mead Papers.

34. Margaret Mead, Letter to Emily Fogg Mead, March 15, 1928, Box A7, file 3, Margaret Mead Papers. Margaret herself had been "the first baby at a new hospital." This note, like her master's research, is evidence of how strongly she both identified and was rivalrous with her mother, despite the fact that she maintained that her grandmother was her principal influence and role model.

35. Her early book reviews are evidence of how strongly she responded to work that evoked places and peoples. Her own most enthusiastic and best-written reviews of books have this quality. There have been a number of articles published that focus on Mead's style, including Dennis Porter's "Anthropological Tales: Unprofessional Thoughts on the Mead/Freeman Controversy," Notebooks in Cultural Anthropology 1 (1984).

36. "American Girl to Study Cannibals," Boston Post, May 24, 1928, clipping, Box L3, file 1, Margaret Mead Papers.

37. "Will Shows Fear of Cannibals," New York Sun, August 22, 1928, clipping, Box L3, file 1, Margaret Mead Papers.

38. Margaret Mead, Letter to Emily Fogg Mead, May 19, 1928, Box A7, file 4, Margaret Mead Papers. The articles were never written.

39. William Morrow, Letter to Margaret Mead, June 20, 1928, Box I2, file 1, Margaret Mead Papers.

40. William Morrow & Co. Coming of Age in Samoa, Order form, 1928, Box L3, File 1, Margaret Mead Papers.

41. "Samoa is the Place for Women . . ." New York Sun, January 23, 1929, clipping, Box L3, file 1, Margaret Mead Papers.

42. Frederick O'Brien, "Where Neuroses Cease from Troubling and Complexes Are at Rest," World, October 21, 1928, clipping, Box L3, file 2, Margaret Mead Papers.

43. "But I Came of Age in Samoa," Esquire, December 1928, cartoon clipping, Box L3, file 1, Margaret Mead Papers.

44. Robert H. Lowie, Review of Coming of Age in Samoa: A Psychological Study of Primitive Youth for Western Civilization by Margaret Mead, American Anthropologist 31, no. 3 (1929).

45. Edward Sapir, "The Discipline of Sex," American Mercury 16 (1929).

46. H. L. Mencken, "Adolescence," American Mercury (November 1929), clipping, file I4, Box 8, Margaret Mead Papers.

47. Roger Sprague, Letter to the Editor: "Samoan Youth," Saturday Review of Literature, November 17, 1928, clipping, Box L1, file 1, Margaret Mead Papers.

48. Mencken, "Adolescence."

49. Robert S. Lynd and Helen Merrell Lynd, Middletown: A Study in Contemporary American Culture (New York: Harcourt, Brace, 1929).

50. According to her mother, Emily Fogg Mead, the others were "Edith Abbott Women in Industry, Mrs. Catt's Woman Suffrage, Dorothy Dix on Prisons, Mary Har-

land's Husbands and Homes, Mrs. Livermore's My Story of the War, and Margaret Sanger's Women and New Race." Emily Fogg Mead, Letter to Margaret Mead, July 19, 1933, Box A7, file 4, Margaret Mead Papers.

51. Nancy C. Lutkehaus, "Margaret Mead and the 'Rustling-of-the-Wind-in-the-Palm-Trees' School of Ethnographic Writing," in *Women Writing Culture*, ed. Ruth Behar (Berkeley: University of California Press, 1995).

52. Margaret Mead, *Coming of Age in Samoa: A Psychological Study of Primitive Youth for Western Civilization* (New York: William Morrow, 1928), 195.

53. Mead, *Coming of Age in Samoa*, 151.

54. Mead, *Coming of Age in Samoa*, 360. This characterization stands in marked contrast to her academic article on Samoa, "The Role of the Individual in Samoan Culture," in which she wrote: "[T]o be young or a woman in Samoa is a sort of guilt in itself, a state of affairs for which perpetual tacit apologies must be made. And the fact that so much of the heavy work, and almost all of the dull, routine and humdrum miscellaneous tasks fall upon the young makes the status of youth a positive and onerous burden." Margaret Mead, "The Role of the Individual in Samoan Culture," *Journal of the Royal Anthropological Institute* 55 (July–December 1928), 485.

55. Margaret Mead, "South Sea Hints on Bringing Up Children," *Parents Magazine* (1929): 48.

56. For the most-cited explications of this idea, see Michel Foucault, *The Care of the Self. The History of Sexuality Vol. 3* (Harmondsworth, UK: Penguin, 1988); Charles Taylor, *Sources of the Self: The Making of Modern Identity* (Cambridge University Press, 1989).

57. John Chynoweth Burnham, *Psychoanalysis and American Medicine, 1894–1918: Medicine, Society and Culture* (New York: International Universities Press, 1967), 89.

58. Steedman, *Strange Dislocations*, 12.

59. Steedman, *Strange Dislocations*, 21–42.

60. Steedman notes that in researching this book she sometimes felt that she was writing a history of "littleness." Steedman, *Strange Dislocations*, 9.

61. Steedman, *Strange Dislocations*, 2.

62. Hans Ulrich Gumbrecht, *In 1926: Living on the Edge of Time* (Cambridge, MA: Harvard University Press, 1997), 393–395.

63. L. C. M., "Books on the Table: Samoan Adolescence," *Argonaut*, January 19, 1929, clipping, Box L3, file 1, Margaret Mead Papers.

64. Mead, *Coming of Age in Samoa*, 213.

65. Untitled review of *Coming of Age in Samoa* by Margaret Mead, *Philadelphia Record*, August 15, 1928, clipping, Box L3, file 1, Margaret Mead Papers.

66. Untitled review of *Coming of Age in Samoa* by Margaret Mead, *Brooklyn Eagle*, August 22, 1929, clipping, Box L3, file 1, Margaret Mead Papers.

67. Caspar Hunt, "The Younger Generation in Samoa," *Travel*, April 1929, clipping, Box L3, file 1, Margaret Mead Papers.

68. "Utopian Marriages, for the Woman," *New York Telegram,* 1930, clipping, Box L3, file 1, Margaret Mead Papers.

69. Mead, "Role of the Individual in Samoan Culture," 495. In a consideration of Mead's later work, Paul Roscoe blames Ruth Benedict for this kind of perverse argumentation, particularly Benedict's assertion that "cultures could reconcile even the most divergent cultural traits into a coherent pattern: 'Taken up by a well-integrated culture, the most ill-assorted acts become characteristic of its peculiar goals, often by the most unlikely metamorphoses.'" Benedict, *Patterns of Culture,* 46, cited in Paul Roscoe, "Margaret Mead, Reo Fortune, and Mountain Arapesh Warfare," *American Anthropologist* 105, no. 3 (2003): 586–587. However, Mead and Benedict read all of each other's work and discussed these ideas with each other. It seems unfair to both of them to blame one for the illogicalities of the other.

70. See, for examples, di Leonardo, *Exotics at Home;* Freeman, *Margaret Mead and Samoa;* Freda Kirchwey, "This Week: Sex in the South Seas," *Nation,* October 24, 1928, clipping, Box L3, file 1, Margaret Mead Papers; Lowie, Review of *Coming of Age in Samoa.*

71. "Adolescence Not a Dangerous Period of Life in Samoa," *St. Louis Globe-Democrat,* December 29, 1929, clipping, Box L3, file 1, Margaret Mead Papers.

72. O'Brien, "Where Neuroses Cease from Troubling and Complexes Are at Rest."

73. Mead, "South Sea Hints on Bringing Up Children," 22.

74. Mead, *Coming of Age in Samoa,* 199.

75. Mead, *Coming of Age in Samoa,* 200.

76. Hunt, "The Younger Generation in Samoa."

77. Aldous Huxley, "The Problem of Faith," *Harpers Magazine,* January 1933, clipping, Box L3, file 2, Margaret Mead Papers.

78. Review of *Coming of Age in Samoa* by Margaret Mead, *Psychoanalytic Review* 16 (1929).

79. Kirchwey, "This Week: Sex in the South Seas."

80. Margaret Mead, "Adolescence in Primitive and Modern Society," in *The New Generation: The Intimate Problems of Parents and Children,* ed. V. F. Calverton and S. D. Schmalhausen (New York: Macauley, 1930), 185.

81. Kirchwey, "This Week: Sex in the South Seas."

82. Well into adulthood, Mead herself was aware of—one might even argue invested in—this version of herself as a little girl. She frequently referred to herself as "your little girl" in her letters to her father and grandmother, and her father wrote to her as "My dear little girl" until she was well over thirty.

83. O'Brien, "Where Neuroses Cease from Troubling and Complexes Are at Rest."

84. Nels Anderson, "In the Light of Samoa," *Survey,* January 15, 1929, clipping, Box L3, file 1, Margaret Mead Papers.

85. Levine, *Unpredictable Past*, 203.

86. Herbert Croly, *The Promise of American Life*, ed. Arthur M. Schlesinger (1909; repr., Cambridge, MA: The Belknap Press of Harvard University Press, 1965), 414.

87. Van Wyck Brooks, "America's Coming of Age," in *Van Wyck Brooks: The Early Years*, 2nd ed., ed. Claire Sprague (Boston: Northeastern University Press, 1993), 97.

88. Brooks, "America's Coming of Age," 95.

89. Croly, *Promise of American Life*, 414.

90. Philip Cushman, *Constructing the Self, Constructing America* (Reading, MA: Addison-Wesley, 1995), 151.

Chapter 4: "Lords of an Empty Creation": Masculinity, Puritanism, and Cultural Stagnation

1. Margaret Mead, Proposal to Social Science Research Council, typescript, 1928, Box I4, file 11, Margaret Mead Papers. The problem and the form of the research were inspired by a conversation she had had with George Cressman, her first husband's young brother.

2. Margaret Mead, *Growing Up in New Guinea: A Comparative Study of Primitive Education* (New York: William Morrow, 1930). Unless otherwise specified, all quotes are from Margaret Mead, *Growing Up in New Guinea: A Comparative Study of Primitive Education* (1930; repr., New York: Perennial, 2001).

3. Frederick Lewis Allen, *Only Yesterday: An Informal History of the 1920s* (New York: Harper & Row, 1964), 284.

4. T. H. Watkins, *The Great Depression: America in the 1930s* (Boston: Little, Brown, 1993), 55.

5. Ann Douglas, *Terrible Honesty: Mongrel Manhattan in the 1920s* (New York: Farrar, Strauss & Giroux, 1995), 32.

6. Lawrence W. Levine, *The Unpredictable Past: Explorations in American Cultural History* (New York: Oxford University Press, 1993), 206–230.

7. Levine, *Unpredictable Past*, 216.

8. According to Susman, "[T]he words most frequently related to the notion of character [were] *citizenship, duty, democracy, work, building, golden deeds, outdoor life, conquest, honor, reputation, morals, manners, integrity,* and above all, *manhood.* Those associated with personality were *"fascinating, stunning, attractive, magnetic, glowing, masterful, creative, dominant, forceful."* Walter Susman, *Culture as History: The Transformation of American Society in the Twentieth Century* (New York: Pantheon Books, 1984), 273–274, 277.

9. Reo Franklin Fortune, *Sorcerers of Dobu* (London: G. Routledge & Sons, 1932).

10. Mead underemphasized the extent to which European contact had affected

Manus society, a weakness in her analysis that was pointed out by contemporary reviewers.

11. Margaret Mead, Letter to Ruth Fulton Benedict, October 18, 1928, AAW Copy 2, B/B61 Boas Papers.

12. Mead to Benedict, October 18, 1928.

13. Margaret Mead, Letter to family and friends, November 22, 1928, Box N40, file 1, Margaret Mead Papers.

14. Margaret Mead, Letter to family and friends, December 16, 1928, Box N40, file 1, Margaret Mead Papers.

15. Margaret Mead, Letter to Franz Boas, January 6, 1929, Film 1263, Reel 15, B/B61 Boas Papers.

16. Mead to family and friends, December 16, 1928.

17. Margaret Mead, Letter to family and friends, February 14, 1929, Box N40, file 1, Margaret Mead Papers.

18. Margaret Mead, "Living with the Natives of Melanesia," *Natural History* 31, no. 1 (1931): 72.

19. Bronislaw Malinowski, *Sex and Repression in Savage Society* (New York: Meridien, 1927).

20. Margaret Mead, Letter to Bronislaw Malinowski, August 9, 1928, Box I2, file 1, Margaret Mead Papers.

21. Bronislaw Malinowski, Letter to Margaret Mead, September 22, 1928, Box I2, file 2, Margaret Mead Papers; Bronislaw Malinowski, Letter to Margaret Mead, September 4, 1929, Box C3, file M, Margaret Mead Papers; Margaret Mead, Letter to Bronislaw Malinowski, August 9, 1928, Box I2, file 1, Margaret Mead Papers.

22. Margaret Mead, Letter to family and friends, March 27, 1929, Box N40, file 1, Margaret Mead Papers.

23. Margaret Mead, "Jealousy: Primitive and Civilized," in *Woman's Coming of Age: A Symposium,* ed. Samuel Schmalhausen and V. F. Calverton (New York: Liveright, 1931), 44.

24. Margaret Mead, "Growing Up in the South Seas," *Forum: The Magazine of Controversy* 87 (May 1932): 285, Box I6, file 12, Margaret Mead Papers.

25. Mead, "Growing Up in the South Seas," 285.

26. Mead, "Growing Up in the South Seas," 288.

27. Mead, *Growing Up in New Guinea* (2001), 161.

28. Ruth Fulton Benedict, "Primitive Life in New Guinea," *New York Times,* November 16, 1930, clipping, Box L3, file 3, Margaret Mead Papers.

29. Melville Herskovitz, "Primitive Childhood," *Nation,* February 4, 1931, clipping, Box L3, file 2, Margaret Mead Papers.

30. Alfred L. Kroeber, Letter to Margaret Mead, October 23, 1930, Box I4, file 9, Margaret Mead Papers.

31. This is a reference to Augustin Krämer, whose general ethnography of Samoa was published in Germany in 1902. Augustin Krämer, *The Samoa Islands: An Outline of a Monograph with Particular Consideration of German Samoa,* trans. Theodore Verhaaren (1902–1903; repr., Honolulu: University of Hawai'i Press, 1994).

32. All quotes this paragraph are from Alfred L. Kroeber, Review of *Growing Up in New Guinea* by Margaret Mead, *American Anthropologist* 33, no. 2 (1931): 248–250.

33. Edith Clarke, "Water Babies," *Saturday Review of Literature,* May 2, 1931, clipping, Box L3, file 3, Margaret Mead Papers.

34. C. W. Hart, Review of *Growing Up in New Guinea* by Margaret Mead, *Man* 32 (June 1932): 146. Note that Fortune spent only six months with the Dobu, a fact that had not bothered Malinowski, who lavished praise in his introduction to *The Sorcerers of Dobu.* Bronislaw Malinowski, "Introduction," in *Sorcerers of Dobu,* ed. Reo Franklin Fortune (London: G. Routledge & Sons, 1932).

35. Hart, Review of *Growing Up in New Guinea* by Margaret Mead. The first English edition contains significant differences from the American editions and later English ones. The reference to Priestley is one sentence inserted in the English edition, presumably to bolster relevance to the British public (169). At various points in the text, "America" is changed to "England." In the first English edition, the four chapters of part 2 are consolidated into two. Most significant, for the purposes of this article, the long section on American fatherhood was cut. Margaret Mead, *Growing Up in New Guinea: A Comparative Study of Primitive Education,* English ed. (London: G. Routledge & Sons, 1931).

36. Editor, Correspondence re: *Growing Up in New Guinea* (cf. *Man* (1932): 174), *Man* 33 (1933). According to Mead's later retrospective on her own publications, Hart's piece was prompted by Malinowski's expressing the opinion that Mead did not know anything about kinship or the Manus language. Margaret Mead, "Introduction," in *Margaret Mead: The Complete Bibliography 1925–1975,* ed. Joan Gordan (The Hague: Mouton, 1976), 5.

37. Margaret Mead, Letter to Alfred Kroeber, May 1, 1931, Box C3, file K, Margaret Mead Papers.

38. Ruth Fulton Benedict, Letter to "Dear Isabel," January 11, 1933, Box O38, file 4, Margaret Mead Papers. By the time Benedict wrote her letter, Fortune's book on the Omaha had also been the subject of negative reviews in the *American Anthropologist,* see Robert H. Lowie, Review of *Omaha Secret Societies* by Reo Franklin Fortune, *American Anthropologist* 35, no. 3 (1933).

39. Mead, *Growing Up in New Guinea* (2001), 212.

40. Margaret Mead, "More Comprehensive Field Methods," *American Anthropologist* 35, no. 1 (1933).

41. Margaret Mead, Letter to Emily Fogg Mead, October 16, 1930, Box A7, file 4, Margaret Mead Papers.

42. Margaret Mead, "An Investigation of the Thought of Primitive Children, with

Special Reference to Animism," *Journal of the Royal Anthropological Institute* 62 (January–June 1932). Unlike many of her peers, Mead did not publish extensively in anthropological journals. When she did, they were likely to be British or Australian journals. This may be because the British and Australians were more sympathetic to her quasi-functionalist approach than were the more historicist Americans. She did, however, publish in other science journals, including *Natural History, Psyche,* and the *Annals of the American Academy of Political and Social Sciences.* For a complete bibliography of her work, see Joan Gordan, *Margaret Mead.*

43. Meritt Hulburd, Letter to Margaret Mead, November 22, 1930, Box I5, file 2, Margaret Mead Papers.

44. Margaret Mead, Stone Age Education—and Ours, typescript, 1930, Box I5, file 2, Margaret Mead Papers.

45. Meritt Hulburd, Letter to Margaret Mead, December 9, 1930, Box I5, file 2, Margaret Mead Papers.

46. Mead, "Growing Up in the South Seas."

47. Isidore Schneider, "Manus and Americans," *New Republic,* November 5, 1930, clipping, Box L3, file 2, Margaret Mead Papers.

48. Ruth Fulton Benedict, Letter to The American Library Association, February 2, 1932, Box I6, file 17, Margaret Mead Papers.

49. Ruth Fulton Benedict, "Psychological Types in the Cultures of the Southwest," in *Proceedings of the XXIII International Congress of Americanists, September 1928* (University of Chicago Press, 1930).

50. Robert S. Lynd and Helen Merrell Lynd, *Middletown: A Study in Contemporary American Culture* (New York: Harcourt, Brace, 1929).

51. George Santayana, *Winds of Doctrine, and Platonism and the Spiritual Life* (Gloucester, MA: P. Smith, 1971).

52. Nathan G. Hale, *Freud and the Americans: The Beginnings of Psychoanalysis in the United States, 1876–1917* (New York: Oxford University Press, 1971), 57–73.

53. Mead, *Growing Up in New Guinea* (2001), 171.

54. Lynd and Lynd, *Middletown* (1929), 149.

55. All quotes in this paragraph to this point from Mead, *Growing Up in New Guinea* (2001), 170–172.

56. Mead, *Growing Up in New Guinea* (2001), 174.

57. Harold E. Stearns, ed., *Civilization in the United States: An Inquiry by Thirty Americans* (New York: Harcourt, Brace, 1922); George W. Stocking, "The Ethnographic Sensibility of the 1920s and the Dualism of the Anthropological Tradition," in *Romantic Motives: Essays on Anthropological Sensibility,* ed. George W. Stocking (Madison: University of Wisconsin Press, 1989), 215.

58. Lynd and Lynd, *Middletown* (1929), 47.

59. Margaret Mead, "Two South Sea Educational Experiments and Their American Implications," *University of Pennsylvania Education Bulletin* 31, no. 36 (1931);

Margaret Mead, "South Seas Tips on Character Training," *Parents Magazine*, March 1932.

60. Margaret Mead, "Standardized America vs. Romantic South Seas," *Scribner's Magazine* (November 1931), 487. Note that, like many of the New York elite, including the Lynds, Sherwood Anderson, Scott Fitzgerald, Mead used the Midwest, in this case, Iowa, as the prototype of an "America" that was the subject of critique.

61. Mead, "Standardized America vs. Romantic South Seas," 491.

62. Mead, "Standardized America vs. Romantic South Seas."

63. Ruth Fulton Benedict, Letter to Emily Fogg Mead, November 11, 1931, Box A7, file 3, Margaret Mead Papers.

64. Mead, *Growing Up in New Guinea* (2001), 10.

65. Mead, "Two South Sea Educational Experiments and Their American Implications," 496.

66. Margaret Mead, "Civil Government for Samoa," *Nation* 132 (February 25, 1931).

67. Margaret Mead, "Are We Mature?" *Thinker* 2 (December 7, 1930), 32.

68. Mead, *Growing Up in New Guinea* (2001), 164. This is clearly a reference to the scene in *Babbitt* in which George Babbitt goes to his minister. Sinclair Lewis, *Babbitt* (New York: Grosset & Dunlap, 1922), 393–395.

69. Mead, *Growing Up in New Guinea* (1930), 107.

70. Margaret Mead, "The Meaning of Freedom in Education," *Progressive Education* 8, no. 2 (1931): 111.

71. Floyd Dell, *Love in the Machine Age: A Psychological Study of the Transition from a Patriarchal Society* (New York: Farrar, 1930).

72. Mead, "Are We Mature?" 32.

73. Mead, *Growing Up in New Guinea* (1930), 174.

Chapter 5: "Every Woman Deviating from the Code": Cultural Lag, Moral Contagion, and Social Disintegration

1. Throughout this chapter, I continue to use "Antler" when referring to Mead's ethnographic material and "Omaha" when referring to the historical record. Like her other work, Mead's work in Nebraska has been repudiated by some scholars. It is not my intention in any of these chapters to evaluate the accuracy of Mead's ethnographies but only to understand how she framed these interpretations in terms of her intellectual heritage, the sociopolitical state of the United States at the time, and her own intellectual trajectory.

2. Micaela di Leonardo, *Exotics at Home: Anthropologies, Others, American Modernities* (University of Chicago Press, 1998).

3. George Stocking, "Ideas and Institutions in American Anthropology: Towards a History of the Interwar Years," in *The Ethnographer's Magic and Other Essays in the History of Anthropology,* ed. George Stocking (Madison: University of Wisconsin Press, 1992), 142.

4. Virginia Yans and Alan Berliner, *Margaret Mead: An Observer Observed* (New York: Mind Matters, 1995), film.

5. Patricia Francis (curator) and Mary Wolfskill (co-curator), "Margaret Mead: Human Nature and the Power of Culture," Library of Congress, 2001, www.loc.gov/exhibits/mead (accessed November 13, 2006).

6. Until I began this research on Mead, I was unaware of this book, as have been almost all anthropologists of my generation to whom I have mentioned it.

7. Margaret Mead, *The Changing Culture of an Indian Tribe* (New York: Columbia University Press, 1932), 16.

8. Margaret Mead, *The Changing Culture of an Indian Tribe* (New York: Capricorn Books, 1966), xxii.

9. Mead, *Changing Culture* (1932), 6.

10. Lewis Merriam, "The Problem of Indian Administration: Report of a Survey Made at the Request of Honorable Hubert Work, Secretary of the Interior" (Baltimore: The Institute for Government Research, 1928).

11. Susan Scheckel, *The Insistence of the Indian: Race and Nationalism in Nineteenth-Century American Culture* (Princeton University Press, 1998), 3.

12. William Fielding Ogburn, *Social Change with Respect to Culture and Original Nature* (New York: B. W. Huebsch, 1922).

13. Richard H. Pells, *Radical Visions and American Dreams: Culture and Thought in the Depression Years* (Urbana: University of Illinois Press, 1998), 25.

14. Lewis Mumford, *Technics and Civilization* (New York: Harcourt, 1934).

15. Mrs. Leonard Elmhirst was the former Dorothy Whitney, the daughter of William C. Whitney and a backer, with her first husband, William Straight, and others, of *New Republic.*

16. Margaret Mead, Letter to Bronislaw Malinowski, August 9, 1930, Box N19, file 11, Margaret Mead Papers.

17. R. H. Barnes, *Two Crows Denies It: A History of Controversy in Omaha Sociology* (Lincoln: University of Nebraska Press, 1984).

18. Margaret Mead, Letter to Ruth Fulton Benedict, July 21, 1930, AAW Copy 2, B/B61 Boas Papers.

19. Mead to Malinowski, August 9, 1930.

20. Margaret Mead, Letter to Franz Boas, July 16, 1930, Box N119, file 11, Margaret Mead Papers.

21. Mead to Boas, July 16, 1930.

22. Mead to Malinowski, August 9, 1930.

23. Mead, *Changing Culture* (1966), 203n12.

24. Thomas Doherty, *Pre-Code Hollywood: Sex, Immorality and Insurrection in American Cinema, 1930–34* (New York: Columbia University Press, 1999), 50.

25. Doherty, *Pre-Code Hollywood,* 53.

26. Clark Wissler, "Foreword," in Mead, *Changing Culture* (1966), iv.

27. Mead, *Changing Culture* (1932), 9.

28. Mead, *Changing Culture* (1932), 6.

29. Ogburn, *Social Change,* 3–40.

30. At this point, Mead was still somewhat ambivalent about her professional identification. Just as she saw "primitive" cultures as natural laboratories from which the modern world could extract knowledge useful for its problems, she saw anthropology as extracting that knowledge in service of the disciplines focused on the modern West—education, psychology, sociology, and history. This attitude was, of course, premised on the strong belief that "primitive" cultures would inevitably die out.

31. Mead, *Changing Culture* (1932), 10.

32. Mead, *Changing Culture* (1932), 15.

33. Mead, *Changing Culture* (1932), 5.

34. Mead, *Changing Culture* (1932), 5.

35. Hortense Powdermaker, Letter to Bronislaw and Elsie Malinowski, December 11, 1930, Stud/11, Malinowksi Papers.

36. As was his habit, Edward Sapir took a swipe at this assumption of Mead's in his article "Cultural Anthropology and Psychiatry," published the same year as *Changing Culture.* He stated, "All *realistic* [my emphasis] field workers in native custom and belief are more or less aware of the dangers" of assuming "the individual informant is near enough to the understandings and intentions of his society." Edward Sapir, "Cultural Anthropology and Psychiatry," *Journal of Abnormal and Social Psychology* 27 (1932).

37. Clark Wissler, Letter to Margaret Mead, August 4, 1930, Box I6, file 10, October, Margaret Mead Papers.

38. Margaret Mead, Letter to Clark Wissler, August 15, 1930, Box I6, file 10, Margaret Mead Papers.

39. Ogburn, *Social Change,* 13.

40. Mead to Wissler, August 15, 1930.

41. Margaret Mead, "The Primitive Child," in *A Handbook of Child Psychology,* ed. Carl Allanmore Murchison (Worcester, MA: Clark University Press, 1931), 669.

42. Mead to Malinowski, August 9, 1930.

43. "Dr. Margaret Mead," 1931, unsourced clipping, Box L3, file 3, Margaret Mead Papers.

44. Barnes, *Two Crows Denies It.*

45 Margaret Mead and Ruth Bunzel, eds., *The Golden Age of American Anthropology* (New York: George Braziller, 1960), 228.

46. Mead, *Changing Culture* (1966), 21.

47. Mead, *Changing Culture* (1966), 25.

48. Mead, *Changing Culture* (1966), 27.

49. Margaret Mead, Letter to Clark Wissler, August 6, 1930, Box I6, file 10, Margaret Mead Papers.

50. Mead, *Changing Culture* (1966), 59.

51. Amy Green has argued that this view of the domestic realm was part and parcel of Stanley Hall's recapitulation theory. Hall argued that [civilized] children proceeded through all the stages of human culture until they reached [modern] civilized adulthood. This theory, she argues, reinforced "the myth of the domestic realm as an eternal, unchanging, and ahistorical shore naturally inhabited by the universal woman." Cited in Phillip Deloria, *Playing Indian* (New Haven, CT: Yale University Press, 1998), 228n39.

52. Mead, *Changing Culture* (1966), 133–134.

53. Mead,*Changing Culture* (1966), 134.

54. Mead, *Changing Culture* (1966), 91.

55. Mead, *Changing Culture* (1966), 140.

56. Mead, *Changing Culture* (1966), 196.

57. Mead, *Changing Culture* (1966), 193.

58. Mead, *Changing Culture* (1966), 163.

59. Mead, *Changing Culture* (1966), 162.

60. Mead, *Changing Culture* (1966), 150.

61. Mead, *Changing Culture* (1966), 150.

62. Ruth Benedict, Letter to Margaret Mead, January 20, 1932, AAW Copy 2, B/B61 Boas Papers.

63. Alfred Tozzer, Review of T*he Changing Culture of an Indian Tribe* by Margaret Mead, *The Annals of the American Academy of Political and Social Science* 165 (January 1933).

64. C. D. F[orde], Review of *The Changing Culture of an Indian Tribe* by Margaret Mead, *Man* 33 (September 1933): 154.

65. Alexander Goldenweiser, Review of *The Changing Culture of an Indian Tribe* by Margaret Mead, *Nation* (1933), clipping, Box L3, file 3, Margaret Mead Papers.

66. Alexander Goldenweiser, Review of *The Changing Culture of an Indian Tribe* by Margaret Mead, *American Anthropologist* 36, no. 4 (1934): 611.

67. Clare Howard, Review of *The Changing Culture of an Indian Tribe* by Margaret Mead, *Barnard College Alumnus Monthly*, December 1932, clipping, Box L3, file 3, Margaret Mead Papers.

68. Ruth Fulton Benedict, "The White Man and the Indian," *New York Herald Tribune Books,* November 12, 1932, clipping, Box L3, file 3, Margaret Mead Papers.

69. The term "broken culture" derived from the story told to Ruth Benedict by an old man and recorded by Mead in a letter to her grandmother soon after she met

"Mrs. Benedict": "'In the beginning there was given to every people a cup of clay. And from this cup they drank their life. Our cup is broken.' Is that not a quaint and poetic way of characterizing the whole culture of the Indians, or any other people for that matter? I would so like to be an Anthropologist," the first recorded commitment to her life's work. Margaret Mead, Letter to "Dear Grandma," March 11, 1923, Box A17, file 3, Margaret Mead Papers.

70. Mead, *Changing Culture*, 221. It is interesting to speculate if Mead drew the analogy to the house from Dewey's essays in the *Nation*, republished in 1930 as *Individualism Old and New*. John Dewey, *Individualism Old and New* (London: George Allen & Unwin, 1931). Mead would have been aware of Dewey's analysis, drawn originally from Van Wyck Brooks, of America as a "house divided against itself." The house analogy sits oddly in *Changing Culture*, and her more dominant disease metaphor would have served as well for the point she was trying to make.

71. Bronislaw Malinowski, Letter to Margaret Mead, March 29, 1930, General Correspondence—Letters M—1925–1938, LSE/Malinowski Papers; Margaret Mead, Letter to Bronislaw Malinowski, January 28, 1930, Box C3, file M, Margaret Mead Papers; Mead to Malinowski, August 9, 1930.

72. In 1960 Ruth Bunzel claimed functionalism for Boas, writing that he believed that "the constituent elements of a culture . . . fitted together into a system of inter-related parts." Ruth Bunzel, "Introduction: Building a Science of Man in America: The Classical Period in American Anthropology, 1900–1920," in *Golden Age*, ed. Mead and Bunzel, 401. This is to some extent a post hoc claim. The rivalry between British and American anthropologists was intense, especially after Radcliffe-Brown was appointed to Chicago in 1931. Boas was notoriously particularistic and severe with students who made overly general claims. However, a "small-f" functionalist framework implicitly underpinned both American and British anthropology in the early twentieth century, although the British were the first to theorize it in terms of an integrated system, after Durkheim, rather than in terms of relations between elements. Stocking, "Ideas and Institutions in American Anthropology."

73. Ogburn, *Social Change*, 200–201.

74. Herbert Croly, *The Promise of American Life* (New York: Houghton Mifflin, 1965), 414.

75. Brooks, *America's Coming of Age*, 95.

76. Ogburn, *Social Change*, 312, 331.

77. See, for example, Hazel Carby's interesting essay on how Zora Neale Hurston located "authentic" black culture in the rural. Hazel Carby, "The Politics of Fiction, Anthropology, and the Folk: Zora Neal Hurston," in *New Essays on Their Eyes Were Watching God*, ed. Michael Awkward (Cambridge University Press, 1990). There are numerous other studies that consider this fraught relationship between authenticity, primitivism, rurality, race, and sexuality; see also, for this period, Elazar Barkan and Ronald Bush, eds., *Prehistories of the Future: The Primitivist Project and the Culture of*

Modernism (Stanford University Press, 1995); Jonathan Fineberg, ed., *Discovering Child Art: Essays on Childhood, Primitivism, and Modernism* (Princeton University Press, 1998); Henricka Kuklick, *The Savage Within: The Social History of British Anthropology, 1885–1945* (Cambridge University Press, 1991); Chip Rhodes, *Structures of the Jazz Age: Mass Culture, Progressive Education, and Racial Discourse in American Modernist Fiction* (New York: Verso, 1998); William J. Rushing, *Native American Art and the New York Avant-garde: A History of Cultural Primitivism* (Austin: University of Texas Press, 1995); Marianna Torgovnick, *Gone Primitive: Savage Intellects, Modern Lives* (University of Chicago Press, 1990).

78. Mead, *Changing Culture* (1932), xix.

79. This was title of a collection of original articles edited by Mead and Ruth Bunzel. Mead and Bunzel, eds., *Golden Age.*

80. Mead had written an article for Schmalhausen and Calverton's collection. Margaret Mead, "Adolescence in Primitive and Modern Society," in *The New Generation: The Intimate Problems of Parents and Children*, ed. V. F. Calverton and S. D. Schmalhausen (New York: Macauley, 1930).

81. Dewey, *Individualism Old and New.*

82. Mumford, *Technics and Civilization.*

83. Dewey, *Individualism Old and New*, 93.

84. Robert Redfield, *Tepoztlan, A Mexican Village: A Study of Folk Life* (University of Chicago Press, 1930).

85. Stuart Chase, *Mexico: A Study of Two Americas* (New York: Macmillan, 1937).

86. Chase, *Mexico: A Study of Two Americas*, 208.

87. Deloria, *Playing Indian.*

88. Deloria, *Playing Indian;* Walter Benn Michaels, *Our America: Nativism, Modernism, and Pluralism* (Durham, NC: Duke University Press, 1995); Scheckel, *Insistence of the Indian.*

89. Lawrence W. Levine, *The Unpredictable Past: Explorations in American Cultural History* (New York: Oxford University Press, 1993), 191.

90. Laura Hapke, *Daughters of the Great Depression: Women, Work and Fiction in the American 1930s* (Athens: University of Georgia Press, 1995).

91. Mead, *Changing Culture*, 220.

92. Mead, *Changing Culture*, 220.

Chapter 6: "Maladjustment of a Worse Order": Temperament, Psychosexual Misidentification, and the Refuge of Private Life

1. "Notes and News," *Oceania* 5, no. 2 (1931): 237.

2. "Notes and News," *Oceania* 7, no. 4 (1933): 106.

3. Gregory Bateson, *Naven: A Survey of the Problems Suggested by a Composite Pic-*

ture of the Culture of a New Guinea Tribe Drawn from Three Points of View (Cambridge University Press, 1936).

4. George Stocking, "Essays on Personality and Culture" in *Malinowski, Rivers, Benedict and Others: Essays on Personality and Culture* (Madison: University of Wisconsin Press, 1986), 3.

5. Jane Howard, *Margaret Mead: A Life* (New York: Simon & Schuster, 1984).

6. David Lipset, *Gregory Bateson: The Legacy of a Scientist* (Englewood Cliffs, NJ: Prentice Hall, 1980). At this point there is no published biography of Fortune. However, a PhD thesis on his life and work is currently in process: Caroline Thomas, "Reo Franklin Fortune: The Historical Ethnography of an Anthropological Career" (doctoral dissertation, University of Waikato, Hamilton, NZ, in prep).

7. Hilary Lapsley, *Margaret Mead & Ruth Benedict: The Kinship of Women* (Amherst: University of Massachusetts Press, 1999).

8. Lois Banner, *Intertwined Lives: Margaret Mead, Ruth Benedict and Their Circle* (New York: Knopf, 2003).

9. James Boon, "Mead's Mediations: Some Semiotics from the Sepik, by way of Bateson, on to Bali," in *Semiotic Mediations: Sociocultural and Psychological Perspectives*, ed. Elizabeth Mintz and Richard J. Parmentier (New York: Academic Press, 1985).

10. Margaret Mead, *Blackberry Winter: My Earlier Years* (New York: William Morrow, 1975), 227–242.

11. Charles Taylor, *Sources of the Self: The Making of Modern Identity* (Cambridge University Press, 1989), 289.

12. Randolph Bourne, "Trans-National America," in *The American Intellectual Tradition: A Sourcebook*, ed. David A. Hollinger and Charles Capper (Oxford University Press, 1997); Waldo David Frank, *Our America* (New York: Boni & Liveright, 1919).

13. Harold E. Stearns, *America Now: An Inquiry into Civilization in the United States by Thirty-six Americans* (New York: The Literary Guild of America, 1938); Harold E. Stearns, ed., *Civilization in the United States: An Inquiry by Thirty Americans* (New York: Harcourt, Brace, 1922).

14. Malcolm Cowley, *Exile's Return: A Literary Odyssey of the 1920s* (1934; repr., London: The Bodley Head, 1951), 214.

15. Richard H. Pells, *Radical Visions and American Dreams: Culture and Thought in the Depression Years* (Urbana: University of Illinois Press, 1998), 100.

16. Pells, *Radical Visions*, 95–97.

17. John Steinbeck, *The Grapes of Wrath* (New York: Viking, 1939).

18. James Agee and Walker Evans, *Let Us Now Praise Famous Men: Three Tenant Families* (Boston: Houghton Mifflin, 1941).

19. Pells, *Radical Visions*, 113–114; Walter Susman, *Culture as History: The Transformation of American Society in the Twentieth Century* (New York: Pantheon Books, 1984), 53.

20. Ruth Fulton Benedict, Letter to Margaret Mead, April 2, 1932, Box B1, file 5, Margaret Mead Papers.

21. Ruth Fulton Benedict, Letter to Margaret Mead, October 9, 1932, in *An Anthropologist at Work: Writings of Ruth Fulton Benedict*, ed. Margaret Mead (Boston: Houghton Mifflin, 1959), 323.

22. Max Bickerton, Letter to Reo Franklin Fortune and Margaret Mead, December 12, 1929, Reo Franklin Fortune Papers, Alexander Turnbull Library.

23. Reo Franklin Fortune, Letter to Bronislaw Malinowski, November 26, 1932, Box N92, file 2, Margaret Mead Papers.

24. Margaret Mead, Letter to Bella Weitzner, October 15, 1931, Box I6, file 10, Margaret Mead Papers.

25. Margaret Mead, Letter to Clark Wissler, October 1, 1931, Box N92, file 1, Margaret Mead Papers.

26. Margaret Mead, Letter to Emily Fogg Mead, November 5, 1931, Box N92, file 2, Margaret Mead Papers.

27. Margaret Mead, Letter to family and friends, January 15, 1932, Box 92, file 3, Margaret Mead Papers.

28. Mead, *Blackberry Winter*, 220.

29. For sympathetic and insightful accounts of Fortune's travels during this period and the impact of these travels on his ethnography, see Lisa Dobrin and Ira Bashkow, "'Pigs for Dance Songs': Reo Fortune's Empathetic Ethnography of the Arapesh Roads," in *Histories of Anthropology Annual, Vol. 2*, ed. Regna Darnell and Frederic W. Gleach (Lincoln: University of Nebraska Press, 2006); Paul Roscoe, "Margaret Mead, Reo Fortune, and Mountain Arapesh Warfare," *American Anthropologist* 105, no. 3 (2003).

30. Margaret Mead, Letter to Emily Fogg Mead, July 31, 1932, Box N92, file 2, Margaret Mead Papers.

31. Bronislaw Malinowski, "Introduction," in *Sorcerers of Dobu*, ed. Reo Franklin Fortune (London: G. Routledge & Sons, 1932), xxiv.

32. C. W. Hart, Review of *Growing Up in New Guinea* by Margaret Mead, *Man* 32 (June 1932).

33. Margaret Mead, Letter to family and friends, 1932: Series IV Bulletin 1, Box N92, file 4, Margaret Mead Papers.

34. Emily Fogg Mead, Letter to Ruth Fulton Benedict, November 26, 1932, Box O38, file 3, Margaret Mead Papers.

35. Mead, *Blackberry Winter*, 223. Nancy McDowell, drawing on Mead's and Fortune's field notes, in conjunction with her experience of a contiguous group plus a short period with the Mundugumor, argues that Mead herself misunderstood their kinship, conflating "descent and affect, structure and sentiment." Nancy McDowell, *The Mundugumor: From the Fieldnotes of Margaret Mead and Reo Fortune* (Washington, DC: Smithsonian Institution Press, 1991), 28.

36. Margaret Mead, Letter to Emily Fogg Mead, October 25, 1932, Box N92, file 2, Margaret Mead Papers. Bateson was "coming" for a long time. The government anthropologist, Chinnery, wrote regular reports, even while the couple was in Aliatoa, of Bateson's imminent arrival.

37. Margaret Mead, Letter to Ruth Fulton Benedict, December 26, 1932, Addition III, Box S4, file 1, Margaret Mead Papers.

38. Cited in Lipset, *Gregory Bateson,* 130.

39. Gregory Bateson, Letter to Bronislaw Malinowski, December 30, 1932, LSE/ Malinowski Papers/7/10.

40. M. V. [Fluff] Cobb, Letter to Margaret Mead, May 5, 1932, Box N92, file 1, Margaret Mead Papers.

41. Mead to Benedict, December 26, 1932.

42. Mead, *Blackberry Winter,* 227.

43. Margaret Mead, Letter to family and friends, February 1, 1933, Box 92, file 3, Margaret Mead Papers.

44. Mead to Benedict, December 26, 1932.

45. Mead to family and friends, February 1, 1933.

46. Margaret Mead, Letter to Ruth Fulton Benedict, January 16, 1933, Addition III, Box S4, file 1, Margaret Mead Papers.

47. Margaret Mead, Letter to Ruth Fulton Benedict, January 28, 1933, Addition III, Box S4, file 1, Margaret Mead Papers.

48. Margaret Mead, Letter to Ruth Fulton Benedict, February 14, 1933, Addition III, Box S4, file 1, Margaret Mead Papers.

49. Bateson to Malinowski, December 30, 1932.

50. Margaret Mead, Letter to Ruth Fulton Benedict, March 9, 1933, Addition III, Box S4, file 1, Margaret Mead Papers.

51. Howard, *Margaret Mead,* 161.

52. Margaret Mead, Letter to Ruth Fulton Benedict, June 15, 1933, Addition III, Box S4, file 1, Margaret Mead Papers.

53. Howard, *Margaret Mead,* 160–161.

54. Reo Franklin Fortune, Letter to Bronislaw Malinowski, January 12, 1937, LSE/ Malinowski/7/8.

55. For sympathetic explications of the "squares" theory, which Mead and Bateson developed and of which this document is a precursor, see Lois Banner, "Mannish Women, Passive Men, and Constitutional Types: Margaret Mead's *Sex and Temperament in Three Primitive Societies* as a Response to Ruth Benedict's *Patterns of Culture,*" *Signs: A Journal of Women in Culture and Society* 28, no. 3 (2003); Gerald Sullivan, "A Four-fold Humanity: Margaret Mead and Psychological Types," *Journal of the History of the Behavioral Sciences* 40, no. 2 (2004); Gerald Sullivan, "Of Feys and Culture Planners: Margaret Mead and Purposive Activity as Value," in *Reading Benedict, Reading*

Mead: Feminism, Race and Imperial Visions, ed. Lois Banner and Dolores Janiewski (Baltimore: Johns Hopkins University Press, 2004).

56. Margaret Mead, Summary of Statement of the Problem of Personality and Culture, typescript, 1933, Box I10, file 4, Margaret Mead Papers.

57. Fortune to Malinowski, January 12, 1937.

58. Margaret Mead, Letter to Ruth Fulton Benedict, June 7, 1933, Box TR1, file 9, Margaret Mead Papers.

59. Mead to Benedict, June 16, 1933.

60. Reo Franklin Fortune, Letter to Gregory Bateson, [early December 1934 or 1935], Addition III, Box S1, file 4, Margaret Mead Papers; Reo Franklin Fortune, Letter to Gregory Bateson, [mid-1933], Addition III, Box S1, file 4, Margaret Mead Papers.

61. Margaret Mead, Letter to Ruth Fulton Benedict, August 26, 1933, Addition III, Box S4, file 1, Margaret Mead Papers.

62. Ruth Fulton Benedict, Letter to Margaret Mead, July 19, 1933, Addition III, Box S5, file 7, Margaret Mead Papers.

63. Ruth Fulton Benedict, Letter to Gregory Bateson, October 26, 1933, Addition III, Box S1, file 3, Margaret Mead Papers.

64. William E. Leuchtenburg, *Franklin Roosevelt and the New Deal 1932–1940* (New York: Harper & Row, 1963), 41–62.

65. Frank had been an intimate of Randolph Bourne at Columbia and went on to be a lifelong friend and familial supporter of Mead. She lived with the Franks throughout the war, and they raised Mary Catherine Bateson during the long periods when Mead and Bateson were out of New York engaged in war work.

66. William C. Manson, "Abram Kardiner and the Neo-Freudian Alternative in Culture and Personality," in *Malinowski, Rivers, Benedict and Others: Essays on Culture and Personality,* ed. George W. Stocking (Madison: University of Wisconsin Press, 1986), 78; Margaret Mead, "Retrospect and Prospect," in *Anthropology and Human Behavior,* ed. T. Gladwin and W. Sturtevant (Washington, DC: Anthropological Society of Washington, 1962), 127–128.

67. Mead to family and friends, January 15, 1932.

68. Mead, *Sex and Temperament,* 279.

69. Mead, *Sex and Temperament,* 281.

70. See, for example, Hortense Powdermaker, "Primitive Ideals for Men and Women," *Saturday Review of Literature,* 1935, Box L4, file 1, Margaret Mead Papers.

71. Mead, *Sex and Temperament,* 283.

72. Mead, *Sex and Temperament,* 284.

73. Mead, *Sex and Temperament,* 290.

74. Mead, *Sex and Temperament,* 295.

75. Mead, *Sex and Temperament,* 291.

76. Mead, *Sex and Temperament,* 295.

77. Mead, *Sex and Temperament*, 301.

78. Mead, *Sex and Temperament*, 291.

79. Mead, *Sex and Temperament*, 298.

80. Mead, *Sex and Temperament*, 293.

81. Mead, *Sex and Temperament*, 292–293.

82. Mead, *Sex and Temperament*, 306.

83. Mead, *Sex and Temperament*, 309.

84. See various letters from Eichelberger to Mead and Benedict in file B4 of the Mead papers. Mead, in turn, took care of her friend, sending her gold for Christmas of 1932. Marie Eichelberger, Letter to Margaret Mead, December 27, 1932, Box B4, file 2, Margaret Mead Papers; Marie Eichelberger, Letter to Ruth Fulton Benedict, Tuesday, n.d., Box B4, file 2, Margaret Mead Papers.

85. Fortune to Bateson, 1935; Fortune to Bateson, 1934 or 1935.

86. Mead, *Sex and Temperament*, 293.

87. Reo Franklin Fortune, Letter to Bronislaw Malinowski, April 20, 1937, LSE/ Malinowski.

88. Mead later wrote: "Both Gregory and I felt we were deviants, each within our own culture. . . . My own interest in children did not fit the stereotype of the American career woman." Mead, *Blackberry Winter*, 240.

89. Micaela di Leonardo, *Exotics at Home: Anthropologies, Others, American Modernities* (University of Chicago Press, 1998), 191.

90. David Lipset, "Re-reading Sex and Temperament: Margaret Mead's Sepik Triptych and Its Ethnographic Critics," *Anthropological Quarterly* 76, no. 4 (2003), 712.

91. Ralph Linton, Review of *Sex and Temperament in Three Primitive Societies* by Margaret Mead, *Madison Capitol Times*, June 6, 1935, clipping, Box L4, file 1, Margaret Mead Papers.

92. Ruth Fulton Benedict, Review of *Sex and Temperament in Three Primitive Societies* by Margaret Mead, *New York Herald Tribune*, June 2, 1935, clipping, Box L4, file 1, Margaret Mead Papers.

93. Richard Thurnwald, Review of *Sex and Temperament in Three Primitive Societies* by Margaret Mead, *American Anthropologist* 38, no. 4 (1936).

94. Margaret Mead, "A Reply to a Review of *Sex and Temperament in Three Primitive Societies*," *American Anthropologist* 39, no. 1 (1937).

95. "Gulliver in New Guinea," *Cincinnati Enquirer*, May 25, 1935, clipping, Box L4, file 1, Margaret Mead Papers; Joseph Wood Krutch, "Men and Women," *Nation*, May 29, 1935, clipping, Box L4, file 1, Margaret Mead Papers.

96. Florence Finch Kelly, "A Challenging View of the Sexes," *New York Times Review of Books*, May 26, 1935, clipping, Box L4, file 1, Margaret Mead Papers.

97. Michael Szalay, *New Deal Modernism: American Literature and the Invention of the Welfare State* (Durham, NC: Duke University Press, 2000), 3.

98. Lawrence W. Levine, *The Unpredictable Past: Explorations in American Cultural History* (New York: Oxford University Press, 1993), 206–230.

99. Charles R. Hearn, *The American Dream in the Great Depression* (Westport: Greenwood Press, 1977), 193.

100. Susman, *Culture as History.*

101. Randolph Bourne, "The Cult of the Best," *New Republic,* January 15, 1916.

102. Laura Browder, *Rousing the Nation: Radical Culture in Depression America* (Amherst: University of Massachusetts Press, 1998), 174–182.

103. Browder, *Rousing the Nation,* 177.

104. Alfred Kroeber, "The Superorganic," *American Anthropologist* 19, no. 2 (1917): 163–213.

105. Edward Sapir, "Culture, Genuine and Spurious," *American Journal of Sociology* 29 (1924): 311.

106. It appears that Hays interviewed Boas extensively before setting up the Production Code Office, and there may have been plans for anthropological involvement in the preproduction phase of film planning. Ruth Fulton Benedict, Letter to Margaret Mead, March 10, 1933, Box B1, file 5, Margaret Mead Papers.

Chapter 7: On Creating a Usable Culture

1. Professor W. G. Minn, verbal testimony, August 10, 1953. Folder 2, New Zealand Special Committee on Moral Delinquency in Children and Adolescents. MS papers 2384, Alexander Turnbull Library, Wellington.

2. Randolph Bourne, "Trans-National America," in *The American Intellectual Tradition: A Sourcebook,* ed. David A. Hollinger and Charles Capper (Oxford University Press, 1997), 175.

3. Margaret Mead, *Sex and Temperament in Three Primitive Societies* (New York: William Morrow, 1935), 290.

4. Margaret Mead, "The Role of the Individual in Samoan Culture," *Journal of the Royal Anthropological Institute* 55 (July–December 1928), 495.

5. Walter Benn Michaels, *Our America: Nativism, Modernism, and Pluralism* (Durham, NC: Duke University Press, 1995).

6. Lois Banner, *Intertwined Lives: Margaret Mead, Ruth Benedict and Their Circle* (New York: Knopf, 2003); Hilary Lapsley, *Margaret Mead & Ruth Benedict: The Kinship of Women* (Amherst: University of Massachusetts Press, 1999).

7. George W. Stocking, "Anthropology and the Science of the Irrational: Malinowski's Encounter with Freudian Psychoanalysis," in *Malinowski, Rivers, Benedict, and Others: Essays on Culture and Personality,* ed. George W. Stocking (Madison: University of Wisconsin Press, 1986).

8. David A. Hollinger, *In the American Province: Studies in the History and Historiography of Ideas* (Bloomington: Indiana University Press, 1985), 57.

9. Hollinger, *In the American Province*, 58.

10. Hollinger, *In the American Province*, 57.

11. Gregory Castle, *Modernism and the Celtic Revival* (Cambridge University Press, 2001); Susan Hegeman, *Patterns for America: Modernism and the Concept of Culture* (Princeton University Press, 1999); Mark Manganaro, *Culture 1922: The Emergence of a Concept* (Princeton University Press, 2002); Michaels, *Our America*.

12. Bourne, "Trans-National America," 180.

13. Randolph Bourne, *Youth and Life* (Boston: Houghton Mifflin, 1913).

14. David A. Hollinger and Charles Capper, *The American Intellectual Tradition: A Sourcebook*, 3rd ed. (New York: Oxford University Press, 1997).

15. Emily Fogg Mead, Letter to Margaret Mead, July 19, 1933, Box A7, file 4, Margaret Mead Papers.

16. Dawn Cook, "100 Most Influential Books of the Century: Booklists for Adults," Boston Public Library, 2000, www.bpl.org/research/AdultBooklists/influential.htm (accessed November 13, 2006).

17. Charles McGrath, ed., *Books of the Century: A Hundred Years of Authors, Ideas and Literature* (New York: Crown, 1999).

18. Mark Henrie, "The Fifty Worst (and Best) Books of the Century," *Intercollegiate Review* 35 (2000).

References

Archival sources

Franz Boas Papers, Library of the American Philosophical Society, Philadelphia
Reo Franklin Fortune Papers, Alexander Turnbull Library, Wellington, New Zealand
Margaret Mead Papers, Library of Congress, Washington, DC
Bronislaw Malinowski Papers, London School of Economics (LSE), London, England

Other sources

Abrahams, Edward. *The Lyrical Left: Randolph Bourne, Alfred Stieglitz and the Origins of Cultural Radicalism in America.* Charlottesville: University Press of Virginia, 1986.

"Adolescence Not a Dangerous Period of Life in Samoa." *St. Louis Globe-Democrat,* December 29, 1929. Clipping, Box L3, file 1, Margaret Mead Papers.

Agee, James, and Walker Evans. *Let Us Now Praise Famous Men: Three Tenant Families.* Boston: Houghton Mifflin, 1941.

Allen, Frederick Lewis. *Only Yesterday: An Informal History of the 1920s.* New York: Harper & Row 1964.

"American Girl to Study Cannibals." *Boston Post,* May 24, 1928. Clipping, Box L3, file 1, Margaret Mead Papers.

Anderson, Benedict. *Imagined Communities: Reflections on the Origin and Spread of Nationalism.* 2nd ed. London: Verso, 1991.

Anderson, Nels. "In the Light of Samoa." *Survey* 62 (January 15, 1929). Clipping, Box L3, file 1, Margaret Mead Papers.

Banner, Lois. *Intertwined Lives: Margaret Mead, Ruth Benedict and Their Circle.* New York: Knopf, 2003.

———. "Mannish Women, Passive Men, and Constitutional Types: Margaret Mead's *Sex and Temperament in Three Primitive Societies* as a Response to Ruth Benedict's *Patterns of Culture.*" *Signs: A Journal of Women in Culture and Society* 28, no. 3 (2003): 833–858.

Banta, Martha. *Imaging American Women: Ideas and Ideals in Cultural History.* New York: Columbia University Press, 1987.

Barkan, Elazar, and Ronald Bush, eds. *Prehistories of the Future: The Primitivist Project and the Culture of Modernism.* Stanford University Press, 1995.

Barnes, R. H. *Two Crows Denies It: A History of Controversy in Omaha Sociology.* Lincoln: University of Nebraska Press, 1984.

Bateson, Gregory. Letter to Bronislaw Malinowski, December 30, 1932. LSE/Malinowski Papers/7/10.

——. *Naven: A Survey of the Problems Suggested by a Composite Picture of the Culture of a New Guinea Tribe Drawn from Three Points of View.* Cambridge University Press, 1936.

Bender, Thomas. *New York Intellect.* Baltimore: Johns Hopkins University Press, 1987.

Benedict, Ruth. Letter to Margaret Mead, January 20, 1932. AAW Copy 2, B/B61 Boas Papers.

Benedict, Ruth Fulton. Letter to Franz Boas, June 26, 1925. Film 1263, Reel 15, B/B61 Boas Papers.

——. Letter to Emily Fogg Mead, November 11, 1931. Box A7, file 3, Margaret Mead Papers.

——. Letter to the American Library Association, February 2, 1932. Box I6, file 17, Margaret Mead Papers.

——. Letter to Margaret Mead, April 2, 1932. Box B1, file 5, Margaret Mead Papers.

——. Letter to Margaret Mead, October 9, 1932. In *An Anthropologist at Work: Writings of Ruth Fulton Benedict,* edited by Margaret Mead, 323. Boston: Houghton Mifflin, 1959.

——. Letter to "Dear Isabel," January 11, 1933. Box O38, file 4, Margaret Mead Papers.

——. Letter to Margaret Mead, July 19, 1933. Addition III, Box S5, file 7, Margaret Mead Papers.

——. Letter to Gregory Bateson, October 26, 1933. Addition III, Box S1, file 3, Margaret Mead Papers.

——. *Patterns of Culture.* New York: Columbia University Press, 1934.

——. "Primitive Life in New Guinea." *New York Times,* November 16, 1930. Clipping, Box L3, file 3, Margaret Mead Papers.

——. "Psychological Types in the Cultures of the Southwest." In *Proceedings of the XXIII International Congress of Americanists, September 1928.* University of Chicago Press, 1930.

——. Review of *Sex and Temperament in Three Primitive Societies* by Margaret Mead. *New York Herald Tribune,* June 2, 1935. Clipping, Box L4, file 1, Margaret Mead Papers.

——. "The White Man and the Indian." *New York Herald Tribune Books,* November 12, 1932. Clipping, Box L3, file 3, Margaret Mead Papers.

Benson, Susan Porter. "Living on the Margin: Working-Class Marriages and Familial Survival Strategies in the United States, 1919–1941." In *The Sex of Things: Gender and Consumption in Historical Perspective*, edited by Victoria de Grazia and Ellen Furlough, 212–243. Los Angeles: University of California Press, 1996.

Bickerton, Max. Letter to Reo Franklin Fortune and Margaret Mead, December 12, 1929. Reo Franklin Fortune Papers, Alexander Turnbull Library.

Blake, Casey Nelson. *Beloved Community: The Cultural Criticism of Randolph Bourne, Van Wyck Brooks, Waldo Frank, and Lewis Mumford.* Chapel Hill: University of North Carolina Press, 1990.

Boas, Franz. Letter to Margaret Mead, July 14, 1925. Box B2, file 3, Margaret Mead Papers.

———. Letter to Ruth Fulton Benedict, July 16, 1925. AAW Copy 2, B/B61 Boas Papers.

———. Letter to Margaret Mead, February 15, 1926. Box N1, file 1, Margaret Mead Papers.

———. *The Mind of Primitive Man.* New York: Columbia University Press, 1911.

———. "New Evidence in Regard to the Instability of Human Types." In *Proceedings of the National Academy of Sciences of the United States of America* 2, no. 12 (1916): 713–718.

Boon, James. "Mead's Mediations: Some Semiotics from the Sepik, by Way of Bateson, on to Bali." In *Semiotic Mediations: Sociocultural and Psychological Perspectives,* edited by Elizabeth Mintz and Richard J. Parmentier, 333–357. New York: Academic Press, 1985.

Bourne, Randolph. "The Cult of the Best." *New Republic* 5 (January 15, 1916): 275–277.

———. "Trans-National America." In *The American Intellectual Tradition: A Sourcebook,* edited by David A. Hollinger and Charles Capper, 170–188. Oxford University Press, 1997.

———. "Trans-National America." *Atlantic Monthly* 118 (1916): 86–97.

———. "Twilight of the Idols." *Seven Arts* 2 (October 1917): 688–702.

———. "The War and the Intellectuals." *Seven Arts* 2 (June 1917): 133–146.

———. *Youth and Life.* Boston: Houghton Mifflin, 1913.

Brooks, Van Wyck. *America's Coming of Age.* New York: B. W. Huebsch, 1915.

———. "America's Coming of Age." In *Van Wyck Brooks: The Early Years,* 2nd ed., edited by Claire Sprague, 79–158. Boston: Northeastern University Press, 1993.

———. "On Creating a Usable Past." *Dial* (1918): 337–341.

———. *The Wine of the Puritans.* London: Sisley's, 1908.

———. "The Wine of the Puritans." In *Van Wyck Brooks: The Early Years,* 2nd ed., edited by Claire Sprague, 1–60. Boston: Northeastern University Press, 1993.

Browder, Laura. *Rousing the Nation: Radical Culture in Depression America.* Amherst: University of Massachusetts Press, 1998.

Bunzel, Ruth. "Introduction: Building a Science of Man in America: The Classical Period in American Anthropology, 1900–1920." In *The Golden Age of American*

Anthropology, edited by Margaret Mead and Ruth Bunzel, 400–402. New York: George Braziller, 1960.

Burnham, John. "The New Psychology." In *1915, The Cultural Moment: The New Politics, the New Woman, the New Psychology, the New Art and the New Theatre in America*, edited by Adele Heller and Lois Rudnick, 117–127. New Brunswick, NJ: Rutgers University Press, 1991.

Burnham, John Chynoweth. *Psychoanalysis and American Medicine, 1894–1918: Medicine, Society and Culture*. New York: International Universities Press, 1967.

"But I Came of Age in Samoa." *Esquire*, December 1928. Cartoon clipping, Box L3, file 1, Margaret Mead Papers.

Caplan, Eric. *Mind Games: American Culture and the Birth of Psychotherapy*. Berkeley: University of California Press, 1998.

Carby, Hazel. "The Politics of Fiction, Anthropology, and the Folk: Zora Neal Hurston." In *New Essays on Their Eyes Were Watching God*, edited by Michael Awkward, 71–93. Cambridge University Press, 1990.

Castle, Gregory. *Modernism and the Celtic Revival*. Cambridge University Press, 2001.

Chabot, C. Barry. *Writers for the Nation: American Literary Modernism*. Tuscaloosa: University of Alabama Press, 1997.

Chase, Stuart. *Mexico: A Study of Two Americas*. New York: MacMillan, 1937.

Clarke, Edith. "Water Babies." *Saturday Review of Literature*, May 2, 1931, 791–792. Clipping, Box L3, file 3, Margaret Mead Papers.

Clayton, Bruce. *Forgotten Prophet: The Life of Randolph Bourne*. Baton Rouge: Louisiana State University Press, 1984.

Clifford, James. "Introduction." In *Writing Culture: The Poetics and Politics of Ethnography*, edited by James Clifford and George Marcus, 1–26. Berkeley: University of California Press, 1986.

———. *The Predicament of Culture: Twentieth Century Ethnography, Literature and Art*. Cambridge, MA: Harvard University Press, 1988.

Clifford, James, and George Marcus, eds. *Writing Culture: The Poetics and Politics of Ethnography*. Berkeley: University of California Press, 1986.

Cobb, M. V. [Fluff]. Letter to Margaret Mead, May 5, 1932. Box N92, file 1, Margaret Mead Papers.

Cook, Dawn. "100 Most Influential Books of the Century: Booklists for Adults." Boston: Boston Public Library, 2000, www.bpl.org/research/AdultBooklists/influential .htm (accessed November 13, 2006).

Cowley, Malcolm. *Exile's Return: A Literary Odyssey of the 1920s*. New York: Viking, 1934.

———. *Exile's Return: A Literary Odyssey of the 1920s*. London: The Bodley Head, 1951.

Croly, Herbert. *The Promise of American Life*. New York: Houghton Mifflin, 1909.

―――. *The Promise of American Life*. Edited by Arthur M. Schlesinger. Cambridge, MA: The Belknap Press of Harvard University Press, 1965.

Cushman, Philip. *Constructing the Self, Constructing America*. Reading, MA: Addison-Wesley, 1995.

Deacon, Desley. *Elsie Clews Parsons: Inventing Modern Life*. University of Chicago Press, 1997.

Dell, Floyd. *Love in the Machine Age: A Psychological Study of the Transition from a Patriarchal Society*. New York: Farrar, 1930.

Deloria, Philip. *Playing Indian*. New Haven, CT: Yale University Press, 1998.

D'Emilio, John, and Estelle Freedman. *Intimate Matters: A History of Sexuality in America*. 2nd ed. New York: Harper & Row, 1997.

Dewey, John. *Individualism Old and New*. London: George Allen & Unwin, 1931.

di Leonardo, Micaela. *Exotics at Home: Anthropologies, Others, American Modernities*. Chicago: University of Chicago Press, 1998.

Dobrin, Lisa, and Ira Bashkow. "'Pigs for Dance Songs': Reo Fortune's Empathetic Ethnography of the Arapesh Roads." In *Histories of Anthropology Annual, Vol. 2*, edited by Regna Darnell and Frederic W. Gleach, 123–154. Lincoln: University of Nebraska Press, 2006.

Doherty, Thomas. *Pre-Code Hollywood: Sex, Immorality and Insurrection in American Cinema, 1930–34*. New York: Columbia University Press, 1999.

Dorreboom, Iris. *The Challenge of Our Time: Woodrow Wilson, Herbert Croly, Randolph Bourne and the Making of Modern America*. Amsterdam: Rodoipi, 1991.

Dorsey, George Amos. *Why We Behave Like Human Beings*. New York: Harper & Brothers, 1925.

Dos Passos, John. *1919*. New York: Harcourt & Brace, 1932.

Douglas, Ann. *The Feminization of American Culture*. New York: Knopf, 1977.

―――. *Terrible Honesty: Mongrel Manhattan in the 1920s*. New York: Farrar, Strauss & Giroux, 1995.

"Dr. Margaret Mead." 1931. Unsourced clipping, Box L3, file 3, Margaret Mead Papers.

Editor. Correspondence re: *Growing Up in New Guinea* (cf. *Man* [1932]: 174). *Man* 33 (1933): 76.

Eichelberger, Marie. Letter to Margaret Mead, December 27, [1932]. Box B4, file 2, Margaret Mead Papers.

―――. Letter to Ruth Fulton Benedict, Tuesday, n.d. Box B4, file 2, Margaret Mead Papers.

Esteve, Mary. "Shipwreck and Autonomy: Rawls, Reisman, and Oppen in the 1960s." *Yale Journal of Criticism* 18, no. 2 (2005): 323–349.

Fineberg, Jonathan, ed. *Discovering Child Art: Essays on Childhood, Primitivism, and Modernism*. Princeton University Press, 1998.

Fitzgerald, Francis Scott. *This Side of Paradise.* New York: Scribner, 1920.

———. *This Side of Paradise.* Edited by James L. W. West. Cambridge University Press, 1995.

F[orde], C. D. Review of *The Changing Culture of an Indian Tribe* by Margaret Mead. *Man* 33 (September 1933): 154.

Fortune, Reo Franklin. Letter to Bronislaw Malinowski, November 26, 1932. Box N92, file 2, Margaret Mead Papers.

———. Letter to Gregory Bateson, [mid-1933]. Addition III, Box S1, file 4, Margaret Mead Papers.

———. Letter to Gregory Bateson, [early December 1934 or 1935]. Addition III, Box S1, file 4, Margaret Mead Papers.

———. Letter to Bronislaw Malinowski, January 12, 1937. LSE/Malinowski/7/8.

———. Letter to Bronislaw Malinowski, April 20, 1937. LSE/Malinowski Papers.

———. *Sorcerers of Dobu.* London: G. Routledge & Sons, 1932.

Foucault, Michel. *The Care of the Self. The History of Sexuality Vol. 3.* Harmondsworth, UK: Penguin, 1988.

Francis, Patricia (curator), and Mary Wolfskill (co-curator). "Margaret Mead: Human Nature and the Power of Culture." Washington, DC: Library of Congress, 2001, www.loc.gov/exhibits/mead (accessed November 13, 2006).

Frank, Waldo David. *Our America.* New York: Boni & Liveright, 1919.

Freeman, Derek. *Margaret Mead and Samoa: The Making and Unmaking of an Anthropological Myth.* Cambridge, MA: Harvard University Press, 1983.

Geertz, Clifford. *Works and Lives: The Anthropologist as Author.* Stanford: Stanford University Press, 1988.

Gifford, Sandford. "The American Reception of Psychoanalysis." In *1915, The Cultural Moment: The New Politics, the New Woman, the New Psychology, the New Art and the New Theatre in America,* edited by Adele Heller and Lois Rudnick, 128–145. New Brunswick, NJ: Rutgers University Press, 1991.

Gilbert, James Burkhart. *Writers and Partisans: A History of Literary Radicalism in America.* New York: Wiley, 1968.

Goldenweiser, Alexander. Review of *The Changing Culture of an Indian Tribe* by Margaret Mead. *Nation* (1933). Clipping, Box L3, file 3, Margaret Mead Papers.

———. Review of *The Changing Culture of an Indian Tribe* by Margaret Mead. *American Anthropologist* 36, no. 4 (1934): 609–611.

Gordan, Joan, ed. *Margaret Mead: The Complete Bibliography, 1925–1975.* The Hague: Mouton, 1976.

Gorman, Paul R. *Left Intellectuals and Popular Culture in Twentieth Century America.* Chapel Hill: University of North Carolina Press, 1996.

"Gulliver in New Guinea." *Cincinnati Enquirer,* May 25, 1935. Clipping, Box L4, File 1, Margaret Mead Papers.

Gumbrecht, Hans Ulrich. *In 1926: Living on the Edge of Time*. Cambridge, MA: Harvard University Press, 1997.

Hale, Nathan G. *Freud and the Americans: The Beginnings of Psychoanalysis in the United States, 1876–1917*. New York: Oxford University Press, 1971.

Hapke, Laura. *Daughters of the Great Depression: Women, Work and Fiction in the American 1930s*. Athens: University of Georgia Press, 1995.

Hart, C. W. Review of *Growing Up in New Guinea* by Margaret Mead. *Man* 32 (June 1932): 146.

Hays, Terence E. "The 'Tiny Islands': A Comparative Impact on the Larger Discipline?" In *American Anthropology in Micronesia: An Assessment*, edited by Robert C. Kiste and Mac Marshall, 484–514. Honolulu: University of Hawai'i Press, 1999.

Hearn, Charles R. *The American Dream in the Great Depression*. Westport: Greenwood, 1977.

Hegeman, Susan. *Patterns for America: Modernism and the Concept of Culture*. Princeton University Press, 1999.

Heller, Adele, and Lois Rudnick. *1915, The Cultural Moment: The New Politics, the New Woman, the New Psychology, the New Art and the New Theatre in America*. New Brunswick, NJ: Rutgers University Press, 1991.

Hemingway, Ernest. *The Sun Also Rises*. New York: Scribner, 1926.

Henrie, Mark. "The Fifty Worst (and Best) Books of the Century." *Intercollegiate Review* 35 (2000): 3–33.

Henriques, Julian, Wendy Hollway, Cathy Urwin, Couse Venn, and Valerie Walkerdine, eds. *Changing the Subject: Psychology, Social Regulation and Subjectivity*. New York: Methuen, 1984.

Herskovitz, Melville. "Primitive Childhood." *Nation* (February 4, 1931): 131–132. Clipping, Box L3, file 2, Margaret Mead Papers.

Hollinger, David A. *In the American Province: Studies in the History and Historiography of Ideas*. Bloomington: Indiana University Press, 1985.

Hollinger, David A., and Charles Capper. *The American Intellectual Tradition: A Sourcebook*. 3rd ed. Oxford University Press, 1997.

Holt, Edwin Bissell. *The Freudian Wish and Its Place in Ethics*. New York: Henry Holt, 1915.

Hoopes, James. *Van Wyck Brooks: In Search of American Culture*. Amherst: University of Massachusetts Press, 1977.

Howard, Clare. Review of *The Changing Culture of an Indian Tribe* by Margaret Mead. *Barnard College Alumnus Monthly*, December 1932. Clipping, Box L3, file 3, Margaret Mead Papers.

Howard, Jane. *Margaret Mead: A Life*. New York: Simon & Schuster, 1984.

Hulburd, Meritt. Letter to Margaret Mead, November 22, 1930. Box I5, file 2, Margaret Mead Papers.

————. Letter to Margaret Mead, December 9, 1930. Box I5, file 2, Margaret Mead Papers.

Hunt, Caspar. "The Younger Generation in Samoa." *Travel,* April 1929. Clipping, Box L3, file 1, Margaret Mead Papers.

Huxley, Aldous. "The Problem of Faith." *Harpers Magazine,* January 1933. Clipping, Box L3, file 2, Margaret Mead Papers.

Huyssen, Andreas. *After the Great Divide: Modernism, Mass Culture, Postmodernism.* Bloomington: Indiana University Press, 1986.

"John Colton." Internet Broadway Database, www.ibdb.com/person.asp?ID=6793 (accessed November 13, 2006).

Kelly, Florence Finch. "A Challenging View of the Sexes." *New York Times Review of Books,* May 26, 1935. Clipping, Box L4, file 1, Margaret Mead Papers.

Kirchwey, Freda. "This Week: Sex in the South Seas." *Nation* (October 24, 1928): 427. Clipping, Box L3, file 1, Margaret Mead Papers.

Krämer, Augustin. *The Samoa Islands: An Outline of a Monograph with Particular Consideration of German Samoa.* Translated by Theodore Verhaaren. 1902–1903, repr.; Honolulu: University of Hawai'i Press, 1994.

Kroeber, Alfred L. Letter to Margaret Mead, October 23, 1930. Box I4, file 9, Margaret Mead Papers.

————. Review of *Growing Up In New Guinea* by Margaret Mead. *American Anthropologist* 33, no. 2 (1931): 248–250.

————. "The Superorganic." *American Anthropologist* 19, no. 2 (1917): 163–213.

Kroes, Rob, ed. *Highbrow Meets Lowbrow: American Culture as an Intellectual Concern.* Amsterdam: Free University Press, 1988.

Krutch, Joseph Wood. "Men and Women." *Nation,* May 29, 1935. Clipping, Box L4, file 1, Margaret Mead Papers.

Kuklick, Henrika. *The Savage Within: The Social History of British Anthropology, 1885–1945.* Cambridge University Press, 1991.

L. C. M. "Books on the Table: Samoan Adolescence." *Argonaut,* January 19, 1929. Clipping, Box L3, file 1, Margaret Mead Papers.

Lapsley, Hilary. *Margaret Mead & Ruth Benedict: The Kinship of Women.* Amherst: University of Massachusetts Press, 1999.

Leuchtenburg, William E. *Franklin Roosevelt and the New Deal 1932–1940.* New York: Harper & Row, 1963.

Levine, Lawrence W. *The Unpredictable Past: Explorations in American Cultural History.* New York: Oxford University Press, 1993.

Lewis, Sinclair. *Babbitt.* New York: Grosset & Dunlap, 1922.

————. *Main Street.* New York: Alfred Knopf, 1920.

————. *Main Street.* New York: Harcourt, Brace & World, 1948.

Linton, Ralph. Review of *Sex and Temperament in Three Primitive Societies* by Margaret Mead. *Madison Capitol Times,* June 6, 1935. Clipping, Box L4, file 1, Margaret Mead Papers.

Lipset, David. *Gregory Bateson: The Legacy of a Scientist.* Englewood Cliffs, NJ: Prentice Hall, 1980.

———. "Re-reading *Sex and Temperament:* Margaret Mead's Sepik Triptych and Its Ethnographic Critics." *Anthropological Quarterly* 76, no. 4 (2003): 693–713.

Lowie, Robert H. Review of *Coming of Age in Samoa: A Psychological Study of Primitive Youth for Western Civilization* by Margaret Mead. *American Anthropologist* 31, no. 3 (1929): 532–534.

———. Review of *Omaha Secret Societies* by Reo Franklin Fortune. *American Anthropologist* 35, no. 3 (1933): 529–533.

Lutkehaus, Nancy C. "Margaret Mead and the 'Rustling-of-the-Wind-in-the-Palm-Trees' School of Ethnographic Writing." In *Women Writing Culture,* edited by Ruth Behar, 210–224. Berkeley: University of California Press, 1995.

Lynd, Robert S., and Helen Merrell Lynd. *Middletown: A Study in Contemporary American Culture.* New York: Harcourt, Brace, 1929.

Lyons, Andrew P., and Harriet Lyons. *Irregular Connections: A History of Anthropology and Sexuality.* Lincoln: University of Nebraska Press, 2004.

MacMaster, Fanny Fogg. Letter to Margaret Mead, December 1, 1932. Box A4, file 6, Margaret Mead Papers.

Malinowski, Bronislaw. Letter to Margaret Mead, September 22, 1928. Box I2, file 2, Margaret Mead Papers.

———. Letter to Margaret Mead, September 4, 1929. Box C3, file M, Margaret Mead Papers.

———. Letter to Margaret Mead, March 29, 1930. General Correspondence—Letters M—1925–1938, LSE/Malinowski Papers.

———. "Introduction." In *Sorcerers of Dobu,* by Reo Franklin Fortune, xv–xxviii. London: G. Routledge & Sons, 1932.

———. *Sex and Repression in Savage Society.* New York: Meridien, 1927.

Manganaro, Mark. *Culture 1922: The Emergence of a Concept.* Princeton University Press, 2002.

———, ed. *Modernist Anthropology: From Fieldwork to Text.* Princeton University Press, 1990.

Manson, William C. "Abram Kardiner and the Neo-Freudian Alternative in Culture and Personality." In *Malinowski, Rivers, Benedict and Others: Essays on Culture and Personality,* edited by George W. Stocking, 72–94. Madison: University of Wisconsin Press, 1986.

McClintock, Anne. *Imperial Leather: Race, Gender, and Sexuality in the Colonial Contest.* London: Routledge, 1995.

McDermott, Ray. "A Century of Margaret Mead." *Teachers College Record* 103, no. 5 (2001): 843–867.

McDowell, Nancy. *The Mundugumor: From the Fieldnotes of Margaret Mead and Reo Fortune.* Washington, DC: Smithsonian Institution Press, 1991.

McGrath, Charles, ed. *Books of the Century: A Hundred Years of Authors, Ideas and Literature.* New York: Crown, 1999.

Mead, Emily Fogg. Letter to Ruth Fulton Benedict, November 26, 1932. Box O38, file 3, Margaret Mead Papers.

———. Letter to Margaret Mead, July 19, 1933. Box A7, file 4, Margaret Mead Papers.

Mead, Margaret. "Adolescence in Primitive and Modern Society." In *The New Generation: The Intimate Problems of Parents and Children,* edited by V. F. Calverton and S. D. Schmalhausen, 169–188. New York: Macauley, 1930.

———. "Are We Mature?" *Thinker* 2 (December 7, 1930): 25–32.

———. *Blackberry Winter: My Earlier Years.* New York: William Morrow, 1975.

———. *The Changing Culture of an Indian Tribe.* New York: Columbia University Press, 1932.

———. *The Changing Culture of an Indian Tribe.* New York: Capricorn Books, 1966.

———. "Civil Government for Samoa." *Nation* 132 (February 25, 1931): 226–228.

———. *Coming of Age in Samoa: A Psychological Study of Primitive Youth for Western Civilization.* 1928, repr.; New York: William Morrow, 1961.

———. "Group Intelligence Tests and Linguistic Disability among Italian Children." *School and Society* 25, no. 642 (1927): 465–468.

———. *Growing Up in New Guinea: A Comparative Study of Primitive Education.* New York: William Morrow, 1930.

———. *Growing Up in New Guinea: A Comparative Study of Primitive Education,* English ed. London: G. Routledge & Sons, 1931.

———. *Growing Up in New Guinea: A Comparative Study of Primitive Education.* New York: Perennial, 2001.

———. "Growing Up in the South Seas." *Forum: The Magazine of Controversy* 87 (May 1932): 285–288. Box I6, file 12, Margaret Mead Papers.

———. *An Inquiry into the Question of Cultural Stability in Polynesia.* New York: Columbia University Press, 1928.

———. "Introduction." In *Margaret Mead: The Complete Bibliography 1925–1975,* edited by Joan Gordan, 1–23. The Hague: Mouton, 1976.

———. "An Investigation of the Thought of Primitive Children, with Special Reference to Animism." *Journal of the Royal Anthropological Institute* 62 (January–June 1932): 172–190.

———. "Jealousy: Primitive and Civilized." In *Woman's Coming of Age: A Symposium,* edited by Samuel Schmalhausen and V. F. Calverton, 35–48. New York: Liveright, 1931.

———. *Kinship in the Admiralty Islands.* New York: American Museum of Natural History, 1934.

———. Letter to "Dear Grandma," March 11, 1923. Box A17, file 3, Margaret Mead Papers.

———. Letter to Ruth Fulton Benedict, August 30, 1924. Addition III, Box S3, file 2, Margaret Mead Papers.

———. Letter to Ruth Fulton Benedict, September 8, 1924. AAW Copy 2, B/B61 Boas Papers.

———. Letter to Franz Boas, January 5, 1925. Box N1, file 1, Margaret Mead Papers.

———. Letter to family and friends, August 1925. Box N4, file 4, Margaret Mead Papers.

———. Letter to family and friends, September 2, 1925. Box N4, file 1, Margaret Mead Papers.

———. Letter to family and friends, September 20, 1925, Box N4, file 1, Margaret Mead Papers.

———. Letter to family and friends, October 31, 1925. Box N4, file 1, Margaret Mead Papers.

———. Letter to family and friends, December 11, 1925. Box N4, file 1, Margaret Mead Papers.

———. Letter to Franz Boas, December 13, 1925. Box N1, file 1, Margaret Mead Papers.

———. Letter to Franz Boas, January 16, 1926. Film 1263, Reel 15, B/B61 Boas Papers.

———. Letter to family and friends, February 9, 1926. Box N4, file 1, Margaret Mead Papers.

———. Letter to Franz Boas, March 14, 1926. Film 1263, Reel 15, B/B61 Boas Papers.

———. Letter to E. S. C. Handy, December 21, 1926. Box I4, file 16, Margaret Mead Papers.

———. Letter to William Fielding Ogburn, April 27, 1927. In *To Cherish the Life of the World: Selected Letters of Margaret Mead*, edited by Margaret M. Caffrey and Patricia A. Francis, 243–244. New York: Basic Books, 2006.

———. Letter to Emily Fogg Mead, March 15, 1928. Box A7, file 3, Margaret Mead Papers.

———. Letter to Emily Fogg Mead, May 19, 1928. Box A7, file 4, Margaret Mead Papers.

———. Letter to Bronislaw Malinowski, August 9, 1928. Box I2, file 1, Margaret Mead Papers.

———. Letter to Ruth Fulton Benedict, October 18, 1928. AAW Copy 2, B/B61 Boas Papers.

———. Letter to family and friends, November 22, 1928. Box N40, file 1, Margaret Mead Papers.

———. Letter to family and friends, December 16, 1928. Box N40, file 1, Margaret Mead Papers.

———. Letter to Franz Boas, January 6, 1929. Film 1263, Reel 15, B/B61 Boas Papers.

———. Letter to family and friends, February 14, 1929. Box N40, file 1, Margaret Mead Papers.

———. Letter to family and friends, March 27, 1929. Box N40, file 1, Margaret Mead Papers.

———. Letter to Bronislaw Malinowski, January 28, 1930. Box C3, file M, Margaret Mead Papers.

———. Letter to Franz Boas, July 16, 1930. Box N119, file 11, Margaret Mead Papers.

———. Letter to Ruth Fulton Benedict, July 21, 1930. AAW Copy 2, B/B61 Boas Papers.

———. Letter to Clark Wissler, August 6, 1930. Box I6, file 10, Margaret Mead Papers.

———. Letter to Bronislaw Malinowski, August 9, 1930. Box N19, file 11, Margaret Mead Papers.

———. Letter to Clark Wissler, August 15, 1930. Box I6, file 10, Margaret Mead Papers.

———. Letter to Emily Fogg Mead, October 16, 1930. Box A7, file 4, Margaret Mead Papers.

———. Letter to Alfred Kroeber, May 1, 1931. Box C3, file K, Margaret Mead Papers.

———. Letter to Clark Wissler, October 1, 1931. Box N92, file 1, Margaret Mead Papers.

———. Letter to Bella Weitzner, October 15, 1931. Box I6, file 10, Margaret Mead Papers.

———. Letter to Emily Fogg Mead, November 5, 1931. Box N92, file 2, Margaret Mead Papers.

———. Letter to family and friends, January 15, 1932. Box 92, file 3, Margaret Mead Papers.

———. Letter to Ruth Fulton Benedict, June 16, 1932. Addition III, Box S3, file 10, Margaret Mead Papers.

———. Letter to Ruth Fulton Benedict, December 26, 1932. Addition III, Box S4, file 1, Margaret Mead Papers.

———. Letter to family and friends, [1932: Series IV Bulletin 1], Box N92, file 4, Margaret Mead Papers.

———. Letter to family and friends, 1932. Box N92, file 4, Margaret Mead Papers.

———. Letter to Ruth Fulton Benedict, January 16, 1933. Addition III, Box S4, file 1, Margaret Mead Papers.

———. Letter to Ruth Fulton Benedict, January 28, 1933. Addition III, Box S4, file 1, Margaret Mead Papers.

———. Letter to family and friends, February 1, 1933. Box 92, file 3, Margaret Mead Papers.

———. Letter to Ruth Fulton Benedict, February 14, 1933. Addition III, Box S4, file 1, Margaret Mead Papers.

———. Letter to Ruth Fulton Benedict, March 9, 1933. Addition III, Box S4, file 1, Margaret Mead Papers.

———. Letter to Ruth Fulton Benedict, June 7, 1933. Box TR1, file 9, Margaret Mead Papers.

———. Letter to Ruth Fulton Benedict, June 15, 1933. Addition III, Box S4, file 1, Margaret Mead Papers.

———. Letter to Ruth Fulton Benedict, August 26, 1933. Addition III, Box S4, file 1, Margaret Mead Papers.

———. Letter to Reo Franklin Fortune, June 19, 1934. In *To Cherish the Life of the World: Selected Letters of Margaret Mead*, edited by Margaret M. Caffrey and Patricia A. Francis, 98–100. New York: Basic Books, 2006.

———. *Letters from the Field, 1925–1965*. New York: Harper & Row, 1977.

———. "Living with the Natives of Melanesia." *Natural History* 31, no. 1 (1931): 62–74.

———. "Margaret Mead." In *A History of Psychology in Autobiography*, edited by Gardner Lindzey, 293–326. New York: Prentice-Hall, 1974.

———. "The Meaning of Freedom in Education." *Progressive Education* 8, no. 2 (1931): 102–111.

———. "The Methodology of Racial Testing: Its Significance for Sociology." *American Journal of Sociology* 31, no. 5 (1926): 657–667.

———. "More Comprehensive Field Methods." *American Anthropologist* 35, no. 1 (1933): 1–15.

———. "The Need for Teaching Anthropology in Normal Schools and Teachers' Colleges." *School and Society* 26, no. 667 (1927): 466–469.

———. "The Primitive Child." In *A Handbook of Child Psychology*, edited by Carl Allanmore Murchison, 669–686. Worcester, MA: Clark University Press, 1931.

———. Proposal to Social Science Research Council. Typescript, 1928. Box I4, file 11, Margaret Mead Papers.

———. "A Reply to a Review of *Sex and Temperament in Three Primitive Societies*." *American Anthropologist* 39, no. 1 (1937): 558–561.

———. "Retrospect and Prospect." In *Anthropology and Human Behavior*, edited by T. Gladwin and W. Sturtevant, 115–149. Washington, DC: Anthropological Society of Washington, 1962.

———. "The Role of the Individual in Samoan Culture." *Journal of the Royal Anthropological Institute* 55 (July–December 1928): 481–495.

———. *Sex and Temperament in Three Primitive Societies*. 1935, repr.; New York: William Morrow, 1961.

———. *Social Organization of Manu'a*. Honolulu: Bernice P. Bishop Museum, 1930.

———. "South Sea Hints on Bringing Up Children." *Parents Magazine* 4 (1929): 20–22, 49–52.

———. "South Seas Tips on Character Training." *Parents Magazine* 3 (March 1932): 231–232.

———. "Standardized America vs. Romantic South Seas." *Scribner's Magazine* 40 (Nov. 1931): 486–491.

———. Stone Age Education—and Ours. Typescript, 1930. Box I5, file 2, Margaret Mead Papers.

———. "Two South Sea Educational Experiments and Their American Implications." *University of Pennsylvania Education Bulletin* 31, no. 36 (1931): 493–497.

———. Summary of Statement of the Problem of Personality and Culture. Typescript, 1933. Box I10, file 4, Margaret Mead Papers.

Mead, Margaret, and Ruth Bunzel, eds. *The Golden Age of American Anthropology.* New York: George Braziller, 1960.

Mencken, H. L. "Adolescence." *American Mercury,* (November 1929): 379–380. Clipping, file I4, Box 8, Margaret Mead Papers.

Merriam, Lewis. "The Problem of Indian Administration: Report of a Survey Made at the Request of Honorable Hubert Work, Secretary of the Interior." Baltimore: The Institute for Government Research, 1928.

Michaels, Walter Benn. *Our America: Nativism, Modernism, and Pluralism.* Durham, NC: Duke University Press, 1995.

Miller, Nina. *Making Love Modern: The Intimate Public Worlds of New York's Literary Women.* New York: Oxford University Press, 1999.

Minn, Professor W. G. Verbal Testimony. August 10, 1953. Folder 2, New Zealand Special Committee on Moral Delinquency in Children and Adolescents. MS papers 2384, Alexander Turnbull Library, Wellington.

Morrow & Co., William. *Coming of Age in Samoa.* Order form, 1928. Box L3, file 1, Margaret Mead Papers.

Morrow, William. Letter to Margaret Mead, June 20, 1928. Box I2, file 1, Margaret Mead Papers.

Mott, F. L. *A History of American Magazines: Vol. 5 Sketches of 21 Magazines, 1905–1930.* Cambridge, MA: The Belknap Press of Harvard University Press, 1957.

Mumford, Lewis. *Technics and Civilization.* New York: Harcourt, 1934.

Munson, Gorham. *The Awakening Twenties: A Memoir–History of a Literary Period.* Baton Rouge: Louisiana University Press, 1985.

"Notes and News." *Oceania* 5, no. 2 (1931): 237.

"Notes and News." *Oceania* 7, no. 4 (1933): 106.

O'Brien, Frederick. "Where Neuroses Cease from Troubling and Complexes Are at Rest." *World* (October 21, 1928). Clipping, Box L3, file 2, Margaret Mead Papers.

Ogburn, William Fielding. *Social Change with Respect to Culture and Original Nature.* New York: B. W. Huebsch, 1922.

Pells, Richard H. *Radical Visions and American Dreams: Culture and Thought in the Depression Years.* Urbana: University of Illinois Press, 1998.

Porter, Dennis. "Anthropological Tales: Unprofessional Thoughts on the Mead/Freeman Controversy." *Notebooks in Cultural Anthropology* 1 (1984): 15–37.

Pound, Ezra. "Provincialism the Enemy." *New Age* 22 (1917): 269, 289, 309.

Powdermaker, Hortense. Letter to Bronislaw and Elsie Malinowski, December 11, 1930. Stud/11, Malinowksi Papers.

———. "Primitive Ideals for Men and Women." *Saturday Review of Literature* (1935): 16. Box L4, File 1, Margaret Mead Papers.

Putnam, James. *Human Motives.* Boston: Little, Brown, 1915.

Rappaport, Roy. "Desecrating the Holy Women." *American Scholar* 55 (1986): 313–347.

Redfield, Robert. *Tepoztlan, a Mexican Village: A Study of Folk Life.* University of Chicago Press, 1930.

Review of *Coming of Age in Samoa* by Margaret Mead. *Psychoanalytic Review* 16 (1929): 115–116.

Rhodes, Chip. *Structures of the Jazz Age: Mass Culture, Progressive Education, and Racial Discourse in American Modernist Fiction.* New York: Verso, 1998.

Roscoe, Paul. "Margaret Mead, Reo Fortune, and Mountain Arapesh Warfare." *American Anthropologist* 105, no. 3 (2003): 581–591.

Rosenzweig, Saul. *The Historic Expedition to America (1909): Freud, Jung, and Hall the King-maker, with G. Stanley Hall as Host and William James as Guest.* 2nd rev. ed. St. Louis: Rana House, 1994.

Rubin, Joan Shelley. *The Making of Middlebrow Culture.* Chapel Hill: University of North Carolina Press, 1992.

Rushing, William J. *Native American Art and the New York Avant-garde: A History of Cultural Primitivism.* Austin: University of Texas Press, 1995.

Ryan, Judith. *The Vanishing Subject: Early Psychology and Literary Modernism.* Chicago University Press, 1991.

"Samoa is the Place for Women . . ." *New York Sun,* January 23, 1929. Clipping, Box L3, file 1, Margaret Mead Papers.

Sandeen, Eric J. "Bourne Again: The Correspondence Between Randolph Bourne and Elsie Clews Parsons." *American Literary History* 1, no. 3 (1989): 489–509.

Santayana, George. "The Genteel Tradition in American Philosophy." Address to the Philosophical Union of the University of California, Berkeley, 1911.

———. *Winds of Doctrine, and Platonism and the Spiritual Life.* Gloucester, MA: P. Smith, 1971.

Sapir, Edward. "Cultural Anthropology and Psychiatry." *Journal of Abnormal and Social Psychology* 27 (1932): 229–242.

———. "Culture, Genuine and Spurious." *American Journal of Sociology* 29 (1924): 401–429.

———. "The Discipline of Sex." *American Mercury* 16 (1929): 413–420.

Scheckel, Susan. *The Insistence of the Indian: Race and Nationalism in Nineteenth-Century American Culture.* Princeton University Press, 1998.

Schlesinger, Arthur M. "Introduction." In Herbert Croly, *The Promise of American Life,* edited by Arthur M. Schlesinger, iii–xxvii. Cambridge, MA: The Belknap Press of Harvard University Press, 1965.

Schneider, David. "The Coming of a Sage to Samoa." *Natural History* 4, no. 6 (1983): 10.

Schneider, Isidore. "Manus and Americans." *New Republic* 15 (November 5, 1930): 330. Clipping, Box L3, file 2, Margaret Mead Papers.

"Scientist Goes on Jungle Flapper Hunt." *New York Sun Times,* November 8, 1925. Clipping, Box L3, file 1, Margaret Mead Papers.

Silverstein, Michael. "Boasian Cosmographic: Anthropology and the Sociocentric Component of Mind." In *Significant Others: Interpersonal and Professional Commitments in Anthropology,* edited by Richard Handler, 131–157. Madison: University of Wisconsin Press, 2004.

Smith-Rosenberg, Caroll. "The New Woman as Androgyne: Social Disorder and Gender Crisis, 1870–1936." In *Disorderly Conduct: Visions of Gender in Victorian America,* 245–349. New York: Oxford University Press, 1985.

Sprague, Roger. Letter to the Editor: "Samoan Youth." *Saturday Review of Literature,* November 17, 1928. Clipping, Box L1, file 1, Margaret Mead Papers.

Stearns, Harold E. *America Now: An Inquiry into Civilization in the United States by Thirty-six Americans.* New York: The Literary Guild of America, 1938.

———, ed. *Civilization in the United States: An Inquiry by Thirty Americans.* New York: Harcourt, Brace, 1922.

Steedman, Carolyn. *Strange Dislocations: Childhood and the Idea of Human Interiority, 1780–1930.* London: Virago, 1995.

Stein, Gertrude. "Why I Do Not Live in America." In *How Writing is Written: Volume II of the Previously Uncollected Writings of Gertrude Stein,* edited by Robert Bartlett Haas, 51. 1928, repr.; Los Angeles: Black Sparrow, 1974.

Steinbeck, John. *The Grapes of Wrath.* New York: Viking, 1939.

Stocking, George. "Ideas and Institutions in American Anthropology: Towards a History of the Interwar Years." In *The Ethnographer's Magic and Other Essays in the History of Anthropology,* edited by George Stocking, 114–177. Madison: University of Wisconsin Press, 1992.

Stocking, George W. "Anthropology and the Science of the Irrational: Malinowski's Encounter with Freudian Psychoanalysis." In *Malinowski, Rivers, Benedict, and Others: Essays on Culture and Personality,* edited by George W. Stocking, 13–49. Madison: University of Wisconsin Press, 1986.

———. "Essays on Personality and Culture." In *Malinowski, Rivers, Benedict, and Others,* 3–12.

———. "The Ethnographic Sensibility of the 1920s and the Dualism of the Anthropological Tradition." In *Romantic Motives: Essays on Anthropological Sensibility*, edited by George W. Stocking, 208–276. Madison: University of Wisconsin Press, 1989.

Stoler, Ann Laura. *Race and the Education of Desire: Foucault's History of Sexuality and the Colonial Order of Things*. Durham, NC: Duke University Press, 1996.

Sullivan, Gerald. "Of Feys and Culture Planners: Margaret Mead and Purposive Activity as Value." In *Reading Benedict, Reading Mead: Feminism, Race and Imperial Visions*, edited by Lois Banner and Dolores Janiewski, 101–114. Baltimore: Johns Hopkins University Press, 2004.

———. "A Four-fold Humanity: Margaret Mead and Psychological Types." *Journal of the History of the Behavioral Sciences* 40, no. 2 (2004): 183–206.

Susman, Walter. *Culture as History: The Transformation of American Society in the Twentieth Century*. New York: Pantheon Books, 1984.

Szalay, Michael. *New Deal Modernism: American Literature and the Invention of the Welfare State*. Durham, NC: Duke University Press, 2000.

Taylor, Charles. *Sources of the Self: The Making of Modern Identity*. Cambridge University Press, 1989.

Thomas, Caroline. "Reo Franklin Fortune: The Historical Ethnography of an Anthropological Career." Doctoral dissertation, University of Waikato, NZ, in prep.

Thurnwald, Richard. "Review of *Sex and Temperament in Three Primitive Societies* by Margaret Mead." *American Anthropologist* 38, no. 4 (1936): 664–667.

Torgovnick, Marianna. *Gone Primitive: Savage Intellects, Modern Lives*. University of Chicago Press, 1990.

Tozzer, Alfred. Review of *The Changing Culture of an Indian Tribe* by Margaret Mead. *The Annals of the American Academy of Political and Social Science* 165 (January 1933): 250.

Turner, Frederick Jackson. "The Significance of the Frontier in American History." Address to the American Historical Association, July 12, 1893, www.uta.fi/FAST/US2/REF/turner.html.

Untitled review of *Coming of Age in Samoa* by Margaret Mead. *Philadelphia Record*, August 15, 1928. Clipping, Box L3, file 1, Margaret Mead Papers.

Untitled review of *Coming of Age in Samoa* by Margaret Mead. *Brooklyn Eagle*, August 22, 1929. Clipping, Box L3, file 1, Margaret Mead Papers.

"Utopian Marriages, for the Woman." *New York Telegram*, 1930. Clipping, Box L3, file 1, Margaret Mead Papers.

Vaughan, Leslie J. *Randolph Bourne and the Politics of Cultural Radicalism*. Lawrence: University of Kansas Press, 1997.

Warner, Marina. *Six Myths of Our Time: Little Angels, Little Monsters, Beautiful Beasts, and More*. New York: Vintage Books, 1995.

Wasserstrom, William. "Preface." In *Van Wyck Brooks: The Critic and His Critics,* edited by William Wasserstrom, vii–xi. Port Washington, NY: Kennikat, 1979.

Watkins, T. H. *The Great Depression: America in the 1930s.* Boston: Little, Brown, 1993.

Wertheim, Arthur F. *The New York Little Renaissance: Iconoclasm, Modernism and Nationalism in American Culture, 1908–1917.* New York University Press, 1976.

"Will Shows Fear of Cannibals." *New York Sun,* August 22, 1928. Clipping, Box L3, file 1, Margaret Mead Papers.

Wissler, Clark. "Foreword." In *The Changing Culture of an Indian Tribe,* by Margaret Mead, iii–v. New York: Capricorn Books, 1966 (1932).

———. Letter to Margaret Mead, August 4, 1930. Box I6, file 10, October, Margaret Mead Papers.

Yans, Virginia, and Alan Berliner. *Margaret Mead: An Observer Observed.* New York: Mind Matters, 1995. Film.

Yellis, Kenneth. "Prosperity's Child: Some Thoughts on the Flapper." *American Quarterly* 21 (1969): 44–64.

Young, Robert J. C. *Colonial Desire: Hybridity in Theory, Culture and Race.* London: Routledge, 1995.

Index

Numbers in **boldface** type refer to
photographs

1919, x, 31
Abbott, Mary Squire, 51
Abrahams, Edward, 54
actualization, 7, 11, 110
Admiralty Islands, 38, 50, 62, 84; *Kinship in
the Admiralty Islands*, 73, 114, 115
Aibom, 118–119
Aliatoa, 115
alienation: Benedict and, 113; condition
of modernity, 1, 4, 16, 21, 29–30, 34, 61,
103, 110; Fortune and, 113; Manus, 69;
Mead's work and, 133, 136
Allotment Scheme. *See* Omaha Allotment
Act (1882)
American Academy of Science, 124
American Anthropologist, 52, 71, 73, 100,
101, 129
American Intellect, 22. *See* genteel tradition
American Mercury, 34
American Museum of Natural History, 14,
69, 87, 113
American Will, 22. *See* genteel tradition
America's Coming of Age, 4, 27, 61
Anderson, Margaret, 32, 33
Anderson, Sherwood, 3, 32, 33, 111
Angel Pavement, 72
Antler, -s, 15, 17, 90, 136; conditions in 1930,
95–96; cultural lag and, 103; history of,
91–95; Mead's reticence about research
on, 83; woman as metaphor for Depres-

sion America, 87, 106; women's lives,
96–99. See also *Changing Culture of an
Indian Tribe, The;* Omaha
Arapesh, 83, 125, 127, 142
Architectural Record, 22
Armory Show, 30
Arnold, Matthew, 24, 29
art of living, 21, 64, 79–80, 141
Atlantic Monthly, 19, 24
Australian Research Council, 65

Babbitt, -ry, 111, 162n68
Baining, 117
Bateson, Gregory, 39, 107, 109, 113; with
Mead and Fortune in New Guinea
(Lake Chambri) and Sydney, 116–125;
role in Mead's separation from Fortune,
128–129
Beard, Charles, 24, 31
Bender, Thomas, 21
Benedict, Ruth, **11;** cultural relativism,
112–113; culture and personality, 126,
132; "culture," modernism and the
writings of, 3, 4, 11, 32, 132; Fortune's
influence on, 39; friend and mentor
to Mead, 3, 39–41, 46, 49, 51, 72, 114,
141; letters to Bateson, 123, 128; Mead's
citation of, 75; Mead's letters to from
New Guinea, 65, 117–119; Mead's letters
to from Sydney, 122; *Patterns of Culture*
draft in the Sepik, 107, 119; professional
support of Mead's career, 72, 75, 88, 123;
reviews of Mead's books, 70, 101, 129;

sexual relationship with Mead, 41, 49, 114, 119, 137
Bernice P. Bishop Museum, 46, 50
biological determinism, 38, 135
Blackberry Winter, 40, 108, 109, 118, 128
Blake, Casey Nelson, 29
Boas, Franz, **9;** anthropological thought, 110, 131–132, 137–139; anti-racism activity, 38; anti-war activity, 31; "culture," modernism and the writings of, 3, 8, 10, 12; fellowship for Fortune, 69; influence on cultural critics, 4, 19, 27, 29, 141; letters to Mead, 49; Mead's letters to, 47, 89, 122; teacher/supervisor of Mead, 38–39, 45–46, 50
Book-of-the-Month Club, 36
Boon, James, 109
Bourne, Randolph, **25;** anthropological influences on, 4, 141; blacklisting, 25; "culture," modernism and the writings of, 3; "culture" and trans-nationalism, 27–29, 110, 131, 139; death of, 31, 33; Dos Passos on, 31; European tour, 24; "Experimental Life," 25–26, 142; friendships, 4, 27; influence on Mead, 32–33, 56, 135, 141; intellectual legacy, 30, 139, 142; *New Republic*, 22, 24, 137; on war, 24–25; *Youth and Life*, 22, 79
Brooks, Van Wyck, **23;** alienation, 29; American culture, 27–28, 29, 35; "culture," modernism and the writings of, 3, 29, 112, 130; friendships, 4; homogenous society, 16; influence on Benedict, Mead, 4, 141; integration, 136; intellectual legacy, 31, 61, 76; masculinity, 12; *New Republic*, 22; organicism, 28, 60, 103; usable past, 28, 139. See also *Freeman; Seven Arts*
Bureau of Ethnology of the Smithsonian Institution, 93
Burnham, John C., 20

Calverton, V. F., 34
Carnegie, Dale, 63

Cattell, James McKean, 31
Chambri. See Tchambuli
Changing Culture of an Indian Tribe, The, 13, 17; chapter on, 83–106; compared to Mead's other books, 14, 15, 129, 136
Chase, Stuart, 104, 105, 111
Chateaubriand, François-René, Vicomte de, 28
child, -hood, 12, 14, 15, 17; adult Mead as, 59, 157n82; American, 70, 74–75, 77, 82; Antler, 98, 99; Antler as, 101; Arapesh, 125; Italian immigrant, 38; Manus, 62–71, 74–76, 78–79, 80, 82; Mead's, 40, 70; Mead's decision to have, 18, 39, 117, 119, 128–129, 139; as metaphor, 28, 54; Mundugumor, **108,** 128; popular culture, 54; psychosexual identification, 127; Samoan, 47, 49, 53–57 *passim,* 76, 80, 134; Samoans as, 56; as solace, 129, 133; squares theory, 102; subjects of research, 41, 64, 65, 80, 83, 92, 102. *See also* daughters; fathers; mothers; sons
civilization, "mother of twentieth century," 1; equivalent to culture, 35, 75, 78, 88, 104, 112; equivalent to society, 33, 62, 132; opposed to primitive, 12, 16, 56–60, 87, 105; opposite of culture, 112. See also *Civilization in the United States; Technics and Civilization*
Civilization in the United States, 35, 78, 112
Clarke, Edith, 71
Clash of Cultures and the Contact of Races, The, 100
Clifford, James, 5, 6
colonial, -ism, 3, 24; Mead's denial of, 52, 136
Columbia University: Boas at, 10, 31; Bourne at, 19, 24; Fortune at, 69, 73; Mead at, 37, 39, 86; network of relationships at, 4
Coming of Age in Samoa, 5–8, 13–17 *passim,* 38; chapter on, 42–61; civilization in, 112; compared to Mead's other books, 65, 70, 75, 80–84 *passim,* 100, 110, 125,

129; cosmopolitanism and, 141–142; homogeneity and, 104–106, 136; royalties from, 87
cosmopolitan, -ism, 18, 26, 30, 33, 35, 110, 139–141. *See also* "Trans-national America"
Cosmopolitan, 32, 51
Cowley, Malcolm, 20, 111
Cressman, Luther, 39, 49–50
Croly, Herbert: Americanization and, 29; art of living, 79; influence on Mead, 60–61, 79, 141; masculinity, 12; Progressive goals, 103, 136; scale of cultural renaissance, 31; unity of nation and individual, 16, 28, 60–61. See also *Promise of American Life*
"Cult of the Best," The, 29. *See also* Arnold, Mathew
cultural critics: in *Changing Culture*, 85–87, 102–106; *Coming of Age*, 60–61; *Growing Up, Sex and Temperament,* 109–112, 130–133; ideas of, 21–32, 75–82 *passim*, 103, 104, 132–141 *passim;* influence on Mead, 16–17, 19; magazines, 32–34, 75–80; modernist literature and, 3; relationships among, 4. *See also* cultural nationalist
cultural determinism, 7, 39, 61, 90, 109, 132. *See also* biological determinism
cultural lag, 17, 85, 86, 103, 104, 105. *See also* Ogburn, William Fielding
cultural nationalist, nativists, 16, 19, 30–35. *See also* cultural critics; Lyrical Left; Young Americans
culture: broken, 17, 102, 105, 106, 165n69; highbrow, lowbrow, 28, 112; middlebrow, 2, 4, 14, 36; traits, 93, 110, 132, 141

daughter, -s: Antler, 94, 98–99; "Disorder and Early Sorrow," 55; Mead as, 32, 41, 77. *See also* fathers; mothers
Dawes Severalty Act (1887), 88
delinquent, 15, 17, 92, 98, 134
Dell, Floyd, 31, 81

Deloria, Phillip, 105
deviant, 57, 81, 129; *Sex and Temperament,* 13, 15, 18, 112, 125–129 *passim,* 133
Dewey, John, 22, 24, 25, 31, 104, 110, 142
di Leonardo, Micaela, 3, 42, 83, 129
Dial, 25, 28, 32, 33–34
Dobu. See *Sorcerers of Dobu*
Doherty, Thomas, 90
Dollard, John, 40, 124, 125, 138
Dorsey, George, 50, 51
Dorsey, James, 93

Eastman, Crystal, 32
Eastman, Max, 32
Eddy, Mary Baker, 63. *See also* mind-cure
Eichelberger, Marie, 128
Eighteenth Amendment, 37
Eliot, T. S., 3, 27, 141
Ellis, Havelock, 37, 44, 51
Elmhirst, Dorothy Whitney (Mrs. Leonard), Committee, 32, 87–88, 148n20. *See also* Straight, Dorothy Whitney
Encyclopedia of the Social Sciences, 64, 83
Esteve, Mary, 25–26
eventuation, 7, 11, 65, 110
Everybody's Magazine, 20
Exile's Return, 111
Exotics at Home, 3
"Experimental Life, The," 25–26, 142

fascism, 17, 85, 105. *See also* National Socialism, Nazism
fathers, fatherhood, 55, 113, 127–128; American and Manus, 64, 70–71, 76–82; Antler, 94–98 *passim. See also* Mead, Edward Sherwood
Firth, Raymond, 115, 128
Fitzgerald, F. Scott, 35, 45, 105
flapper, 2, 16, 42–45
Fletcher, Alice, 88, 92, 93
Forde, C. Daryl, 100, 101
Fortune, Reo Franklin: Arapesh research, 115–116; Bateson and, 116, 117, 128–129; employment prospects, 87, 116, 117;

intellectual impact, 39–41; Manus research, 65–66, 68, 73, 88; marriage to Mead, 49–50; Mead, Bateson and, **121,** 118–128; Mundugumor research, 116; in New York, 69, 114; Omaha research, 88; personal values, 113–114, 116; in reviews, 71–72, 116; in *Sex and Temperament,* 128; in Sydney, 107, 115, 122–123. See also *Sorcerers of Dobu*
Forum: The Magazine of Controversy, 74
Frank, Lawrence, 4, 124
Frank, Waldo, 3, 12, 24, 29–35 *passim,* 110, 137
Freeman, 35
Freeman, Derek, 6
Freud, Sigmund, 2, 12, 16, 37; American visit, 19–22, 34, 44, 54; Malinowski and, 68, 102; Mead's conversion to, 40, 125; Mead's use of, 76, 102, 138; popular ideas about, 57, 61
Fromm, Eric, 40, 124, 125, 138
Frontier Mentality, 22
functionalism, dys-: American society, 65, 104–105; anthropological, 71, 85, 102, 104, 138; Antler society, 13, 94; Mead and, 17, 39, 68, 79, 137; Ogburn, 103; Progressive, 60, 85

Geertz, Clifford, 6
genteel tradition, 12, 19, 22, 34, 36, 76. *See also* Santayana, George
Gibson Girl, 43, 44
Gifford, Sandford, 20
Gilbert, James, 30
Goethe, Johann, 54
Goldenweiser, Alexander, 31, 100–101
Gone with the Wind, 63
Good Housekeeping, 20
Greenwich Village, 16, 20, 23, 44
Gregory, Alyse, 32
Growing Up in New Guinea, 13–17 *passim;* chapter on, 62–82; compared to Mead's other books, 84, 100, 106, 125, 129;

completion of, 87, 91; reviews of, 106, 114, 116, 129
Gumbrecht, Hans, 55

Haddon, A. C., 39
Hammonton, New Jersey, 38
Handbook of Child Psychology, The, 92
Handy, E.S.C., 50
Hanover Conference on Human Relations, 124–125
Hapgood, Hutchins, 31
Harlem Renaissance, 37
Hart, C. W., 71–72, 114, 116
Hays Office, 133, 173n106
Hegeman, Susan, 3–4, 11, 140
Hersokovitz, Melville, 70
heterogeneous, culture, nation, society, 26, 80, 119, 135–136. *See also* homogenous
heterosexual, -ity, 2, 44–45, 81, 125, 130
hidden motives, 20
Hollinger, David, 30, 33, 139–142 *passim*
homogenous, culture, nation, society, 18, 27; functionalism and, 106, 135–138; human nature and, 126; methodological implications of, 91–93; nostalgia for, 43, 113; Samoa as, 56, 59, 61, 78
homosexual, -ality, 55, 81, 126–130. *See also* inversion
Hoover, President Herbert, 62, 63, 100
Horney, Karen, 40, 138
How to Win Friends and Influence People, 63
Howard, Clare, 101
Howard, Jane, 40
Hurston, Zora Neale, 3
Huxley, Aldous, 58
Huyssen, Andreas, 12

illness, 98, 101, 136; damaged ankle, 115–116; influenza, 31; malaria, 116–117; mental, 119–120; as paradigm, 91; scorpion bite, 119; smallpox, 88, 94; tuberculosis, 99; undiagnosed, 116 imperialism, 3, 10, 17, 91. *See also* colonial

Individualism Old and New, 104

influenza epidemic, 1918, 31

integrated, dis-, culture, nation, society: Antlers as, 87, 94, 102; Benedict and, 112; cultural critics and, 17, 23, 103, 111; Depression thought, 130; functionalism and, 13, 18, 85, 87, 103–105; in Mead's work, 135, 137–138; personal development and, 85; "primitive" societies as, 87, 94, 103–105; Progressivism and, 17, 34, 60, 85, 103; repression of difference in, 126

interiority, 6, 53–58 *passim*

International Congress of Anthropological and Ethnological Sciences, 125

inversion, 2, 81, 126–127. *See also* homosexual

James, William, 142, 148n22

Johnson Acts. *See* National Origins Acts

Journal of the Royal Anthropological Institute, 73

Karawop, 115, 116

Key, Ellen, 44

Kinship in the Admiralty Islands, 73, 114–115

Kirchwey, Freda, 58–61 *passim*

Kroeber, Alfred L., 52, 70–72, 114, 132

Ku Klux Klan, 43

La Flesche, Francis, 93

League of Nations, 34

Levine, Lawrence, 42, 60, 63–64, 130

Lewis, Frederick Allen, 43, 45

Lewis, Sinclair, 35, 162n68

Life Begins at Forty, 64

Lippman, Walter, 22, 31

Little Review, 33

Living Newspapers, The, 131

Lorengau, 66

"lost generation," 111

Love in the Machine Age, 81

Lowie, Robert, 35, 52, 93

Luhan, Mabel Dodge, 32

Lynd, Helen and Robert, 52, 75–78 *passim,* 86, 110, 124

Lyrical Left, 23, 134, 135. *See also* cultural critics; cultural nationalist; Young Americans

machine age, 2, 12, 43, 74, 78–81; as metaphor, 104

Macy, Nebraska, 83, 88

magazines: "little," 24, 32–34, 52, 82, 140; mass circulation, 20, 36, 44, 45, 59, 60, 65, 138, 140; Mead's reading, 6, 7, 32; Mead's writing for, 6, 51; reviews in, 51, 52, 75, 100. *See also* specific titles

Main Street, 35, 45; "Main Street" (metaphor), 29, 45

maladjustment, Antler society as, 99, 101, 136; causes of, 2, 20, 81, 86, 103, 127

malaga, 49

Manganaro, Marc, 3, 11, 140

Mann, Thomas, 55

Manu'a, 47, 66

Manus: books on, 88; boy as personification, 15, 17; chapter on, 62–82; compared to other cultures, 89, 116, 141

Marcus, George, 6

masculinity: modernity and, 2, 12, 41; Depression and, 54, 80; Fortune and, 113; in *Growing Up,* 16–17; in *Sex and Temperament,* 125, 128

Masses, 31

materialism: Manus, 76; in Mead's work, 7; in modernist thought, 16, 64–65, 85, 103, 130, 131

McMaster, Fanny Fogg, 37

McMillan, Margaret, 54

Mead, Edward Sherwood, 32, 37–38, 40–41, 86

Mead, Emily Fogg, 38, 40

Mencken, H. L. (Henry Louis), 12, 33–36 *passim,* 52

Mental Hygiene Association, movement, 20
Merriam, Lewis, 85
Mexico: A Study of Two Americas, 104–105
Mexico and Southwest, 112
Michaels, Walter Benn, 137, 140
Midwest, American, 17, 27, 37, 83, 111, 162n60
Mignon, 54, 55, 58
Miller, Nina, 2, 30
mind-cure, 3, 63
Mind of Primitive Man, The, 8
Modern Quarterly, 34
modernism, modernist: aesthetic criteria, 33–34; anthropology and, 3–4, 11, 140–141; communitarianism and, 33; cultural nationalism and, 1, 16, 36, 110, 112, 137, 140; masculinity and, 12; Mead and, 6, 11, 79; primitivism and, 14, 87
modernity: anthropology and, 3, 4, **7**, 104; cultural lag and, 103; ethnicity and, 43; flapper and, 43, 60; masculinity and, 12; nostalgia and, 53; self and, 14, 53; sex and, 135, 138
"More Comprehensive Field Methods," 73
Morrow, William (person; publishing company), 35, 50–51, 53, 69, 100
mothers, motherhood, 36, 77, 98, 99, 102, 105, 129. *See also* Mead, Emily Fogg
Mumford, Lewis, 22, 35, 86, 104
Muncie, Indiana, 75
Mundugumor, 108, 116, 125–128 *passim,* 142

Nathan, George Jean, 34
Nation, 58, 70, 100, 101
National Academy of Sciences, 38
National Origins Acts, (1921, 1924), 37, 38
National Socialism, Nazism, 135, 139. *See also* fascism
Naven, 107
Nebraska, 13, 38, 83–93 *passim*
New Age Illustrated, 59

New Deal, 105, 124
New Republic, 22–25, 32, 104, 136, 137, 148n20, 150n63
New Woman, New Women, 1–2, 44
New York League of Girls' Clubs, 50
New Zealand, 39, 49, 65, 113, 115, 134

Oceania (journal), 107
Ogburn, William Fielding, 5, 17, 40, 85–**86, 92,** 103
Omaha (Native Americans), 7, 13–14, 38, **97,** 126, 141; chapter on, 83–106
Omaha Allotment Act (1882), 88, 93–98 *passim*
"On Creating a Usable Past," 28
Only Yesterday, 43
Oppenheim, James, 33
organic, 28, 34, 60–61, 103–104, 113
Our America: Frank, Waldo, 35; Michaels, Walter Benn, 9, 140

Parkinson, Mrs. Phoebe, 68
Parsons, Elsie Clews, 3, 4, 13, 22, 32, 35, 88, 132, 141
Paterson Strike Pageant, 30
Patterns of Culture, 4, 11, 107, 108, 112, 119, 132
Peri, (Pere) village, 66
personality: biology and, 18; cultural critics and, 60, 79, 141; culture and, 7, 14, 39, 75, 126; Mead's, 59; modernity and, 6, 36, 80; Mundugumor, 125; squares theory, 120–122; temperament, individuality and, 91–92
personification, 14–15, 55, 105
Pitt Rivers, William, 100
Pound, Ezra, 30
preachment yarn, 90
Priestly, J. B., 72
"Primitive Child, The," 92–93
Progressive, Progressivism, Croly, 19, 21, 79, 136–137; Depression and, 85; dissolution of, 34, 103–104; in Mead's work, 60–61; psychoanalysis, 20

Progressive Education movement, theory, 75, 80
Prohibition, 37, 43, 124
Promise of American Life, The, 19, 21–22, 103
provincialism, 30, 33, 35–36, 43, 139
psychoanalysis, psychology: Americans and, 16, 20, 35, 54, 61, 76, 111; Antler, 89; *Coming of Age* as, 75; ethnology and, 90, 92–93; Fortune and, 39, 49; Mead and, 5, 18, 39, 40, 45, 47, 49, 83, 109, 138; modernity and, 3, 8, 12, 55–57, 130; progressive education theory and, 80; squares theory, 120–122
psychosexual identification, 126–130, 139
Puritan, -ical, -ism: America as, 16; cultural critics and, 21–23 *passim,* 30–34 *passim,* 111; Manus as, 15, 70, 76, 82. *See also* genteel tradition; *Wine of the Puritans, The*
Putnam, Frederic, 93
Putnam, James, 20

Rabaul, 66, 68, 115, 117
race, 3; Antlers, 89–90, 105–106; Brooks and, 28; culture and, 8–12; National Origins Acts, 37; in Pago Pago, 46; squares theory, 120, 122
Radcliffe-Brown, A. R., 39, 65, 79, 118
Rankine, Annette, Mrs., 32
Reed, John, 31
repression: genteel tradition and, 12, 34, 36; Manus and, 69, 76, 82; New Women and, 2; psychoanalysis and, 20–22, 138; Samoa and, 16, 57–61 *passim*
Rockefeller Foundation, 124
Rodman, Henrietta, 32
Rourke, Constance, 4

Sacco, Nicola and Vanzetti, Bartolomeo, 37
Samoa: chapter on, 42–61; compared to other societies, 64, 79–80, 105, 126, 134, 137; fieldwork conditions in, 38, 89; as homogenous society, 16. See also *Coming of Age in Samoa*

Santayana, George, 12, 19, 22, 27, 76. *See also* genteel tradition
Sapir, Edward: attacks on Mead's work, 52; on culture, 132; Mead's lover, 39, 46, 49; modernism, 3, 4, 10; research plans, 92, 93
Saturday Evening Post, 74
Saturday Review of Literature, 32, 52
Scheckel, Susan, 85, 105
Schmallhausen, Samuel, 104
Science Service, 51
Scientific American, 65
Scopes Trial, 52
Sepik, region, River, 107, 108, 109, 113
Seven Arts, 24–25, 30, 32, 33
Sex and Temperament in Three Primitive Societies, 7, 13–18 *passim;* chapter on, 107–133; compared to Mead's other books, 83–84; cultural critics influence on, 141; influence of, 142; integration and, 136; psychologists influence on, 40, 138; squares theory, 139
Smart Set, 34, 51
Social Change with Respect to Culture and Original Nature, 86–87, 90
Society of Americanists Conference, 49
sons, 77–78
Sorcerers of Dobu, 39, 65, 69, 107, 116
Southwest, American, 112
squares theory, 18, 122, 139
standardization, 2, 7, 65, 78–80
Stearns, Harold, 32, 35, 78, 111, 112
Steedman, Carolyn, 14–15, 54–55
Stein, Gertrude, 1
Stein, Leo, 20
Stocking, George, 83, 108
Straight, Dorothy Whitney, 22, 32. *See also* Elmhirst, Dorothy Whitney
Sulka, 117
Susman, Walter, 130, 158n8

Tau, 47, 57
taupou, 46, 47
Taylor, Charles, 7–8, 14, 109

Taylorism, 64, 78
Tchambuli, 118, 125, 130, 142
Technics and Civilization, 87, 104
temperament: art of living and, 80; culture and, 7, 11, 13–14, 110, 133; dance as indicator of, 47; deviance and, 18, 47; personality, individuality and, 91–92, 109–110, 112; psychosexual identification and, 125–129; squares theory, 120–122, 139. See also *Sex and Temperament in Three Primitive Societies*
Tennessee Anti-Evolution Act (1925), 37
Thayer, Scofield, 32, 33
This Side of Paradise, 45
Thurnwald, Richard, 129
Tozzer, Alfred, 52, 100
"Trans-National America," 24, 26, 30
Turner, Frederick Jackson, 22, 147n51

University of Cambridge, 39, 50, 107, 113, 116, 117, 128
University of New Zealand, 49
University of Sydney, 65, 115, 123

Vanity Fair, 32, 34
Veblen, Thorstein, 142

Watson, James Sibley, 33
Watson, John B., 51
Why We Behave like Human Beings, 36
Wilhelm Meister, 54
Wilson, Edmund, 111
Wilson, Woodrow (President), 22, 24, 26
Wine of the Puritans, The, 27–28
Wissler, Clark, 87–92 *passim,* 95, 115
Woman's Journal, 65
Woodbridge, Frederick, 24

You Can't Take It with You, 64
Young, Robert, 8, 9, 10, 12
Young Americans, 23, 29, 135. *See also* cultural critics; cultural nationalist; Lyrical Left
Youth and Life, 19, 22, 25, 32
Yuet River, 116

About the Author

MAUREEN A. MOLLOY is a professor of women's studies at the University of Auckland. She has a PhD in anthropology and has published on the relationships between academic ideas and popular culture across a range of fields, including policy studies and feminist theory and practice. She is currently engaged in a study of globalization and the fashion industry.

Production Notes for
Molloy / On Creating a Usable Culture

Designed by Leslie Fitch and the University of Hawai'i Press
Production Staff with Minion text and display in Caslon

Composition by Josie Herr

Printed on 60# Text White Opaque, 426 ppi